PSYCHOLOGY OF MOTIVATION

PSYCHOLOGY OF MOTIVATION

LOIS V. BROWN
EDITOR

Nova Science Publishers, Inc.
New York

Copyright © 2007 by Nova Science Publishers, Inc.

NOTICE TO THE READER

LIBRARY OF CONGRESS CATALOGING-IN-PUBLICATION DATA

Psychology of motivation / Lois V. Brown, editor.
    p.cm.
Includes index.
ISBN-13: 978-1-60021-598-8 (hardcover)
ISBN-10: 1-60021-598-X (hardcover)
1. Motivation (Psychology) I. Brown, Lois V.
BF503.P79   2007
153.8--dc22   2007010129

Published by Nova Science Publishers, Inc. ✦ New York

CONTENTS

PREFACE

In psychology, motivation refers to the initiation, direction, intensity and persistence of behavior. Motivation is a temporal and dynamic state that should not be confused with personality or emotion. Motivation is having the desire and willingness to do something. A motivated person can be reaching for a long-term goal such as becoming a professional writer or a more short-term goal like learning how to spell a particular word. Personality invariably refers to more or less permanent characteristics of an individual's state of being (e.g., shy, extrovert, conscientious). As opposed to motivation, emotion refers to temporal states that do not immediately link to behavior (e.g., anger, grief, happiness). This new book presents that latest research in this field.

Chapter 1 - Motivated behaviors are simultaneously fascinating and difficult to understand. Our fellow humans often exhibit behaviors that appear to have no underlying logic or reasonable explanation. This chapter attempts to identify the important contributors to motivated behaviors. We begin by defining motivation and its relationship with need states. Next the complicated processes of habituation and sensitization are discussed, followed by an analysis of selective attention. The role of memory systems in directing successful motivated behaviors is addressed along with identification of the brain structures that appear to be involved. In this regard there is much to be learned. The chapter concludes with summaries of current research findings concerning the brain angiotensin system's importance in memory consolidation and retrieval. This section includes descriptions of the impact of currently prescribed antihypertensive medications such as angiotensin converting enzyme (ACE) inhibitors and angiotensin receptor blockers (ARBs) on cognition. The overall goal of this chapter is to assist the reader to better understand and appreciate the complex issue of human motivated behaviors from the perspective of research contributions made using both human and animal subjects.

Chapter 2 - Inner desires and motives often result in confrontation with what is requested by others or considered socially appropriate, and even with one's own goals. Regulating internally-generated impulses is therefore an important ability for accomplishing goals and instructions as well as complying with social norms. In Psychology, this ability has been linked to the concept of self-regulation. The term "self-regulation" refers to those processes by which people exercise control over their emotional and behavioral responses in order to accomplish their own goals and/or to adapt to the cognitive and social demands of specific situations. The type of processes implicated in such ability involve modulating the intensity, frequency and duration of verbal and motor responses, activating and/or inhibiting behaviors according to situational demands in the absence of external monitoring, delaying acting upon a desired object or goal and modulating emotional reactivity (Fonagy & Target, 2002; Thompson, 1994; Kopp, 1992). Thus, it is no surprise that the ability to self-regulate is been shown to relate to important aspects of socialization during childhood, as emotionality, delay of gratification, compliance, moral development, social competence, empathy, adjustment, and academic performance (Eisenberg et al., 2004). As a matter of fact, self-regulation is thought to be "essential for transforming the inner animal nature into a civilized human being" (Vogs & Baumeister, 2004, p. 1).

Although increased evidence shows that some regulatory operations may be carried out in an automatic, nonconscious mode (Fitzsimons & Bargh, 2004), most definitions of self-regulation place the emphasis on processes exerted by the self in a conscious and deliberate way which activation entails some effort. Within this framework, the ability to self-regulate has been linked to executive aspects of attention (Posner & Rothbart, 1998; Rueda, Posner & Rothbart, 2004). According to this view, the brain network underlying executive attention constitutes the neural basis for action monitoring and is activated in situations that involve conscious detection, inhibitory control and resolution of conflict produced by dominant but inappropriate responses.

Based on the motivational properties of emotions, other studies highlight the effect of affective variables over attentional processes. Affects appear to exert their influence either by facilitating the processing of relevant information in a substantially automatic mode (Öhman, 1997) or, in a more elaborated way, by demanding additional involvement of control processes on affective-relevant situations (Gross, 2002). In addition, motivational variables and strategies are shown to modulate aspects of self-regulation. There is evidence of the influence of promotion-approach versus prevention-avoidance styles on processes of decision making, generation of alternatives, probability estimates and evaluation of outcomes (Higgins & Spiegel, 2004).

In this chapter, the authors stress the contribution of control processes related to attention for emotional and behavioral regulation, placing emphasis on the specific neural systems involved in such processes. In addition, we analyze the influence of motivational and emotional variables on the functioning of attentional control in an effort to understand their interdependence for regulating behavior.

Chapter 3 - In this chapter the authors outline a recently developed "Feeling-is-for-Doing" perspective for the influence of specific emotions on decision-making and behavior. This perspective holds that discrete emotions present functional psychological mechanisms involved in orchestrating goal-directed behavior. Studies corroborating the basic premises of this perspective are presented, along with results indicating that investigating the impact of specific emotions on people's decisions is indeed illustrative of the fundamental motives underlying their behavior. The Feeling-is-for-Doing perspective is then related to and compared with other theories about emotional influences on decision-making.

Chapter 4 - This chapter represents a summary of a programme of research conducted over the past ten years focusing on the motivations, explanations, and correlates of dietary preference and behaviour. While there is a significant body of literature attesting to the psychophysiological correlates and of different dietary practices, as well as a clinical literature on pathological dietary behaviours and avoidances, there is only a relatively small body of research investigating the psychological motivations for adopting different practices. In a number of studies we have sought to locate diet into existing theories of choice and behaviour in social psychology, focusing particularly on the motivational foundation of social values, materialism, and beliefs about hierarchy and tradition. In this chapter we bring together the findings of this range of studies to try to give an overall picture of how dietary behaviour can be fitted into the broad context of social psychology. As well as discussing the role that values, materialism, and other beliefs and attitudes account for a range of dietary behaviours we have as a specific interest the foundations of the 'decision' to consume or abstain from consuming meat, and animal-derived products. As well as acting as a microcosm for broader dietary behaviour, meat abstention also represents a social 'deviant' practice in many Western cultures, as it is adopted by a minority.

Chapter 5 - The aim of this chapter is to provide an overview of recent research that integrates two key theories of motivation: the theory of planned behavior and self-determination theory. The chapter will adopt an evidence-based approach to evaluate how the integration of these theories provides a more complete model of motivation. After an overview of the component theories, two theoretical premises for theoretical integration will be discussed: (1) self-determination theory provides a formative explanation for the origin of the antecedents of intentional behavior and (2) self-determination theory constructs operate at a generalized contextual level and reflect the origin or *locus of causality* of an action while theory of planned behavior constructs are situational and reflect expectations regarding engagement in a specific future behavior. Empirical evidence for the integration of these theories is then presented in the form of a meta-analysis of 13 published studies. The meta-analytically derived correlations corrected for sampling and measurement error will then be used as a basis for a path analysis examining the pattern of relations among the variables from the integrated theory. The implications of the integrated models for future research and interventions are discussed.

Chapter 6 - Motivation lies at the root of many risk-related behaviors, including alcohol abuse, problem gambling, risky sex, and disordered eating behaviors. This chapter provides a review of empirical work examining risk-related behaviors from the perspective of Self-Determination Theory. Theoretical implications for incorporating self-determination in prevention and treatment of risk-related behavior are also considered.

Self-Determination Theory presents a humanistic perspective on motivation, assuming that individuals intrinsically strive to fulfill basic needs for competence, relatedness, and autonomy. In negotiating the environment, externally regulated behaviors are internalized and integrated into the self. Individual differences in motivational orientations emerge as a function of exposure to different environments with some individuals tending to operate more autonomously and others generally more oriented toward extrinsically controlling factors. A considerable volume of basic research has supported the main tenets of Self-Determination Theory and a growing body of literature has begun to explore its application to risk-related behaviors.

A large proportion of the chapter focuses on etiology, reviewing multiple connections between self-determination and risk behaviors with emphasis on social motivations and influences. Research related to alcohol abuse, problem gambling, risky sexual behavior, and disordered eating behaviors are reviewed in turn. Discussion and review of prevention and treatment implications focus primarily on correction of normative misperceptions, mandated treatment, and motivational interviewing. Finally, theoretical discussion is presented regarding the conceptualization of self-determination and intrinsic motivation related to potentially "addictive" healthy and unhealthy behaviors.

Chapter 7 - Prospective memory is defined as memory for actions to be performed in the future, such as remembering to take a medication or remembering to mail a bill. A cognitive approach has yielded significant advances in our understanding of prospective memory processes. However, in this chapter, we argue that further insight can be gained by integrating motivational constructs. Specifically, the authors outline a new, goal-based motivational-cognitive model of prospective memory in which goal-related prospective memories are viewed as benefiting from both effortful and automatic processing throughout all phases of the prospective memory task. Drawing on contemporary goal frameworks, the new model views goals as knowledge structures with associative links to prospective memories. As a result of these associative connections, goal-related prospective memories are predicted (a) to be perceived as more important, (b) to benefit from greater use of mnemonic strategies, (c) to show greater accessibility in memory, (d) to show preferential allocation of attention during retrieval and performance, and (e) to benefit from automatic retrieval processes. Consequently, these processes are predicted to contribute to superior performance for goal-related prospective memories. In this chapter, we also review evidence that supports our new model. By guiding research into the motivational processes contributing to prospective memory, we hope to contribute to a more complete and ecologically valid understanding of prospective memory performance.

Chapter 8 - Psychological theories on motivation generally focus on one single attitude object, or goal, at a time. However, people always hold multiple goals simultaneously. Therefore, motivation with respect to one goal should be considered within the context of other goals that are part of the individual's personal goal system. Some goals coincide when the attainment of one goal leads to goal progress of another. Others goals may be in conflict with one another. A conflict in goals occurs when various equally desired end states are mutually exclusive, either because they draw from similar limited resources or because they are logically incompatible. Conflict in goals may lead to mixed emotions about a goal and to feelings of ambivalence. Empirical research within the field of health behavior strongly suggests that examining behavior within the context of the personal goal structure adds significantly to our understanding of behavioral change.

Chapter 9 - During the past 20 years, there's been an abundance of research that has addressed the distinction between implicit and explicit cognitive processes. Implicit processes are those that can occur spontaneously and without conscious intent or awareness; explicit processes are those that occur with such intent and awareness. Recently, several of these studies have included addressing the effects of various motivational pursuits – in particular, goal-directed pursuits.

Researchers who investigate the implicit nature of goal-directed pursuits usually propose that such endeavors are represented as organized knowledge structures housed within a person's overall network of underlying associations. As a result, these structures can be activated in the same way that other concepts are activated. In other words, if appropriate cues are presented in the environment, these structures become activated; in turn, they operate toward completion, and both the activation and the operation can occur without the need for conscious awareness and/or maintenance.

As examples, consider two experiments. In one experiment, participants who were incidentally exposed to words related to the goal of achievement (e.g., succeed, attain, master), tended to perform better on a task, compared to participants who were not primed with the same words (Bargh, Gollwitzer, Lee-Chai, Barndollar, & Trotschel, 2001). In a second experiment, participants who were asked to concentrate on specific characteristics of a close friend, tended to express more willingness to help in a subsequent situation, compared to participants who were not asked to concentrate on characteristics of a friend (Fitzsimons & Bargh, 2003). In these experiments, the goals that were activated were achievement and helpfulness, respectively. In both cases, the goals apparently operated without the need for conscious awareness or maintenance.

Chapter 10 - Research into why individuals do or do not engage in important health behaviors is often approached from the perspective of expectancy-value theories of motivation. Such theories suggest that the motivation to engage in a behavior is regulated by the outcome expectancies for the behavior and the value of the outcome. However, the relationship of expectancies and values to stable individual differences known to affect motivation are often overlooked. In this chapter the links between procrastination, a behavioral style known to be linked to poor health behaviors, and household safety behaviors were examined using an expectancy-value theory (EVT) framework. Adults (N = 254) recruited from the community and the Internet completed self-report measures of procrastination, health self-efficacy, household safety behaviors, previous experiences with household accidents, and questions about the importance of keeping their homes free from potential accidents. Despite the fact that chronic procrastinators were more likely to have experienced a household accident that could have been prevented, procrastination was negatively related to the performance of household safety behaviors. Procrastination was also negatively related to health-self-efficacy and household safety value. Hierarchical regression testing the EVT variables found support for the predictive value of both outcome expectancies (self-efficacy) and value, but not their product, in explaining household safety behaviors after controlling for procrastination. Separate path analyses tested whether self-efficacy and valuing household safety mediated the relationship between procrastination and household safety behaviors. Safety value and self-efficacy each partially mediated the procrastination-household safety behaviour relationship after controlling for procrastination. These findings suggest that EVT may be useful for explaining motivations for household safety behaviors in general, and may also provide insight into the lack of motivation for these behaviors demonstrated by procrastinators.

Chapter 11 - Organisms need information about their own organism's state, and about the surrounding in order to survive and reproduce. Even the simple organisms, such as protozoans utilize instantly available information that is provided by oncoming stimulation. The very first form of stimulus seeking – testing movements - develops in Platyhelminthes. The further evolution of stimulus seeking behavior is discussed in terms of the theory of integrative levels. The new qualities emerging at the developing levels of integration change both mechanisms of behavior, and it's form. The major steps of information seeking behavior evolution are: orienting reflex, locomotor exploration, investigatory responses, perceptual exploration, manipulatory responses, play, and cognitive curiosity. The analysis of each behavioral activity is conducted on the basis of comparative method. The cognitive activity is presented as an product of exploratory activity and play evolution. Therefore, the multi factorial nature of motivation of information seeking is finally discussed.

Chapter 12 - Personal norms are the main motivator of intention to perform pro-social behaviour. They reflect the beliefs people have about what is right and what is wrong. Schwartz's norm activation model states that awareness of consequences and ascription of responsibility are related to personal norms, but it is not clear how, as the norm activation model can be interpreted as a moderator and a mediator model. In this chapter we compared both interpretations of the norm activation model and found that our data support a mediator model. This means that personal norms are influenced by awareness of consequences and ascription of responsibility. Targeting awareness of consequences and ascription of responsibility would activate personal norms which increases the behavioural intention.

Chapter 13 - HIV has become a worldwide pandemic. Indeed, there are a number of factors that are involved in the transmission and progression of HIV to AIDS. Therefore, this chapter first identifies the various behaviors that have contributed to the risk of contracting HIV. Although HIV testing is an essential component in the detection and transmission of HIV, individuals who are most at-risk of contracting HIV often fail to pursue such testing. This is unfortunate because knowledge of one's seropositivity can assist in the management of this disease, and reduce transmission of HIV to others. This chapter will highlight scientific advances in the detection of HIV, as well as methods of motivating individuals to effectively manage this potentially fatal condition.

Chapter 14 - The familiar experience of a conflict between our actions and our normative beliefs was termed *akrasia* by the ancient Greeks. Philosophical theories of akrasia are helpful in illuminating situations of unwilling addiction as well as other disorders of motivation. The phenomenon of akrasia creates problems for theories of rational action, and this difficulty has meant that some philosophical approaches to akrasia have been forced to deny that akrasia really exists at all. If genuine akrasia is to be adequately characterised, it may be helpful to examine these attempts and their outcomes.

In: Psychology of Motivation
Editor: Lois V. Brown, pp. 1-3

ISBN: 978-1-60021-598-8
© 2007 Nova Science Publishers, Inc.

Expert Commentary A

RESEARCH ON FUNDAMENTAL MOTIVES

Kenneth R. Olson

Motives refer to what people desire and value. Steven Reiss and colleagues have identified 16 fundamental human motives (Reiss & Havercamp, 2005) that are purported to be universal. The development of a psychometrically sound measure of these motives, the Reiss Profile of Motivation Sensitivities, affords a variety of research possibilities. Comparisons of this scale with measures of related psychological variables would provide additional information regarding construct validity of the Reiss Profile and further our understanding of the nature of the fundamental motives.

A variable that appears related to motives is the widely studied general motivational orientation of approach versus avoidance. Individuals with an approach orientation are primarily motivated by positive incentives and potential rewards, whereas individuals with an avoidance orientation are motivated to avoid potentially negative and aversive outcomes. Fundamental motives should be related to fundamental motivational orientations. Correlations of the Reiss Profile with measures of approach and avoidance would identify the motives that are primarily approach oriented and the motives that are avoidance oriented.

The constructs of motives, values, and goals also share conceptual similarities. Each refer to psychological constructs that are meaningful and desirable to people and that serve to direct their behavior. Future research that compares the Reiss Profile with measures of values and goals would clarify similarities and differences between specific fundamental motives, values, and goals and the extent of their relationship to each other.

Schwartz (1994) identified ten basic human values that people view as important in life. These values were present across diverse cultures and exhibited a two-dimensional structure. The first value dimension involved openness to change versus preservation of the status quo. The second dimension involved self-enhancement versus self- transcendent values. Reiss has noted that the fundamental motives he identified are related to the construct of values.

Values are also closely related to the construct of goals. Schwartz defined values as desirable trans-situational goals that serve as guiding principles in people's lives. Grouzet et al. (2005) identified the structure of goal contents across 15 cultures. The 11 types of goals were defined by two primary dimensions underlying the goals: (1) intrinsic (e,g., self-acceptance, affiliation) versus extrinsic (e.g., financial success, image), and (2) self-transcendent (e.g., spirituality) versus physical (e.g., hedonism). The first dimension refers to goals oriented toward inherent psychological needs as opposed to external rewards or praise. The second dimension represents goals that are primarily concerned with maintaining and enhancing one's physical pleasure and survival as opposed to those concerned with something higher. This dimension is also akin to what religious writings refer to as conflicts between the spirit and the flesh. The second dimension of self- transcendent versus physical goals bears a close conceptual similarity to Schwartz's self- transcendent versus self-enhancement values.

Relations between fundamental motives and basic goals can be logically expected. The motives that underlie and impel people's behavior should be reflected in the goals that they formulate and pursue. The following motive-goal relations can be hypothesized to exist between the Reiss Profile motives and the goals identified by Grouzet et al.(2005): social contact—affiliation, tranquility—safety, acceptance—conformity, romance—hedonism, status—popularity, idealism—community feeling. Conversely, some of the goals (e.g., spirituality) and some of the motives (e.g., curiosity, vengeance) do not seem to have a clear counterpart.

The relation of the Reiss Profile motives to the two underlying goal dimensions is also an issue for future research. For example, the motives of honor, idealism, and family are considered the "higher" motives that are related to self-actualization (Reiss & Havercamp, 2005), and these motives are also statistically related to a measure of purpose in life (Olson & Chapin, in press). These findings suggest that these three motives would be related to the goals of the self-transcendent dimension.

One factor that may limit the relation between motives and goals is the impact of external situational influences. People may fail to adopt goals that are congruent with their underlying motives in the face of perceived pressure from society or significant others. For example, an individual may choose a career goal based on pressure to achieve high salary or occupational prestige rather than considering the extent to which the career would satisfy important personal motives. Research has documented the benefits to well- being from congruence between motives and goals, and the detrimental psychological effects of motive-goal incongruence. Research is needed to determine the extent to which fundamental motives channel the adoption and pursuit of basic human goals.

Previous research has identified underlying dimensions of basic values, goals, and motivational orientations. The construct of fundamental motives would also seem ripe for exploration of underlying dimensions. Factor analysis of motive correlations from several studies may identify underlying dimensions of the 16 Reiss Profile motives.

The research suggested thus far involves the existing Reiss Profile scale. Additions to the current methodology of assessment would serve to advance motive research. The Reiss Profile is a self-rating measure. Development of an other-rating form of the Reiss Profile would expand the range of potential research. Thus, for example, spouses' self- rated motive profiles could be compared to both their partners' self-ratings and to their partners' ratings of their spouse. Some spouses may view their partners' fundamental motives quite differently than partners view their own motives. The relationship of these ratings to marital satisfaction could also be studied.

An other-rating form of the Reiss Profile would also allow historical research similar to that employed with measures of personality traits, such as the Big Five traits. For example, experts on U.S. presidents have used other-rating forms to rate the personality traits of the presidents so that a composite trait profile of the presidents could be compiled. These traits ratings have also been correlated with historians' ratings of presidential greatness in order to determine the traits most closely associated with greatness. A similar approach could be used to assess the fundamental motives of presidents (and other persons).

Development of a short form of the Reiss Profile would also be beneficial. The current scale that measures 16 motives contains 128 items (8 items per motive). A shorter version that retained acceptable reliability and validity would expand the scope of potential research. It would allow measurement of the fundamental motives in studies where constraints regarding time or large numbers of scales limits the number of items that can be administered. This would expand the promising potential of the Reiss Profile to research that could otherwise not be undertaken.

REFERENCES

Grouzet, F., et al. (2005). The structure of goal contents across 15 cultures. *Journal of Personality and Social Psychology, 89,* 800-816.

Olson, K., R., & Chapin, B. (in press). Relations of fundamental motives and psychological needs to well-being and intrinsic motivation. In *Issues in the psychology of motivation,* P. R. Zelick (Ed.). Hauppauge, New York: Nova Science Publishers.

Reiss, S., & Havercamp, S. M. (2005). Motivation in developmental context: A new method for studying self-actualization. *Journal of Humanistic Psychology, 45,* 41-53.

Schwartz, S. H. (1994). Are there universal aspects in the structure and contents of human values? *Journal of Social Issues, 50,* 19-45.

In: Psychology of Motivation
Editor: Lois V. Brown, pp. 5-28

ISBN: 978-1-60021-598-8
© 2007 Nova Science Publishers, Inc.

Chapter 1

MOTIVATED BEHAVIORS: THE INTERACTION OF ATTENTION, HABITUATION AND MEMORY

John W. Wright and Roberta V. Wiediger

Departments of Psychology, Veterinary and Comparative Anatomy,
Pharmacology and Physiology, and Programs in Neuroscience and Biotechnology
Washington State University, Pullman, Washington, USA

ABSTRACT

Motivated behaviors are simultaneously fascinating and difficult to understand. Our fellow humans often exhibit behaviors that appear to have no underlying logic or reasonable explanation. This chapter attempts to identify the important contributors to motivated behaviors. We begin by defining motivation and its relationship with need states. Next the complicated processes of habituation and sensitization are discussed, followed by an analysis of selective attention. The role of memory systems in directing successful motivated behaviors is addressed along with identification of the brain structures that appear to be involved. In this regard there is much to be learned. The chapter concludes with summaries of current research findings concerning the brain angiotensin system's importance in memory consolidation and retrieval. This section includes descriptions of the impact of currently prescribed antihypertensive medications such as angiotensin converting enzyme (ACE) inhibitors and angiotensin receptor blockers (ARBs) on cognition. The overall goal of this chapter is to assist the reader to better understand and appreciate the complex issue of human motivated behaviors from the perspective of research contributions made using both human and animal subjects.

INTRODUCTION

Behavioral scientists view motivated behaviors as arising from a physiological and/or psychological need or desire. This need or desire activates and directs the individual toward appropriate goals that will hopefully satisfy this arousal. Much research effort has been devoted to basic motivated need states such as hunger, thirst, and sexual desire. The physiological and neurological substrates of these motivated behaviors have been reasonably well mapped out (reviewed in Bear et al., 2007). Higher order motivated behaviors such as the need to achieve, belong, create, be happy are much more difficult to study and thus many theories have been formulated to guide research in these areas including those that suggest people achieve such goals by employing rational problem solving strategies (Cognitive theories), by forming expectations concerning the achievement of their goals (Expectancy theories), or by shaping and ordering the desired goals according to social pressures and personal relationships (Social Need theories) (reviewed in Lefton and Brannon, 2006).

The present chapter begins with a discussion of how motivated behaviors are initiated according to needs. How that need state becomes goal-directed, and when achieved how a reward system reinforces the sequence of successful behaviors. This behavioral solution is stored in long-term memory so that it can be recalled at a later time under similar circumstances, thus providing future behavioral advantage to the individual (Figure 1). In the same way unsuccessful behavioral strategies are remembered and not repeated under similar circumstances. The roles of emotional affect and selective attention impact such motivated behaviors and are also considered. An attempt is made to describe the neuroanatomy and neurochemistry that underlie and mediate these processes; however, there are many gaps in our understanding of these systems. This chapter concludes with a consideration of how we are capable of adapting goal-directed behaviors in the face of rapidly changing social and technological environments. In this regard the notion of neural plasticity and the brain angiotensin system are of major importance and will be discussed in some detail.

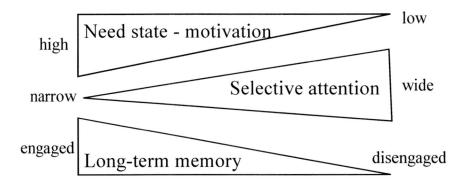

Figure 1. The relationship among a motivated need state, selective attention, and long-term memory. When a need state is high selective attention is very focused on stimuli that are related to satisfying the need and retrieval of relevant information from long-term memory is engaged.

INITIATION OF MOTIVATED BEHAVIORS

1. What are Motivated Behaviors?

The word motivation comes from the same root word as motion (L. motio, fr motus: "to move, a proposal for action"). So motivation invigorates and energizes behavior. But does this explain such behaviors? Most people have short-term and long-term goals that guide and encourage those behaviors believed important in achieving specific goals. It has been said that even a profound lack of ambition requires careful planning. Over the years behavioral scientists have repeatedly changed their definitions of motivation. During this process a notion of what is, and what is not, motivated behavior has evolved. For example, Sigmund Freud believed that the nervous system possesses a reserve of libido or sexual energy. As this libido energy builds up it requires release. If the normal behavioral outlet is blocked or frustrated, it will take an alternative path of expression. This notion led Freud to suggest that should a person be unable to release the libido energy in an acceptable way, irrational and self-damaging behaviors may surface in the form of nervous ticks, coughs, and repetitive motions (Freud, 1908). The famous ethologist, Konrad Lorenz (1950), came to a similar conclusion and believed there to be a "reservoir" of instinctional energy. With buildup over time this energy is released through appropriate outlets such as mating with a partner, or if blocked this energy is released through "displaced behaviors" that may look inappropriate in a particular situation. For example, a young bull elk may not succeed against older bucks in retaining sexually receptive cows during rutting season. He resorts to the displaced behaviors of using his horns to flip soil and brush in the air, or chewing on branches and the bark of trees. Both Freud and Lorenz assumed that once initiated the process of energy buildup and resulting behavioral outlet cannot be terminated. We now realize that many behaviors are simply cancelled and are never directly or indirectly expressed.

2. The Role of Need State

An alternative approach to understanding motivation comes from Walter Cannon's (1929) notion of "homeostasis". This concept assumes that an ongoing attempt is made to maintain many bodily functions at optimal levels. For example, blood glucose level rises following a meal and then begins to slowly fall as cells utilize the glucose. Once glucose has fallen to a lower threshold level it is detected by hypothalamic glucose receptors and the individual experiences hunger. This feeling of hunger energizes and directs attention and behaviors toward obtaining another meal, and so on. Cannon's approach provides only a partial explanation. Human motivated behaviors are not strictly homeostatic since needs are often anticipated prior to the body's detection of a "need state". For example, we may prepare a lunch in the morning in anticipation of a drop in blood glucose during the work day. We may carry an umbrella or coat in anticipation of rain and cold weather later on that same day. On long hikes we carry water and supplies appropriate for the duration of the trip. Cannon's homeostatic notion led to drive-reduction theory (Hull, 1943) that suggests animals and humans strive to reduce needs and drives whenever possible. Thus, we drink to reduce thirst, eat to reduce hunger, have sexual relations to reduce sexual drive, live in less polluted locations to reduce exposure to contaminated environments, and so on. The major short-coming of drive theory is that it does not lend itself to higher order motivated behaviors. In this regard, rather than seeking a constant state of reduced drive level, humans frequently seek increased levels of stimulation. Thus, the optimal state may be a moderate, or even high level of stimulation, rather than as little as possible.

3. Incentive Theory

An explanation for such behaviors as described above led to "incentive" theories of motivation. According to these theories many behaviors are exhibited not because of a need state but because of environmental stimuli that attract us or induce us to action. For example, you consume a delicious large meal and are satiated, but upon seeing the dessert tray you eat a large piece of pie. Thus, many motivated behaviors arise from a need state that drives behavior plus incentives that modify these drives.

4. Intrinsic and Extrinsic Motivations

This brings us to the current notion of intrinsic and extrinsic motivations. An intrinsic motivation encourages behaviors for their own sake. An extrinsic motivation is dependent upon the consequential rewards and punishments resulting from the behavior. Thus, if candy bar consumption occurs because of a threshold drop in blood glucose, this is an intrinsically based motivation. However, if you eat a food that you don't care for in order to please your spouse, this is an extrinsically derived motivation. When we describe ourselves as "highly motivated" we are usually considering extrinsic motivation. A persistence to succeed at school, in a new career or occupation, at mastering a new hobby, are likely motivated by external rewards received, or expected to be received, by these goal-directed behaviors rather than any intrinsic satisfaction (McClelland et al., 1989). In this way primary motivational need states for food, water, shelter, are based on biological needs. Secondary motivations arise from learned experiences within one's environment and do not directly satisfy biological needs but may facilitate these needs.

One of the most famous and frequently utilized approaches to the understanding of motivations is Abraham Maslow's (1970; 1971) hierarchy of needs. Maslow understood the distinction between primary and secondary motivations and extended this concept to include a sequencing and prioritization of these motives. In this way, the basic biological needs formed the foundation of his pyramid, safety and security needs the next level, belongingness and love the next level, esteem needs concerned with accomplishment, success and prestige came next, and finally at the top of the pyramid, "self actualization" suggesting the accomplishment of one's full potential regarding creativity and productivity. This model has been used extensively in businesses and corporations around the world as a means to understand and encourage successful and motivated behaviors by employees. This theory makes use of both intrinsic and extrinsic motivations in the construction of the hierarchy.

THE DECISION TO IGNORE IRRELEVANT STIMULI

1. How do we Sort out Important Information?

Humans are built to focus attention on relevant environmental events and exclude irrelevant events. Our eyes, ears, and nose can quickly be oriented to maximize attention to stimuli within the environment that stand out from the background. Such a system utilizes these distal receptors in a way that provides a survival advantage in dangerous environments and situations. Selective attention processing of relevant information is important to survival. Thus, we are often bombarded with a wealth of incoming information but we selectively attend to only a fraction of these stimuli. Those stimuli that we attend to are deemed the most relevant and important at that instant in time and all other stimuli are ignored or receive limited attention. This is an ongoing process during our waking hours. In a hostile environment we are designed to be on full alert to stimuli that indicate danger or possible harm. Because of the way our brain is configured we respond equivalently to physical, psychological, or environmental threats. An example of physical harm could be a stalker, a "peeping Tom", or mugger who attacks. Psychological threats come in many forms, hard negotiations over business deals, problems raising teenage children, spousal dissatisfaction, pressure from a job supervisor, etc. Environmental threats may include abrupt temperature changes, humidity swings, floods, earthquakes, thunderstorms, etc. All of these require various levels of focused attention and decision making concerning a plan to reduce their physiological, psychological and environmental impact. With experience we are able to predict with increasing precision when and from where in our environment such threats may occur. This ability to predict the occurrence of a possible threat is accompanied by better coping strategies.

2. Habituation and Sensitization

One mechanism all animals, including humans, use to sort out irrelevant stimuli is the process of habituation. Habituation is defined as a decrease in responsiveness to a repeatedly presented stimulus (Harris, 1943; Thorpe, 1966). The practical importance of habituation resides in the simultaneous ability to rapidly "tune out" irrelevant stimuli while permitting heightened attention to the remaining relevant stimuli. For example, a buck grazes near the edge of a forest. A twig snaps and the deer raises his head, ears erect, eyes scanning for danger, body tense, ready to escape. Sensing no threat he returns to grazing. Again a twig snaps and he scans for any possible danger but soon returns to grazing. Through subsequent potential threatening similar stimuli the buck returns to grazing sooner and sooner. Since there appears to be no danger in the environment the buck can attend to other important needs. Now let's say a new sound occurs, perhaps a nearby falling limb. The buck again is alert and then returns to its grazing. This is called sensitization. A new potential threatening stimulus reinstates the partially habituated responses. These events represent a very adaptive pattern of behavior that balances vigilance with the need to satisfy basic needs. Humans make use of these processes during a normal day. For example, reading a novel in a coffee shop would be impossible without "tuning out" extraneous stimuli. However, a sudden unusual noise or loud voice can momentarily divert one's attention and then if there are no continuing distracters, you return to your novel. If you pause from reading this chapter you may temporarily refocus your attention to sounds that you have habituated to. Perhaps distant city noises, a room fan, the ticking of a nearby clock, etc.

3. Selective Attention to Relevant Stimuli

The phenomena of habituation and sensitization contribute to the process of selective attention, i.e. ignoring or filtering irrelevant stimuli and focusing on only the most relevant stimuli to the need or task at hand (Figure 2). Although this process resembles habituation it is different since the intensity of selective processing is increased. Selective attention has an important advantage in that it results in faster reaction time and shorter time to task completion (Posner et al., 1980). Selective attention experiments have been conducted using brain scan techniques. In one such experiment Petersen and colleagues (1988) asked subjects to view a computer screen as an image was flashed for about ½ second. After a short delay a second image was flashed. Each image consisted of small squares or rectangles that could vary in color and moved across the screen at different rates of speed. Although the speed, shape, and color of the objects could change from the first image to the second, the subject was asked to decide whether the images were the same or different under one of two sets of instructions. When selective attention was being tested subjects were asked to pay attention to just one feature, for example shape or color or speed in making the decision. During the divided attention condition subjects were asked to monitor all features and make their decision based on a change in any feature. As the task requirements moved from attention directed at one feature that could be quickly discriminated, to many features that required more time, brain processing spread from the primary visual cortex to both primary and association visual cortices. Thus, attention increased brain activity but as the complexity of the task increased additional brain areas were activated. The investigators concluded that reaction time increases as the task becomes more complex and recruits more brain areas. Along these lines there are many jobs that require multitasking, the process of simultaneously attending to more than one task during a given period of time. There is considerable controversy over whether multitasking compromises the quality of performance for any one task. Brain scan data suggest that as processing increases in complexity the time required to make reasonable decisions also increases, suggesting that multitasking has the potential to negatively impact performance.

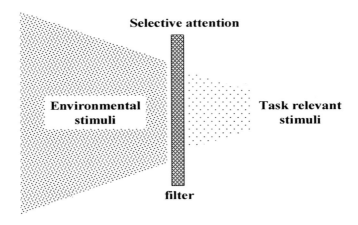

Figure 2. Selective attention can be represented as a variable filter that sorts out task relevant environmental stimuli on a second-to-second basis. This filter can be rapidly modified to accommodate a variety of need states and goals attended to sequentially or in combination.

4. Brain Mediation of Attention

To maintain attention several brain neurochemical pathways are involved that utilize acetylcholine (Ach), dopamine (DA), norepinephrine (NE) and 5-hydroxytryptamine (5-HT). The majority of cell bodies of these neurons are located in the brain stem and project axons to subcortical and cortical locations. For example, NE neurons in the locus ceruleus of the brain stem send axons to the neocortex, and thalamus. These pathways potentiate attention to relevant sensory input and simultaneously reduce attention to low level input. Thus, changes in the neural activity of locus ceruleus neurons correlate with vigilance (Aston-Jones et al., 1998). In this way an increased release of NE within these brain structures appears to enhance the signal-to-noise ratio for relevant environmental stimuli. This system makes possible quick response times to environmental threats and dangers.

INFLUENCE OF MEMORY SYSTEMS ON MOTIVATED BEHAVIORS

1. What Types of Memories do we Use?

Human memory can be divided into short-term memory (also known as primary or working memory) lasting only a few seconds but longer with rehearsal, and long-term memory (secondary or reference memory) that lasts weeks, months, and perhaps years. Short-term memory occurs with information that is perceived to be temporarily valuable. For example, you look up the telephone number of your dentist to make a "check-up appointment". Before you have a chance to dial the number the directory slaps shut. Unless you were actively rehearsing the phone number you will probably have to look it up again. This usually indicates that you did not intend to consolidate this number into long-term memory. Thus, it was a "throw away" piece of information as opposed to the new telephone number of a close friend or relative that you want to remember. Long-term memory can be further divided into *explicit memory* (also known as declarative memory) and *implicit memory* (procedural memory) (Barco et al., 2006; Figure 3). Procedural memory typically consists of motor skills that have been repetitively learned. For instance, how to strike a match, tie your shoes, ride a bicycle, swim the backstroke. Thus, these procedural memories usually have a significant motor component and are very difficult to adequately explain in words or writing but are most often shown to others. When we teach a youngster how to tie his/her shoe laces we begin by demonstrating the skill. Later we may use a "reminder story" to cue the appropriate sequence of steps. For example, "the rabbit races around the tree and into its hole and then it makes a bow with one ear, wraps the other ear around the bow and dives back into its hole to make a bow of its other ear." In this way each movement is cued by the story.

In contrast with implicit memories that are difficult to explain in words, explicit memories consist of autobiographical information and factual knowledge that is rehearsed, encoded and remembered via verbal and written language. These memories permit uniqueness with respect to our family background, differing experiences, and individual training. However, there are also many shared pieces of information and knowledge that shape and define our memories such as mathematical formulas and historical dates that have been placed in long-term memory. These shared memories permit communication among friends, family and colleagues regarding many tasks that require solutions such as how to build a boat, bake a cake, sew a skirt, interpret a map, determine the yards of concrete to fill driveway forms, etc. Both short-term and long-term memories are essential to a successful and productive life.

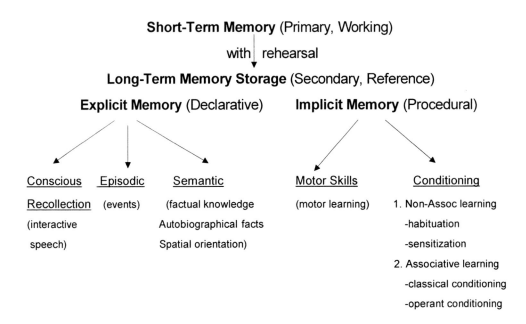

Types of Memory

Short-Term Memory (Primary, Working)

with rehearsal

Long-Term Memory Storage (Secondary, Reference)

Explicit Memory (Declarative)   **Implicit Memory** (Procedural)

Conscious   Episodic   Semantic   Motor Skills   Conditioning

Recollection   (events)   (factual knowledge   (motor learning)   1. Non-Assoc learning

(interactive   Autobiographical facts   -habituation

speech)   Spatial orientation)   -sensitization

                                                                       2. Associative learning

                                                                          -classical conditioning

                                                                          -operant conditioning

Figure 3. With rehearsal short-term memory may result in long-term memory consolidation. The major categories of long-term memory storage are explicit and implicit memories. Subcategories under each are listed.

Disruption of memory due to concussion, brain injury/tumor, encephalitis, stroke, alcoholism/drug abuse may result in amnesia. These traumas typically produce limited amnesia. The memory loss can be categorized as *retrograde amnesia*, i.e. a loss of memory for events prior to the insult; and *anterograde amnesia*, a difficulty with forming new memories following the insult. There can also be combinations of these two forms of amnesia. For example a concussion or head injury patient may present a severe retrograde amnesia for several hours or days prior to the injury, coupled with difficulty remembering events that occurred immediately following the injury.

2. Brain-Mediated Immediate and Delayed Rewards

The basic drives of thirst, hunger, and sex are associated with persistent need states that can be satisfied with water, food, and receptive mate. However, there are instances when the need cannot be immediately met, i.e. water, food, or a sexual partner, is not available. These so-called "consummatory behaviors" are often fixed in form and stereotypic while a delay forces more adaptive and flexible behaviors of searching, foraging, planning, in order to locate the reward. Thus, when the goal cannot be immediately achieved humans and animals make use of past experiences in order to increase the likelihood of a successful behavioral strategy. Such memories are formed by previously learned behaviors under similar sets of circumstances. These learned behaviors can be categorized under *instrumental* and *classical* conditioning paradigms. Under the former type of learning behaviors that increase the probability of satisfying the need are more likely to be retained in memory and used in the future. In contrast, those behaviors that are unsuccessful will be less likely to occur under similar circumstances.

The hypothalamus appears to be intimately involved in controlling motivated behaviors. It is anatomically positioned to detect hormonal changes in the blood stream and in the cerebrospinal fluid. Hypothalamic motivation centers have been identified for thirst, hunger, temperature regulation, circadian rhythms, sex and aggression. These hypothalamic centers are modulated by higher level structures including the limbic system and neocortex (Figure 4). For example, despite being very hungry many of us have food aversions often learned due to a bad experience with a particular food. A very common experience is becoming sick after eating a dish of potato salad at a picnic on a warm summer day. This bout with food poisoning may result in refusal to eat potato salad for many months or years after the incident. How is this mediated? It appears that despite signals from the hypothalamus to engage consummatory repetitive behaviors, these higher centers override this command. Along these lines, it has been shown that electrical stimulation of the amygdala can inhibit aggressive behaviors initiated by the hypothalamus (reviewed in Squire et al., 2003).

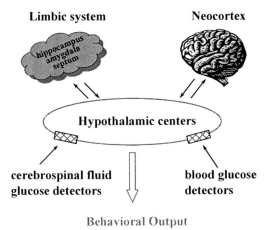

Figure 4. The hypothalamus is responsible for detecting changes in glucose levels in the blood stream and in the cerebrospinal fluid as related to identifying hunger. Similarly, hypothalamic osmodetectors are concerned with body water balance and thirst. The hypothalamus also monitors hormone levels concerned with circadian, sexual and emotional behaviors.

Beginning in the mid 1950s Olds and Milner initiated a series of experiments using electrical stimulation of the brain of rats that began to pinpoint reward pathways. Often these animals learned new behaviors in order to receive electrical stimulation to these pathways. This suggested that the effect of the stimulation was rewarding, and in fact the behaviors that achieved this electrical stimulation increased in probability when placed in similar circumstances at a future time. More recent investigations have indicated similar findings when electrical stimulation is delivered to the midbrain central gray, the locus ceruleus, substantia nigra, caudate nucleus, or nucleus accumbens (Phillips, 1984). These sites have in common proximity to catecholamine releasing neurons especially DA synthesizing neurons. Results such as these led Wise (1982) to propose that drugs of abuse activate these same reward mediating structures and pathways to increase excitement in a mesolimbic DA system.

3. Memory Modifies Motivated Behaviors

As mentioned in the previous section a bad experience with tainted food, water or a sexual partner can lead to profound changes in future behaviors associated with that reward. The mechanisms mediating these changes in behavior appear to be stored in long-term memory. But how can this happen and when and where might these memories be stored? Brain anatomy suggests an explanation to how memories can modify motivated behaviors. Specifically, the striatum, including the putamen and caudate nuclei, receive input from limbic structures including amydala, hippocampus, and prefrontal cortex (Figure 5). In turn, the striatum projects to the lateral hypothalamus, and globus paladus. The pallidum projects to other basal ganglia structures and brain stem motor nuclei that result in connections with the prefrontal cortex and thalamus, thus completing a limbic-striatum-pallidum circuit. Some years ago Mogenson and colleagues (1980) argued that this circuit translates motivational behavior into action. Several limbic structures, most notably the hippocampus along with the prefrontal cortex, are primarily involved in encoding, storing, and retrieving memories and may serve to translate our basic motivations into more complicated and calculated behavioral responses.

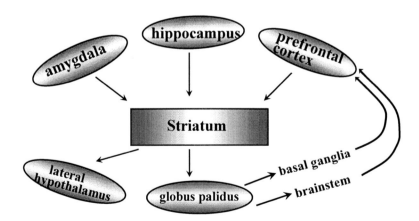

Figure 5. The striatum receives information from limbic structures including the amygdala, hippocampus and prefrontal cortex, and sends information to the lateral hypothalamus and globus palidus. Feedback loops via the basal ganglia and brainstem complete the return pathway to the prefrontal cortex. In this way those brain areas that mediate emotion and motivation are integrated with problem solving and motor structures and pathways.

4. Hippocampal Long-Term Potentiation and Delayed Rewards

Since the 1970s considerable research has been devoted to the phenomenon of long-term potentiation (LTP) and its role in memory storage (Bliss & Coolingridge, 1993). LTP was first discovered by Bliss and Lomo (1973) in the rabbit hippocampus and is produced by applying short but strong excitatory stimulation (tetanus) to presynaptic neurons. This tetanus activates postsynaptic N-methyl D-aspartate (NMDA) receptors resulting in calcium entry and a sustained higher level of activation in these neurons, i.e. a new potentiated level. This phenomenon is thought by many researchers to serve as a basic mechanism of memory encoding and storage in the hippocampus and perhaps in other memory storing structures of the brain. Presumably, if a critical need state is not satisfied then memory mechanisms are activated in order to guide productive behavioral strategies in the direction of locating the reward and satisfying the need state (Figure 1). In order for these memories to be stored it appears that hippocampal LTP may have to be activated to facilitate the underlying electrophysiology and neurochemistry that mediate memory formation. Blockade of NMDA receptors and the formation of hippocampal LTP has a detrimental effect on memory storage, as does the inhibition of protein synthesis (reviewed in Bear et al., 2007). These findings point to an important role for the hippocampus in the storage of information relevant to modifying motivated behaviors.

MEMORY CONSOLIDATION AND MOTIVATED BEHAVIORS

How do we adapt to changes in our lives brought on by new acquaintances, new jobs, new technologies, and new ways of doing familiar tasks? The answer to this question has its basis in the phenomena of neural plasticity. For many years neuroscientists believed that the adult mammalian central nervous system was incapable of neural regeneration, i.e. the formation of new neurons. There was also doubt over the occurrence of synaptic plasticity, the formation of new synapses in the brain. Recently it has become clear that several brain structures evidence neural and synaptic plasticity in the adult mammal. This section begins by describing an emerging model of how memory appears to be consolidated and stored. This requires an understanding of several biochemical cascades made possible by matrix metalloproteinases (MMPs), and tissue inhibitors of matrix metalloproteinases (TIMPs), acting on scaffolding proteins. The following sections discuss the potential roles of the brain angiotensin system, angiotensin converting enzyme (ACE) inhibitors, and angiotensin receptor blockers (ARBs) in memory formation, cognitive processing, and motivation.

1. Current Theories of Memory Consolidation

Previously we described the·contribution of hippocampal LTP to memory formation, and the fact that once glutamate binds to NMDA receptors calcium entry into the neuron occurs. This calcium signal is an important prerequisite to changes in synaptic spine shape, number, and protein synthesis that underlie synaptic reconfiguration (Kelleher et al., 2004). There is growing evidence that systems consolidation involves shifts in the storage location of the consolidated memories from the hippocampus and/or amygdala through association cortex to final storage in the prefrontal cortex and medial temporal lobe (Frankland & Bontempi, 2005). Once the memory has been transmitted to the prefrontal cortex and/or medial temporal lobe it is assumed to represent a permanent and long-lasting "engram" (i.e. memory trace). However, this assumption has been challenged by the reconsolidation theory originally posited some years ago (Misanin et al., 1968; Rubin & Franks, 1969; Rubin, 1976). This reconsolidation theory suggests that the permanence of a long-term memory trace can be disrupted with memory retrieval/reactivation (Nader, 2003). This retrieval process is hypothesized to return the trace to a labile state thus allowing for modification and updating. In support of this theory there appears to be many similarities between the initial consolidation process and the reconsolidation process including: 1) both can be blocked by anisomycin (a generalized protein inhibitor); 2) both appear to require activation of CREB and Zif-268 (reviewed in Lee et al., 2004). There is also recent evidence that consolidation requires brain-derived neurotrophic factor (BDNF) a powerful growth factor, while reconsolidation is dependent upon activation of the scaffolding protein Zif-268 (Lee et al., 2004). An understanding of systems consolidation requires that we discuss several enzyme cascades that are important in permitting the initial consolidation of the memory trace and perhaps the reconsolidation of the memory trace as well. The proteins involved in this process include MMPs, TIMPs, and scaffolding proteins.

The MMPs are a family of proteolytic enzymes important to restructuring of the extracellular matrix and scaffolding proteins (Stamenkovic, 2003). At present over 25 MMPs have been identified and all appear to require activation by serine proteinases. In this way a propeptide must be cleaved off in order to reveal the catalytic domain of the MMP. This activates the MMP and unleashes its enzymatic activity. Several MMPs have been implicated in the processes of angiogenesis (formation of new blood vessels) blastocyte implantation and ovulation (steps involved in the fertilized egg implanting within the uterus), and wound healing (reviewed in Ennis & Matrisian, 1994). Extracellular matrix degradation by MMPs is controlled and accomplished by three important mechanisms: 1) regulation of gene transcription; 2) regulation of pro-enzyme activation; and 3) via the presence of TIMPs. Most MMPs are non-constituitively expressed however, gene transcription may occur via growth factor stimulation, oncogene products, phorbol esters, as well as cell-to-cell and cell-to-ECM interactions. It is also entirely possible for MMPs to activate other MMPs (Yong et al., 1998). These characteristics of MMPs make them very attractive candidates concerning their potential contributions to the phenomena of memory consolidation, reconsolidation, retrieval, and they are thus important to motivated behaviors.

Tissue inhibitors of metalloproteinases 1-4 form a family of secreted glycoproteins (Maskos & Bode, 2003). MMP proteolytic activities can be inhibited by TIMPs that form tight non-covalent complexes with them (Bode et al., 1999; Jeng et al., 2001). Imbalance between the normal levels of MMP activity promotes remodeling, while an inhibition of their actions by TIMPs may result in pathology (Lukes et al., 1999). These imbalances have been seen in arthritis, athrosclerosis, Alzheimer's disease, cancer, Guillain-Barre syndrome, ischemia, infarctions, and other disease states (reviewed in Jeng et al., 2001; Kaczmarek et al., 2002). The hippocampus and cerebellum have been implicated as having the greatest expression of MMPs of any brain structures. Backstrom et al., (1996) reported MMP-9 mRNA and protein in pyramidal neurons of the human hippocampus and dentate gyrus.

Valliant and colleagues (1999) have reported reasonably high levels of MMP-2 and lower levels of MMP-9 in adult rat cerebellum, especially in Purkinje and granular neurons.

Nedivi et al., (1993) were the first to record increased dentate gyrus levels of TIMP-1 mRNA following seizures. Subsequently elevated TIMP-1 mRNA and protein were measured in the hippocampus with seizure (Jaworski et al., 1999). Enhanced MMP-9 mRNA expression was seen in both the dendritic layers and neuronal cell body primarily within the dentate gyrus. These results were interpreted to suggest that MMP-9 expression is involved in activity-dependent remodeling, perhaps via influencing synaptic connections, and are thus relevant to the process of neural plasticity.

There is a wealth of research findings concerning a role for the hippocampus in spatial learning and memory. The importance of this structure is supported by the observation that hippocampal damage results in a compromised ability to solve tasks that demand recognition of spatial cues and strategies (Morris et al., 1990; Sutherland & McDonald, 1990). Once the hippocampus is activated it appears that neural plasticity occurs in the form of LTP along with concomitant changes in synaptic morphology in the dentate gyrus and subfields of the hippocampus (reviewed in Bennington & Frank, 2003; Wright et al., 2002). There is considerably less information concerning the possible extracellular matrix modifications that may occur and mediate memory consolidation. A model that illustrates the presumed steps necessary for memory consolidation is offered in Figure 6. This hypothetical model presents possible relationships among extracellular matrix and MMP molecules and several receptor systems in the control of neural plasticity. Cell surface receptors such as integrins and neural cell adhesion molecules interact with receptor tyrosine kinases at pre- and post-synaptic appositions to influence receptor and cytoskeletal functions. Glutamate release activates NMDA receptors ultimately facilitating calcium entry into the cell. Reconfiguration of extracellular matrix molecules appears to be triggered by calcium signaling. Cellular signaling may also occur via other avenues as well. Activation of cholinergic receptors by acetylcholine is involved in memory consolidation, however recent evidence strongly suggests that pharmacological blockade of cholinergic receptors resulting in inhibition of learning memory can be overcome by the concomitant activation of other receptor systems most notably brain angiotensin receptors. Thus, the brain angiotensin receptor system appears to provide a parallel pathway for initiation of extracellular matrix rearrangement and neural plasticity.

2. The Brain Angiotensin System and Memory

There is accumulating evidence that angiotensins, by direct action or as modulators, influence the roles of other neurotransmitters important in cognitive processing, depression, mood change, and responses to stress. Pharmacological manipulation of brain angiotensins can result in altered mental acuity, antidepressant-like and anxiolytic-like effects (reviewed in Gard, 2002; Gard and Rusted, 2004). Angiotensins have also been implicated in the enhancement of learning acquisition and memory consolidation (reviewed in Wright and Harding, 1997, 2004). The present section considers available evidence linking brain angiotensins with altered cognitive processing, learning and memory. There is growing recognition that the complexity of the brain angiotensin system has been significantly underestimated.

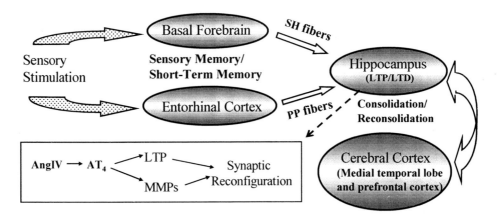

Figure 6. A pathway model describing how sensory stimulation may activate sensory and short-term memories in basal forebrain and entorhinal cortex structures resulting in the formation of long-term potentiation and memory consolidation in the hippocampus. Septo-hippocampal and perforant pathway fibers appear to be of major importance concerning information flow into the hippocampus. The AngIV/AT$_4$ receptor system may facilitate memory consolidation in the hippocampus by at least two mechanisms. Activation of this system facilitates hippocampal LTP and promotes the activation of MMPs that may initiate new plasticity by causing reconfiguration of the ECM. There is reason to suggest that consolidated memories located in the medial temporal lobe and prefrontal cortex can be reactivated in the hippocampus, modified and reconsolidated, thus providing an efficient and rapid mechanism for updating existing memories. Adapted from Wright and Harding (2004).

Formation of Angiotensin Ligands

The protein angiotensinogen serves as a precursor protein to angiotensin peptides (Figure 7). The decapeptide angiotensin I (AngI) is formed by the protease renin (EC 3.4.23.15) acting upon the amino terminal of angiotensinogen. AngI is a substrate for angiotensin converting enzyme (ACE: EC 3.4.15.1), a zinc metalloprotease that hydrolizes the carboxy terminal dipeptide His-Leu to form AngII (Johnston, 1990). AngII is converted to AngIII by glutamyl aminopeptidase A (AP-A: EC 3.4.11.7, or A-like activity) that cleaves the Asp residue at the N-terminal (Chauvel et al., 1994; Rich et al., 1984; Wilk and Healy, 1993). AngII can also be converted to Ang(1-7) by Carb-P cleavage of Phe (reviewed in Wright & Harding, 1997). Membrane alanyl aminopeptidase N (AP-N: EC 3.4.11.2) cleaves Arg at the N-terminal of AngIII to form AngIV. AngIV can be further converted to Ang(3-7) by carboxypeptidase P (Carb-P) and propyl oligopeptidase (PO) cleavage of the Pro-Phe bond. Endopeptidases such as chymotrypsin are capable of cleaving the Val, Tyr, and Ile residues along with dipeptidyl carboxypeptidase that cleaves the His-Pro bond, reducing AngIV and Ang(3-7) to inactive peptide fragments and amino acid constituents (Johnston, 1990; Saavedra, 1992; Speth et al., 2003; Unger et al., 1988).

AngI is considered inactive while AngII and AngIII are full agonists at the AT$_1$ and AT$_2$ receptor subtypes (reviewed in deGasparo et al., 2000). AngIV binds with low affinity at the AT$_1$ and AT$_2$ receptor subtypes (Bennett and Snyder, 1976; Glossman et al., 1974; Harding et al., 1992), but with high affinity and specificity at the AT$_4$ receptor subtype (Bernier et al., 1994; Harding et al., 1992; Jarvis et al., 1992). A specific binding site for Ang(1-7) has been reported (Ferrario 2003; Neves et al., 2003; Santos et al., 2000), but not fully elucidated.

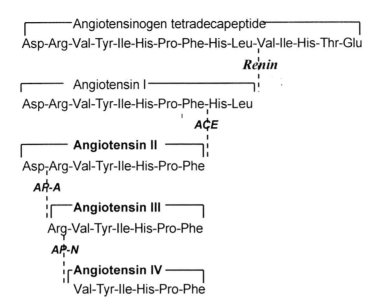

Figure 7. Peptide structures and enzymes involved in the conversion of the tetradecapeptide portion of angiotensinogen to angiotensin I through angiotensin IV. Biologically active angiotensins include angiotensins II, III, IV. Adapted from Wright and Harding (2004).

Angiotensin IV and the AT₄ Receptor Subtype in Memory

The renin-angiotensin system (RAS) mediates several physiologies and behaviors including blood pressure, sodium and body water balance, cyclicity of reproductive hormones and sexual behaviors, and pituitary gland hormones. These functions appear to be under the control of the AT_1 receptor subtype (Allen et al., 2000; deGasparo et al. 2000; Gard, 2002; Thomas and Mendelsohn, 2003). A second subtype, the AT_2, has also been implicated in the regulation of blood pressure, renal function, and vascular growth (deGasparo and Siragy 1999; deGasparo et al. 2000; Speth et al. 1995). The octapeptide AngII has traditionally been considered the end-product of the RAS and therefore the active ligand at these receptors subtypes. Accumulating evidence now indicates that additional shorter chain angiotensins also serve as effector peptides in this system. These peptides include the heptapeptide des Asp[1]-AngII referred to as angiotensin III (AngIII) (Vauquelin et al. 2002; Wright and Harding, 1997), the hexapeptide des Asp[1], des Arg[2]-AngII referred to as AngIV (Albiston et al., 2003; deGasparo et al., 2000; Thomas and Mendelsohn, 2003; Wright and Harding, 1994, 1997, 2004; Wright et al., 1995), and the heptapeptide des Phe[8]-AngII referred to as Ang(1-7) (Ferrario, 2003; Ferrario et al., 1997; Santos et al., 2000). The proposed functions mediated by AngIV include influences upon blood flow (Coleman et al., 1998; Kramar et al., 1997; Møeller et al., 1999; Slinker et al., 1999), kidney natriuresis (Hamilton et al., 2001; Handa et al., 1998), expression of plasminogen activator inhibitor (PAI-1) in endothelial cells (Kerins et al., 1995: Mehta et al., 2002) and in epithelial cells of the kidney proximal tubule (Gesualdo et al., 1999), and memory facilitation (reviewed in Albiston et al., 2003; Bohlen und Halback, 2003; Wright et al., 2002). The functions thus far identified for Ang(1-7) include vasopressin, nitric oxide (NO), and prostaglandin release, and facilitation of baroreceptor reflex sensitivity (Santos, 2000).

Our laboratory has measured facilitated Morris water maze performance in scopolamine, or mecamylamine, pretreated rats with icv treatment of AngIV analogs (Olson et al., 2004; Pederson et al. 1998; Wright et al., 1999). This suggests a role for AngIV in the facilitation of cognitive processing noted during treatment with ACE inhibitors. It has also been established that Ang(1-7) and AngI(3-10) levels are elevated during treatment with ACE inhibitors (Lawrence et al., 1990). Both AngII(2-7) and AngI(3-10) bind at the AT_4 receptor subtype with affinities nearly comparable to that of native AngIV (Sardinia et al., 1993). Also, conversion of Ang(1-7) to a ligand that acts at the AT_4 receptor is not only possible, but likely.

3. ACE Inhibitors and Cognition

With the advent of ACE inhibitors to treat hypertension, congestive heart failure, and following cardiac infarction, came the anecdotal observations that these medications also facilitated cognitive functioning and feelings of well-being. Croog et al. (1986) employed 626 mild to moderated hypertensive male patients in randomized double-blind trials over a 24-week study. Patient self-reports indicated improved mental acuity at work, less sexual dysfunction, and increased sense of well-being on captopril. There was no change with propranolol treatment, and a decline in those patients placed on methyldopa. Blood pressure was equivalently controlled in all three treatment groups. Deicken (1986) and Zubenko et al., (1984) have reported captopril-induced mood elevating effects in depressed patients. Barnes et al. (1992) posited that elevated brain AngII levels may interfere with acetylcholine (Ach) release that in turn interferes with cognitive processing (Bartus et al., 1982). According to this hypothesis ACE inhibitors may facilitate cognitive functioning by reducing the synthesis of AngII thus removing an inhibitory influence upon Ach release (Barnes et al., 1990). In support of this hypothesis Costall and colleagues (1989) treated mice with captopril or ceranapril and measured a habituatory response of moving from a brightly lit area to the darker area of a light/dark box. The muscarinic acetylcholine receptor antagonist scopolamine impaired habituation, while captopril and ceranapril were both effective at countering this scopolamine effect (Barnes et al., 1992). Scopolamine has also been shown to delay the time required for rats to locate a submerged platform in the Morris water maze task (Morris, 1984). Treatment with ceranapril offset this scopolamine-induced impairment such that escape times were not different from controls. In further support, Barnes and colleagues (Barnes et al., 1991a,b) reported high binding densities for [^{3}H]-ceranapril in rat striatum and hippocampus, and human caudate, attributed to ACE in the mirovasculature and perhaps at extravascular sites. Intravenous pretreatment with captopril reduced subsequent [^{3}H]-ceranapril binding in most areas of the brain, except the striatum and brain stem, measured 20 min following treatment. Barnes and colleagues (1989) have also reported AngII-induced interference with potassium-mediated release of [^{3}H]-Ach from rat entorhinal cortex slices. This AngII effect could be blocked by the AT_1 receptor antagonist sarthran. Along these lines, Mondadori and Etienne (1990) found that captopril and enalapril reduced electroshock-induced amnesia in mice. These animals were trained to avoid the dark compartment of a two-chamber passive avoidance apparatus by the application of foot shock in the dark side immediately following an electroconvulsive shock. Recall of the conditioned response was facilitated in those mice given ACE inhibitors one hour prior to the conditioning trial. Flood and Morley (1993) reported similar results using an active avoidance task in mice. Barnes et al. (1990, 1991b) have shown that reasonably low doses of losartan and the AT_2 receptor antagonist P123177 improved scopolamine-impaired performance in the previously described habituation test. Similarly, DeNoble (1991) measured impaired performance on a passive avoidance task in rats icv treated with renin. This impairment could be offset with ACE inhibitor treatment or by the application of the AT_1 receptor antagonists EXP3312 or EXP3880, but not PD123177. The proposal that ACE inhibitors enhance learning has been challenged by Chen and Mendelsohn (1992) who reported that a high oral dose of ceranapril in rats inhibited ACE at the CVOs, but not within blood-brain barrier protected structures. This suggests that ceranapril does not cross the blood-brain barrier.

4. Angiotensin Receptor Blockers and Cognition

AT_1 receptor antagonists (losartan, olmosartan, valsartan, irbesartan) have been increasingly prescribed to control essential hypertension since FDA approval several years ago (Oparil et al., 2001; Basile and Chrysant, 2006). In addition to reducing blood pressure these compounds have been noted to improve cognitive functioning (Gard and Rusted, 2004; Trenkwalder, 2002). It appears likely that such improvement in cognition, especially memory consolidation and retrieval, occur at least in part due to AngIV facilitation of AT_4 receptors coupled with decreased AT_1 receptor activation. Thus, the negative impact of AT_1 receptor activation on memory encoding and consolidation is greatly reduced with ARB treatment.

CONCLUSION

Available research findings concerning the roles of attention, habituation and memory in facilitating and guiding motivated behaviors are presently reviewed. At the simplest level motivated behaviors are designed to satisfy basic intrinsic need states such as thirst, hunger and safety needs, as well as reproductive behaviors. An understanding of higher order need states, driven by extrinsic motivation and involving memory systems, requires more complicated analyses. The use of memory recall concerning previously employed strategies under similar circumstances increases the probability of successful solutions. Several theories of memory consolidation are presented including those concerning the brain angiotensin system. The involvement of the angiotensin IV/AT_4 receptor system appears to be critical to successful encoding, consolidation and retrieval of relevant memories. A great deal of valuable information is presently being accumulated from research programs investigating the positive cognitive effects of antihypertensive medications such as ACE inhibitors and angiotensin receptor blockers. Future research efforts must be directed at achieving a better understanding of how the brain contributes to the initiation, interpretation, and termination of motivated behaviors.

ACKNOWLEDGMENTS

The work from our laboratory presented in this chapter was supported by NIH grant RO1-HL64245-03, NSF grant IBN-0091337, the Edward E. and Lucille I. Lainge Endowment for Alzheimer's Disease Research, and funds provided for medical and biological research by the State of Washington Initiative Measure No. 171. We thank Mrs. Ruth day for secretarial assistance provided during the course of writing this manuscript.

REFERENCES

Albiston, A.L., Mustafa, T., McDowall, S.G., Mendelsohn, F.A., Lee, J., and Chai, S.Y. (2003). AT(4) receptor is insulin-regulated membrane aminopeptidase: potential mechanisms of memory enhancement. *Trends in Endocrinology and Metabolism,* 14: 72-77.

Allen, A.M., Oldfield, B.J., Giles, M.E., Paxinos, G., McKinley, M.J., and Mendelsohn, F.A. (2000). Localization of angiotensin receptors in the nervous system. Pages 79-124, in Quirion, R., Bjorklund, A., and Hodfelt, T. (Eds.), *Handbook of Chemical Neuroanatomy.* Elsevier, Amsterdam.

Aston-Jones, G., Rajkowski, J., Ivanova, S., Usher, M., and Cohen, J. (1998). Neuromodulation and cognitive performance: Recent studies of noradrenergic locus ceruleus neurons in behaving monkeys. *Advances in Pharmacology,* 42: 755-759.

Backstrom, J.R., Giselle, P.L., Cullen, M.J., and Tőkés, Z.A. (1996). Matrix metalloproteinase-9 (MMP-9) is synthesized in neurons of the human hippocampus and is capable of degrading the amyloid-β peptide (1-40). *Journal of Neuroscience,* 16: 7910-7919.

Barco, A., Vailey, C.H., and Kandel, E.R. (2006). Common molecular mechanism in explicit and implicit memory. *Journal of Neurochemistry,* 97: 1520-1533.

Barnes, J.M., Barnes, N.M., Costall, B., Coughlan, J., Horovitz, Z.P., Kelly, M.E., Naylor, R.J., and Tomkins, D.M. (1989). ACE inhibition and cognition. In MacGregor, G.A. and Sever, P.S. (Eds.), *Current Advances in ACE Inhibition.* Churchill Livingston Press, New York, pp. 159-171.

Barnes, J.M., Barnes, N.M., Costall, B., Coughlan, J., Kelly, M.E., Naylor, R.J., Tomkins, D.M., and Williams, T.J. (1992). Angiotensin-converting enzyme inhibition, angiotensin, and cognition. *Journal of Cardiovascular Pharmacology,* 19 (Suppl.6): 563-571.

Barnes, N.M., Champaneria, S., Costall, B., Kelly, M.E., Murphy, D.A., and Naylor, R.J. (1990). Cognitive enhancing actions of DuP 753 detected in a mouse habituation paradigm. *Neuroreport,* 1: 239-242.

Barnes, N.M., Cheng, C.H., Costall, B., Naylor, R.J., Williams, T.J., and Wischik, C.M. (1991a). Angiotensin converting enzyme density is increased in temporal cortex from patients with Alzheimer's disease. *European Journal of Pharmacology,* 20: 289-292.

Barnes, N.M., Costall, B., Kelly, M.E., Murphy, D.A., and Naylor, R.J. (1991b). Cognitive enhancing actions of PD123177 detected in a mouse habituation paradigm. *Neuroreport,* 2: 351-353.

Bartus, R.T., Dean, R.L., Beer, B., and Lippa, A.S. (1982). The cholinergic hypothesis of geriatric memory dysfunction. *Science,* 217: 408-417.

Basile J.N., and Chrysant S. (2006). The importance of early antihypertensive efficacy: The role of angiotensin II receptor blocker therapy. *Journal of Human Hypertension,* 20:169-175.

Bear MF, Connors BW, and Paradiso MA. (2007). *Neuroscience, Exploring the Brain.* Lippincott Williams & Wilkins, Philadelphia, PA, third edition, pp. 510-531.

Benington, J.H., and Frank, M.G. (2003). Cellular and molecular connections between sleep and synaptic plasticity. *Progress in Neurobiology,* 69: 71-101.

Bennett, Jr. J.P., and Snyder, S.H. (1976). Angiotensin II binding to mammalian brain membranes. *Journal of Biological Chemistry,* 251:7423-7430.

Bernier, S.G., Fournier, A., and Guillemette, G. (1994). A specific binding site recognizing a fragment of angiotensin II in bovine adrenal cortex membranes. *European Journal of Pharmacology,* 271: 55-63.

Bliss, T.B.P., and Collingridge, G.L. (1993). A synaptic model of memory: Long-term potentiation in the hippocampus. *Nature,* 361:31-39.

Bliss, T.B.P., and Lomo, T.J. (1973). Long-lasting potentiation of synaptic transmission in the dentate area of the anaesthetized rabbit following stimulation of the perforant path. *Journal of Physiology,* 232:331-356.

Bode, W., Fernandez-Catalan, C., Tschesche, H., Grams, F., Nagase, H., and Maskos, K., (1999). Structural properties of matrix metalloproteinases. *Cellular and Molecular Life Sciences,* 55, 639-652.

Bohlen und Halback, O.V. (2003). Angiotensin IV in the central nervous system. *Cell and Tissue Research,* 311: 1-9.

Cannon, E.B. (1929). Organization for physiological homeostasis. *Physiological Review,* 9:399-431.

Chauvel, E.N., Llorens-Cortes, C., Coric, P., Wilk, S., Roques, B.P., and Fournie-Zaluski, M.C. (1994). Differential inhibition of aminopeptidase A and aminopeptidase N by new-amino thiols. *Journal of Medicinal Chemistry,* 37: 2950-2957.

Chen, B.Z., and Mendelsohn, F.A.O. (1992). Effect of acute and chronic administration of ceranapril on angiotensin converting enzyme in plasma, kidney, lung, brain-regions and cerebrospinal-fluid of rats. *Neuropharmacology,* 31: 929-935.

Coleman, J.K., Krebs, L.T., Hamilton, T.A., Ong, B., Lawrence, K.A., Sardinia, M.F., Harding, J.W., and Wright, J.W. (1998). Autoradiographic identification of kidney angiotensin IV binding sites and angiotensin IV-induced renal blood flow changes in rats. *Peptides,* 19: 269-277.

Costall, B., Coughlan, J., Horovitz, Z.P., Kelly, M.E., Naylor, R.J., and Tomkins, D.M. (1989). The effects of ACE inhibitors captopril and SQ29852 in rodent tests of cognition. *Pharmacology, Biochemistry, and Behavior,* 33: 573-579.

Croog, S.H., Levine, S., Testa, M.A., Brown, B., Bulpitt, C.J., Jinkins, C.D., Klerman, G.L., and Williams, G.H. (1986). The effects of antihypertensive therapy on the quality of life. *The New England Journal of Medicine,* 314: 1657-1664.

deGasparo, M., Catt, K.J., Inagami, T., Wright, J.W., and Unger, T. (2000). International Union of Pharmacology. XXIII. The angiotensin II receptors. *Pharmacological Review,* 52: 415-72.

deGasparo, M., and Siragy, H.M. (1999). The AT$_2$ receptor: Fact, fancy and fantasy. *Regulatory Peptide,* 81: 11-24.

Deicken, R.F. (1986). Captopril treatment of depression. *Biological Psychiatry,* 12: 1425-1428.

DeNoble, V.J., DeNoble, K.F., Spencer, K.R., Chiu, A.T., Wong, P.C., and Timmermans, B.M. (1991). Non-peptide angiotensin II receptor antagonist and angiotensin-converting enzyme inhibitor: effect on a renin-induced deficit of a passive avoidance response in rats. *Brain Research,* 561: 230-235.

Ennis B.W., and Matrisian L.M. (1994). Matrix degrading metalloproteinases. J. *Neurooncology,* 18: 105-109.

Ferrario, C.M. (2003). Contribution of angiotensin-(1-7) to cardiovascular physiology and pathology. *Current Hypertension Report,* 5: 129-134.

Ferrario, C.M., Chappell, M.C., Tallant, E.A., Brosnihan, K.B., and Diz, D.I. (1997). Counterregulatory actions of angiotensin-(1-7). *Hypertension,* 30: 535-541.

Flood, J.F., and Morley, J.E. (1993). Dose-response differences in the ability of ramipril to improve retention in diabetic mice. *European Journal of Pharmacology,* 240: 311-314.

Frankland, P. W., and Bontempi, B. (2005). The organization of recent and remote memories. *Nature Reviews Neuroscience,* 6, 119-130.

Freud S. (1908/1963). "Civilized" sexual morality and modern nervousness. In P. Rieff (Ed.), *Freud, Sexuality and the Psychology of Love.* New York: Collier Books pp. 20-40. (Original work published 1908).

Gard, P.R. (2002). The role of angiotensin II in cognition and behaviour. *European Journal of Pharmacology,* 438: 1-14.

Gard, P.R., and Rusted, J.M. (2004). Angiotensin and Alzheimer's disese: therapeutic prospects. *Expert Review of Neurotherapeutics,* 4:87-96.

Gesualdo, L., Ranieri, E., Monno, R., Rossiello, M.R., Colucci, M., Semeraro, N., Grandaliano, G., Schena, F.P., Ursi, M., and Cerullo, G., (1999). Angiotensin IV stimulates plasminogen activator inhibitor-1 expression in proximal tubular epithelial cells. *Kidney International,* 56: 461-470.

Glossmann, H., Baukal, A., and Catt, K.J. (1974). Angiotensin II receptors in bovine adrenal cortex. Modification of angiotensin II binding by guanyl nucleotides. *Journal of Biological Chemistry,* 249: 664-666.

Hamilton, T.A., Handa, R.K., Harding, J.W., and Wright, J.W. (2001). A role for the AT$_4$/angiotensin IV system in mediating natriuresis in the rat. *Peptides,* 22: 935-944.

Handa, R.K., Krebs, L.T., Harding, J.W., and Handa, S.E. (1998). Angioensin IV AT$_4$-receptor system in the rat kidney. *The American Journal of Physiology,* 274: F290-F299.

Harding, J.W., Cook, V.I., Miller-Wing, A.V., Hanesworth, J.M., Sardinia, M.F., Hall, K.L., Stobb, J.W., Swanson, G.N., Coleman, J.K., Wright, J.W., and Harding, E.C. (1992). Identification of an AII (3-8) AIV binding site in guinea pig hippocampus. *Brain Research,* 583: 340-343.

Harris, J.D. (1943). Habituatory response decrement in the intact organism. *Psychological Bulletin,* 40:385-422.

Hull, C.L. (1943). *Principles of Behavior: An Introduction to Behavior Theory.* New York: D. Appleton Press.

Jarvis, M.F., Gessner, G.W., and Ly, C.G., (1992). The angiotensin hexapeptide 3-8 fragment potently inhibits [^{125}I] angiotensin II binding to non-AT$_1$ or -AT$_2$ recognition sites in bovine adrenal cortex. *European Journal of Pharmacology*, 219: 319-322.

Jaworski, J., Biedermann, I.W., Lapinska, J., Szklarczyk, A., Figiel, I., Konopka, D., Nowicka, D., Filipkowski, R.K., Hetman, M., Kowalczyk, A., and Kaczmarek, L. (1999). Neuronal excitation-driven and AP-1-dependent activation of timp-1 gene expression in rodent hippocams. *Journal of Biological Chemistry*, 274, 28106-28112.

Jeng, A., Gonnell, N., and Skiles, J. (2001). The design, structure, and therapeutic application of matrix metalloproteinase inhibitors. *Current Medicinal Chemistry*, 8, 425-474.

Johnston, C.I. (1990). Biochemistry and pharmacology of the renin-angiotensin system. *Drugs*, 39: 21-31.

Kaczmarek, L., Lapinska-Dzwonek, J., and Szymczak, S. (2002). Matrix metalloproteinases in the adult brain physiology: a link between c-Fos, AP-1 and remodeling of neuronal connections? *EMBO Journal*, 21, 6643-6648.

Kelleher, III, R.J., Govindarajan, A., and Tenegawa, S. (2004). Translational regulatory mechanisms in persistent forms of synaptic plasticity. *Neuron*, 44, 59-73.

Kerins, D.M., Hao, Q., and Vaughan, D.E. (1995). Angiotensin induction of PAI-1 expression in endothelial cells is mediated by the hexapeptide angiotensin IV. *The Journal of Clinical Investigation*, 96: 2515-2520.

Kramár, E.A., Harding, J.W., and Wright, J.W. (1997). Angiotensin II-, and IV-induced changes in cerebral blood flow: Roles of AT$_1$, AT$_2$, and AT$_4$ receptor subtypes. *Regulatory Peptides*, 68: 131-138.

Lawrence, A.C., Evin, G., Kladis, A., and Campbell, D.J. (1990). An alternative strategy for the radioimmunoassay of angiotensin peptides using amino-terminal-directed antisera: measurement of eight angiotensin peptides in human plasma. *Journal of Hypertension*, 8: 715-724.

Lee, J.L.C., Everitt, B.J., and Thomas, K.L. (2004). Independent cellular processes for hippocampal memory consolidation and reconsolidation. *Science*, 304, 839-843.

Lefton, LA, and Brannon, L. (2006). *Psychology*. Pearson/Allyn and Bacon, Boston MA, ninth edition, pp. 416-424.

Lorenz, K. (1950). The comparative method in studying innate behaviour patterns. *Symposia of the Society for Experimental Biology*, 4:221-268.

Lukes, A., Mun-Bryce, S., Lukes, M., and Rosenberg, G.A. (1999). Extracellular matrix degradation by metalloproteinases and central nervous system diseases. *Molecular Neurobiology*, 19, 267-284.

Maskos, K., and Bode, W. (2003). Structural basis of matrix metalloproteinase and tissue inhibitors of metalloproteinases. *Molecular Biotechnology*, 25, 241-266.

Maslow, A.H. (1970). *Motivation and Personality*. New York: Harper & Row, second edition.

Maslow, A.H. (1971). *The farther Reaches of Human Nature*. New York: Viking Press.

McClelland, D.C., Koestner, R., and Weinberger, J. (1989). How do self-attributed and implicit motives differ? *Psychological Review*, 96:690-702.

Mehta, J.L., Li, D.Y., Yang, H., and Raizada, M.K. (2002). Angiotensin II and IV stimulate expression and release of plasminogen activator inhibitor-1 in cultured human coronary artery endothelial cells. *Journal of Cardiovascular and Pharmacology*, 39: 789-794.

Misanin, J.R., Miller, R.R., and Lewis, D.J. (1968). Retrograde amnesia produced by electroconvulsive shock after reactivation of a consolidated memory trace. *Science*, 160, 203-204.

Møeller, I., Clune, E.F., Fennessy, P.A., Bingley, J.A., Albiston, A.L., Mendelsohn, F.A., and Chai, S.Y. (1999). Up regulation of AT_4 receptor levels in carotid arteries following balloon injury. *Regulatory Peptides,* 83: 25-30.

Mogenson, J.G., Jones, D.L., and Yim C.Y. (1980). From motivation to action: Functional interface between the limbic system and the motor system. *Progress in Neurobiology, 14:69*-97.

Mondadori, C., and Etienne, P. (1990). Nootropic effects of ACE inhibitors in mice. *Psychopharmacology,* 100: 301-307.

Morris, R.G. (1984). Development of a water-maze procedure for studying spatial learning in the rat. *Journal of Neuroscience and Methods, 11*: 47-60.

Morris, R.G.M., Schenk, F., Tweedie, F., and Jarrard, L.E. (1990). Ibotenate lesions of hippocampus and/or subiculum: dissociating components of allocentric spatial learning. *European Journal of Neuroscience,* 2, 1016-1028.

Nader, K. (2003). Memory traces unbound. *Trends in Neuroscience,* 26, 65-72.

Nedivi, E., Hevroni, D., Naot, D., Israeli, D., and Citri, Y. (1993). Numerous candidate plasticity-related genes revealed by differential cDNA cloning. *Nature*, 363, 718-722.

Neves, L.A., Averill, D.B., Ferrario, C.M., Chappell, M.C., Aschner, J.L., Walkup, M.P., and Brosnihan, K.B. (2003). Characterization of angiotensin-(1-7) receptor subtype in mesenteric arteries. *Peptides*, 24, 455-462.

Olson, M.L., Olson, E.A., Qualls, J.H., Stratton, J.J., Harding, H.W., and Wright, J.W. (2004). Norleucine[1]-Angiotensin IV alleviates mecamylamine-induced spatial memory deficits. *Peptides*, 25: 233-241.

Oparil, S., Williams D., Chrysant S.G., Marbury T.C., and Neutel M.M. (2001). Comparative efficacy of almesartan, losartan, valsartan, and irbesartan in the control of essential hypertension. *Journal of Clinical Hypertension,* 3:283-291.

Pederson, E.S., Harding, J.W., and Wright, J.W. (1998). Attenuation of scopolamine-induced spatial learning impairments by an angiotensin IV analog. *Regulatory Peptides,* 74: 97-103.

Petersen, S.E., Fox, P.T., Posner, M.I., Mintum M, Raichle M.E. (1988). Positron emission tomographic studies of the cortical anatomy of single-word processing. *Nature,* 331:585-589.

Phillips, A.G. (1984). Brain reward circuitry: A case for separate systems. *Brain Research Bulletin,* 12:195-201.

Posner, M.I., Snyder C.R.R., and Davidson B.J. (1980). Attention and the detection of signals. *Journal of Experimental Psychology, General*, 109:160-174.

Rich, D.H., Moon, B.J., and Harbeson, S. (1984). Inhibition of aminopeptidases by amastatin and bestatin derivatives, effect of inhibitor structure on slow-binding processes. *Journal of Medicinal Chemistry,* 27: 417-422.

Rubin, R.D. (1976). Clinical use of retrograde amnesia produced by electroconvulsive shock. A conditioning hypothesis. *Canadian Psychiatric Association Journal*, 21, 87-90.

Rubin, R.D., and Franks, C. (1969). New application of ECT. In R.D. Rubin and C. Franks (Eds), *Advances in Behavior Therapy.* San Diego, CA: Academic Press, pp. 37-44.

Saavedra, J.M. (1992). Brain and pituitary angiotensin. *Endocrine Reviews,* 13: 329-380.

Santos, R.A., Campagnole-Santos, M.J., and Andrade, S.P. (2000). Angiotensin(1-7): an update. *Regulatory Peptides,* 91: 45-62.

Sardinia, M.F., Hanesworth, J.M., Krebs, L.T., and Harding, J.W. (1993). AT_4 receptor binding characteristics: D-amino acid- and glycine-substituted peptides. *Peptides,* 14: 949-954.

Slinker, B.K., Wu, Y., Brennan, A.J., Campbell, K.B., and Harding, J.W. (1999). Angiotensin IV has mixed effects on left ventricle systolic function and speeds relaxation. *Cardiovascular Research,* 42: 660-669.

Speth, R.C., Brown, T.E., Barnes, R.D., and Wright, J.W. (2003). Brain angiotensinergic activity: The state of our current knowledge. *Proceeding of the Western Pharmacology Society,* 46: 11-15.

Speth, R.C., Thompson, S.M., and Johns, S.J. (1995). Angiotensin II receptors: Structural and functional considerations. In Mukhopadhyay, A.K. and Raizada, M.K., (Eds.), *Current concepts: Tissue renin angiotensin systems as local regulators in reproductive and endocrine organs.* New York, Plenum Press, pp. 169-192.

Squire, L.R., Bloom, F.E., McConnell, S.K., Roberts, J.L., Spitzer, N.C. and Zigmond, M.J. (2003). *Fundamental Neuroscience.* San Diego, Academic Press, pp. 1315-1321.

Stamenkovic, I. (2003). Extracellular matrix remodeling: the role of matrix metalloproteinases. *Journal of Pathology,* 200, 448-464.

Sutherland, R.J., and McDonald, R.J. (1990). Hippocampus, amygdala and memory deficits in rats. *Behavioural Brain Research,* 37, 57-79.

Thomas, W.G., and Mendelsohn, F.A.O. (2003). Molecules in focus: Angiotensin receptors: form and function and distribution. *International Journal of Biochemistry Cell Biology,* 35: 774-779.

Thorpe, W.H. (1966). *Learning and instinct in animals.* Cambridge, MA, Harvard University Press, 1966.

Trenkwalder, P. (2002). Potential for antihypertensive treatment with an AT_1-receptor blocker to reduce dementia in the elderly. *Journal of Human Hypertension,* 16: S71-S75.

Unger, T., Badoer, E., Ganten, D., Lang,, R.E., and Rettig, R. (1988). Brain angiotensin: pathways and pharmacology. *Circulation,* 77: 140-154.

Vaillant, C., Didier-Bazes, M., Hutter, A., Belin, M.F., and Thomasset, N. (1999). Spatiotemporal expression patterns of metalloproteinases and their inhibitors in the postnatal developing rat cerebellum. *Journal of Neuroscience,* 19: 4994-5004.

Vauquelin, G., Michotte, Y., Smolders, I., Sarre, S., Ebinger, G., Dupont, A., and Vanderheyden, P. (2002). Cellular targets for angiotensin II fragments: pharmacological and molecular evidence. *Journal of Renin-Angiotensin-Aldosterone System,* 3: 195-204.

Wilk, S., and Healy, D.P. (1993). Glutamyl aminopeptidase (aminopeptidase A), the BP-1/6C3 antigen. *Advances in Neuroimmunology,* 3: 195-207.

Wise, R. (1982). Neuroleptics and operant behavior: the anhedonia hypothesis. *Behavioral Brain Sciences,* 5:39-87.

Wright, J.W., and Harding, J.W. (1994). Brain angiotensin receptor subtypes in the control of physiological and behavioral responses. *Neuroscience and Biobehavioral Reviews,* 18: 21-53.

Wright, J.W., and Harding, J.W. (1997). Important roles for angiotensin III and IV in the brain renin-angiotensin system. *Brain Research Review,* 25: 96-124.

Wright, J.W., and Harding, J.W. (2004). The brain angiotensin system and extracellular matrix molecules in neural plasticity, learning, and memory. *Progress in Neurobiology,* 72: 263-293.

Wright, J.W., Kramar, E.A., Meighan, S.E., and Harding, J.W. (2002). Extracellular matrix molecules, long-term potentiation, memory consolidation and the brain angiotensin system. *Peptides, 23*: 221-246.

Wright, J.W., Krebs, L.T., Stobb, J.W., and Harding, J.W. (1995). The angiotensin IV system: Functional implications. *Frontiers in Neuroendocrinology,* 16: 23-52.

Wright, J.W., Stubley, L, Pederson, E.S., Kramar, E.A., Hanesworth, J.M., and Harding, J.W. (1999). Contributions of the brain angiotensin IV-AT$_4$ receptor subtype system to spatial learning. *Journal of Neuroscience,* 19: 3952-3961.

Yong, V.W., Krekoski, C.A., Forsyth, P.A., Bell, R., and Edwards, D.R. (1998). Matrix metalloproteinases and diseases of the CNS. *Trends in Neuroscience,* 21, 75-80.

Zubenko, G.S., and Nixon, R.A. (1984). Mood elevating effect of captopril in depressed patients. *American Journal of Psychiatry,* 141: 110-111.

In: Psychology of Motivation
Editor: Lois V. Brown, pp. 29-45

ISBN: 978-1-60021-598-8
© 2007 Nova Science Publishers, Inc.

Chapter 2

ATTENTION AND MOTIVATION INTERDEPENDENCE IN SELF-REGULATION. A NEUROCOGNITIVE APPROACH

M. Rosario Rueda[*], Alberto Acosta and Milagros Santonja
Universidad de Granada, Spain

ABSTRACT

Inner desires and motives often result in confrontation with what is requested by others or considered socially appropriate, and even with one's own goals. Regulating internally-generated impulses is therefore an important ability for accomplishing goals and instructions as well as complying with social norms. In Psychology, this ability has been linked to the concept of self-regulation. The term "self-regulation" refers to those processes by which people exercise control over their emotional and behavioral responses in order to accomplish their own goals and/or to adapt to the cognitive and social demands of specific situations. The type of processes implicated in such ability involve modulating the intensity, frequency and duration of verbal and motor responses, activating and/or inhibiting behaviors according to situational demands in the absence of external monitoring, delaying acting upon a desired object or goal and modulating emotional reactivity (Fonagy & Target, 2002; Thompson, 1994; Kopp, 1992). Thus, it is no surprise that the ability to self-regulate is been shown to relate to important aspects of socialization during childhood, as emotionality, delay of gratification, compliance, moral development, social competence, empathy, adjustment, and academic performance (Eisenberg et al., 2004). As a matter of fact, self-regulation is thought to be "essential for transforming the inner animal nature into a civilized human being" (Vogs & Baumeister, 2004, p. 1).

Although increased evidence shows that some regulatory operations may be carried out in an automatic, nonconscious mode (Fitzsimons & Bargh, 2004), most definitions of

---

[*] Corresponding author: M. Rosario Rueda, Dpto. Psicología Experimental, Universidad de Granada – Spain. Phone: +34 958 249609; Email: rorueda@ugr.es

self-regulation place the emphasis on processes exerted by the self in a conscious and deliberate way which activation entails some effort. Within this framework, the ability to self-regulate has been linked to executive aspects of attention (Posner & Rothbart, 1998; Rueda, Posner & Rothbart, 2004). According to this view, the brain network underlying executive attention constitutes the neural basis for action monitoring and is activated in situations that involve conscious detection, inhibitory control and resolution of conflict produced by dominant but inappropriate responses.

Based on the motivational properties of emotions, other studies highlight the effect of affective variables over attentional processes. Affects appear to exert their influence either by facilitating the processing of relevant information in a substantially automatic mode (Öhman, 1997) or, in a more elaborated way, by demanding additional involvement of control processes on affective-relevant situations (Gross, 2002). In addition, motivational variables and strategies are shown to modulate aspects of self-regulation. There is evidence of the influence of promotion-approach versus prevention-avoidance styles on processes of decision making, generation of alternatives, probability estimates and evaluation of outcomes (Higgins & Spiegel, 2004).

In this chapter, we stress the contribution of control processes related to attention for emotional and behavioral regulation, placing emphasis on the specific neural systems involved in such processes. In addition, we analyze the influence of motivational and emotional variables on the functioning of attentional control in an effort to understand their interdependence for regulating behavior.

ATTENTION AND SELF-REGULATION

Selecting information and controlling thoughts and actions have been a major function of attention from the earliest theoretical models (Broadbent, 1958; James, 1890). Attentional selection has an important adaptive role in individuals' interactions with the environment. Orienting attention over a scene and selecting the object or location to attend to is necessary for carrying out desired actions. Likewise, attention can be directed internally to coordinate memories, thoughts, and emotions.

A widely accepted theory of attention proposes that the attentional system exerts its influence by modulating the functioning of systems involved in information processing (Posner & Raichle, 1994). Many of the studies that provide evidence of the regulatory aspect of attention show modulation of sensory systems. Studies using functional Magnetic Resonance Imaging (fMRI) and cellular recording have demonstrated that a number of brain areas such as the superior parietal lobe and temporal parietal junction play a key role in modulating activity within primary and extrastriate visual systems when attentional orienting occurs (Corbetta & Shulman, 2002; Desimone & Duncan, 1995). In addition, other neuroimaging studies have suggested that the regulatory effects of attention apply just as well to brain areas involved in processing the semantics of words, storing information in memory and generating emotions such as fear and sadness (Posner & Raichle, 1994, 1998).

Attention can be automatically driven by external stimulation or endogenously controlled in accordance with the goals and wishes of the individual. Norman and Shallice (1986) developed a cognitive model for distinguishing between automatic and controlled processes. According to their model, psychological processing systems rely on a number of hierarchically organized schemas of action and thought used for routine actions. These schemas are automatically triggered, and contain well-learned responses or sequences of actions. However, a different mode of operation involving the Supervisory Attention System is required when situations call for more carefully elaborated responses. These are situations that involve 1) novelty, 2) error correction or troubleshooting, 3) some degree of danger or difficulty, and 4) overcoming strong habitual responses or tendencies.

Maurizio Corbetta and Gordon Shulman have also stressed the dichotomy between top-down or goal-directed and bottom-up or stimulus-driven forms of attentional selection (Corbetta & Shulman, 2002). In their view, this dichotomy is expressed in two brain pathways for attentional selection and control. The top-down system includes parts of the intra-parietal and superior frontal cortex and is involved in selecting stimuli and responses based on goals and intentions. The second system is activated by relevant stimulation in a more automatic way, as when stimuli are salient or unexpected, and includes the temporo-parietal cortex and inferior frontal cortex of the right hemisphere. These two forms of attentional selection are thought to interact in normal behavior, as when attentional control is required for processing significant information.

In line with these views, in the literature about emotion, many authors have acknowledged the existence of automatic and controlled modes of processing affective information. For example, Mandler (1984, pp. 118-119) argued that emotional experience is conscious by definition. In his opinion, perception of changes in the autonomic nervous system (arousal) and the interpretation of the emotional situation are consciously integrated. Arousal serves as the signal that calls for a more careful and attentive evaluation of the environment in emotionally-salient situations. From a more functional perspective, Oatley and Jenkins (1992) consider that emotions sign the occurrence of events that are relevant to individuals' goals and cause the insertion and maintenance of this information in consciousness. Emotions are often linked to distinctive action tendencies that must be reorganized according to the priorities of particular situations. Attentional control is seen as the key system for this behavioral readjustment.

Brain Networks Underlying Attentional Functions

The concept of brain network refers to a group of brain areas that are connected to one another and carry out different operations related to a common particular function. Traditional methods used to examine brain activity together with the recent emergence of functional neuroimaging have allowed many cognitive tasks to be analyzed in terms of the brain areas they activate. In the field of attention, a large bulk of data has supported the existence of three brain networks that contribute to attention-related functions (Posner & Dehaene, 1994; Posner & Petersen, 1990). These networks carry out the functions of alerting, orienting and executive control. Alerting is the most elementary aspect of attention and describes the state of wakefulness and arousal of an organism; orienting is the selection of information from sensory input; executive control involves the mechanisms for resolving conflict among thoughts, feelings and responses. The three brain networks have been shown to differ in their functional anatomy, as well as the neurochemical modulators that influence their efficiency (Posner, Rueda & Kanske, 2007).

The alerting function has been associated with activation of frontal and parietal regions particularly of the right hemisphere. A traditional way to study alertness has been to use warning signals prior to the presentation of targets. The influence of warning signals on the level of alertness is thought to be due to modulation of neural activity by the norepinephrine system (Marrocco & Davidson, 1998; Everitt & Robbins, 1997; Stewart, Burke & Marrocco, 2001).

Orienting involves directing attention toward the source of sensory signals. This may be done overtly as when head or eyes are also oriented, or may occur covertly without any head or eye movements. The orienting system for visual events has been associated with posterior brain areas including the superior parietal lobe and temporal parietal junction as well as the frontal eye fields. Event-related fMRI studies have suggested that the superior parietal lobe is associated with orienting following the presentation of a cue indicating where in space a person should attend (Corbetta, Kincade, Ollinger, McAvoy & Shulman, 2000). However, when a target occurs at a location different from the one that is cued (uncued location) and attention has to be disengaged from the cued location and moved to the new position, there is activity in the temporal parietal junction (Corbetta et al., 2000). Moreover, lesions of the parietal lobe and superior temporal lobe have been consistently related to difficulties in orienting (Losier & Klein, 2001). In addition, pharmacological studies carried out with animals that have been trained to use cues to direct attention to targets have shown the cholinergic system to modulate covert orienting responses (Stewart, Burke & Marrocco, 2001; Davidson & Marrocco, 2000).

Executive control is required in situations that involve planning, error detection, novelty and difficult processing or conflict situations in which overcoming habitual actions is needed. The function of the conflict network seems to be modulated by the dopaminergic system (Posner, Rueda & Kanske, 2007). Executive functions are often studied by tasks that involve conflict, such the Stroop and flanker tasks. In the Stroop task subjects must respond to the ink color (e.g. red) of a word while ignoring the color word name (e.g. blue). In the flanker task (Eriksen & Eriksen, 1974), the target is surrounded by irrelevant stimuli (flankers) which suggest an incorrect response. Resolving conflict in these types of situations activates the anterior cingulate cortex (ACC) and lateral prefrontal cortex (Fan, Flombaum, McCandliss, Thomas & Posner, 2003). Imaging studies carried out with tasks designed to analyze different operations involved in executive attention indicate that lateral areas of the prefrontal cortex are involved in representing specific information over time, while medial areas are more related to the detection and monitoring of conflict (Casey, Thomas, Welsh, et al., 2000; Botvinick, Braver, Barch, Carter & Cohen, 2001; Botvinick, Nystrom, Fissell, Carter, & Cohen, 1999; MacDonald, Cohen, Stenger & Carter, 2000).

Executive Attention and Self-Regulation

Among the three attentional networks, executive control is the network involved in the volitional and controlled aspect of the attentional system. Its functions include resolving into appropriate actions the kinds of situations described by Norman and Shallice as requiring cognitive control (Posner & DiGirolamo, 1998).

An important cognitive mechanism related to the functioning of the executive attention network is the conscious detection of targets (Posner & Raichle, 1994). Conscious detection plays a special role in selecting a target stimulus from among alternatives and monitoring for conflict situations in which a response tendency must be overcome. Moreover, detection is a controlled process that engages attention in a way that resists interference by other signals. Imaging studies have shown that, independently of the characteristics defining a target stimulus (color, motion, form, etc.), particular brain areas, including parts of the intraparietal and superior frontal cortices, are specifically activated by detected targets as contrasted to passive viewing of the same type of stimuli (Corbetta & Shulman, 2002). A type of detection particularly interesting for action monitoring is the detection of erroneous responses. A behavioral indicator of error detection and correction is the slowing of reaction time immediately following the commission of an error. An electrophysiological component, the error-related negativity (ERN), is also consistently recorded following the subject's detection of an error (Gehring, Gross, Coles, Meyer, & Donchin, 1993). Further, the distribution of the activity associated with the ERN on the scalp has been linked to activity originating in the anterior cingulate cortex (van Veen & Carter, 2002).

Another important mechanism for action regulation is inhibitory control. Inhibition can be applied to different stages of information processing. Interference suppression is required for impeding the processing of irrelevant information, as when targets are presented among distracters. Inhibition is also necessary for withholding responses that, although prompted by current stimulation, might not be appropriate. Interference suppression is usually studied with experimental paradigms that involve conflict. The most common way to measure response inhibition is by using tasks in which participants are required to inhibit their response to a particular stimulus while having to respond to related stimuli (Go/No-Go Tasks). Under Go/No-Go instructions, promptness to respond can be manipulated by varying the proportion of Go trials, or by presenting a No-Go signal at varying time intervals after the Go stimulus (the Stop-signal Paradigm). The efficiency of inhibition is measured behaviorally by the number of omissions and false alarms, but it can be also measured using physiological indices, such as muscular preparation or brain activity. In adults, No-go conditions are shown to activate parts of the dorsolateral and medial frontal cortex on both hemispheres as well as the orbitofrontal cortex (Casey et al., 1997; Watanabe et al., 2002; Bunge et al., 2002).

These mechanisms of control are also present when regulating affective information. It is usually assumed that the final product of an emotional episode is the affective experience associated to it, the conscious feeling of which may involve the executive attention network. On the other hand, there is evidence that early processing of affective information occurs in an automatic non-conscious way. When the relevance of this information is low according to current goals, further processing of that information is thought to be prevented by the control system thru inhibition. The involvement of mechanisms of conscious detection and inhibition is especially important in social interactions. Intentions, motives and desires implicated in inter-personal interactions are quite heterogeneous and social competence often depend on detecting them with efficacy and having the ability to flexibly determine the most appropriate responses.

Evidence from Cognitive and Emotional Studies

Activation of the anterior cingulate gyrus have been linked to a variety of specific functions in attention (Posner, Rueda & Kanske, 2007), working memory (Duncan et al., 2000), emotion (Bush, et al, 2000), pain (Rainville, Duncan, Price Carrier, & Bushnell, 1997) and monitoring for conflict (Botvinick et al., 2001) and error (Holroyd & Coles, 2002). In tasks like the Stroop and flanker, which activate the anterior cingulate and lateral prefrontal areas, conflict is introduced by the need to respond to one aspect of the stimulus while ignoring another. Resolving these situations constitute a particular form of cognitive regulation that requires the controlled coordination of the mechanisms discussed above.

In emotional studies, the anterior cingulate is often seen as part of a network involved in the cognitive regulation of emotions. The interaction between this structure and the lateral and medial prefrontal cortex provide a brain circuitry for self-regulation. The lateral prefrontal cortex is implicated in the generation, maintenance, and selection of regulatory strategies whereas the ACC appear to be involved in the online monitoring of the regulation process (Ochsner & Gross, 2004). Several data coming from neuroimaging studies seem to support such idea. In one of these studies, participants were exposed to erotic films with the requirement to regulate any resulting arousal while their brain activity was registered using fMRI (Beauregard, Levesque & Bourgoulin, 2001). Results revealed significant activation of the ACC. Interestingly, the cingulate activity was found to be related to the regulatory instruction. In a different study, cognitive reappraisal of photographs producing negative affect showed a correlation between extent of cingulate activity and the reduction in negative affect (Ochsner, Bunge, Gross & Gabrieli, 2002). Similarly, in a study in which hypnotism was used to control the perception of pain, the cingulate activity reflected the perception, not the strength, of the physical stimulus (Rainville et al, 1997). These results show a role for this anatomical structure in regulating limbic activity related to emotion and provide evidence for a role of the cingulate as a part of the network controlling affect (Ochsner & Gross, 2005; Bush, et al., 2000).

In addition, large lesions of the anterior cingulate either in adults (Damasio, 1994) or children (Anderson, Damasio, Tranel & Damasio, 2000) result in great difficulty in regulating behavior, particularly in social situations. Smaller lesions may produce only a temporary inability to deal with conflict in cognitive tasks (Turken & Swick, 1999; Ochsner et al., 2001).

Evidence from Temperament and Developmental Studies

Links between attention and self-regulation have also been found in temperament research. In temperament studies, individual differences in reactivity and regulation are commonly measured using questionnaires.

Factor analyses of mostly parent-reported questionnaires have provided evidence for three broad factors of temperament in childhood: Surgency/Extraversion, Negative Affect and Effortful Control (Rothbart, Ahadi, Hershey & Fisher, 2001; Rothbart & Bates, 2006). Extraversion and negative affect represent early developing temperamental reactivity systems which are related to the onset, intensity and duration of responses to external and internal stimulation. These two reactivity factors are associated to patterns of activation/approach and inhibition/withdraw responses respectively that parallel two general motivational systems that will be discussed later. The third factor, effortful control is a later developing dimension that relates to individual differences in self-regulatory abilities used for modulating reactivity (Rothbart & Rueda, 2005). Effortful control allows individuals to regulate their behavior in relation to current and future needs, as in situations that involve coping with immediate punishment or avoiding instant reward in the face of a more rewarding situation in the future. Thus, the first two broad temperament constructs represent generalized characteristics of individuals' positive and negative emotionality and the motivational impulses derived from them. The third construct stands for individuals' efforts to control such impulses according to instructions, goals or social norms.

It has been argued that the executive attention network constitutes the neural system underlying effortful control (Rueda, Posner & Rothbart, 2005; Rothbart & Rueda, 2005). Several studies have shown a positive relation between performance on cognitive tasks related to executive attention and parent or self-reported effortful control (Gerardi-Caulton, 2000; González, Fuentes, Carranza & Estévez, 2001; Rothbart, Ellis, Rueda & Posner, 2003; Chang & Burns, 2005). Eisenberg and her colleagues have also found that 4 to 6-year old boys with good attentional control tend to deal with anger by using non-hostile verbal methods rather than overt aggressive methods (Eisenberg, Fabes, Nyman, Bernzweig, & Pinulas, 1994).

In line with these data, the work by Kochanska and colleagues over the past decade has shown that effortful control plays an important role in the development of conscience. In studies of temperament and conscience, the early internalization of moral principles appears to be facilitated in fearful preschool-aged children, especially when their mothers use gentle discipline (Kochanska, 1997). In addition, internalized control is greater in children who are high in effortful control (Kochanska, Murray, & Harlan, 2000; Kochanska, Murray, Jacques, Koenig, & Vandegeest, 1996). Individual differences in effortful control are also related to aspects of metacognitive knowledge, such as theory of mind. Tasks that require inhibitory control are correlated with performance on theory of mind tasks even when other factors, such as age, planning skills, and receptive vocabulary are factored out (Carlson, Moses, & Claxton, 2004).

All these data point to the idea that effortful control serves as the basis for the development from more reactive to more self-regulative behavior. Executive attention contributes to this development by providing the attentional flexibility required to manage negative affect, consider potential actions in light of moral principles, and coordinate reactions that are under voluntary control (Rothbart & Rueda, 2005).

MOTIVATION AND ATTENTION

Peter Lang has proposed the existence of two general motivational systems (e.g. Lang, Davis & Öhman, 2000). One, the aversive system, has a protective and defensive function, while the second, the appetitive system, mediates approaching behavior and relates to needs for feeding, nurturing and procreating. The aversive system activates negative emotions as fear and anxiety, whereas positive emotions are associated to the appetitive system. According to Lang and colleagues (Lang, Bradley & Cuthbert, 1997) motivated behavior can be described using two basic dimensions, one representing its affective valence (positive or negative) and the second representing its intensity (arousal).

Brain Circuitries Supporting Defensive and Appetitive Responses

In consonance with the basic and primitive nature of affects, appraising the affective significance of information has been related to early-evolving subcortical brain structures.

The amygdala appears to be implicated in the rapid detection and encoding of arousing information, especially that with negative valence, including potential threats and fearful stimulation. Activation of the amygdala has been related to learning and expressing fear as well as processing emotional information contained in both faces and non-social stimulation (see reviews by Phelps, 2006; and Compton, 2003). On the other hand, another subcortical structure, the striatum, is implicated in the automatic encoding and representation of implicit sequences of thoughts and actions that lead to positive outcomes. For example, the nucleus accumbens, a striatal structure, is activated by the anticipation of monetary rewards (Knutson, Adams, Fong & Hommer, 2001). In general, the striatum seems to play an important role in learning sequences of stimulation that lead to rewards and hence have a reinforcing value (Rolls, 2000).

Additionally, brain regions of the frontal lobe have been involved in more elaborate aspects of processing emotions. Converging lesion and neuroimaging data indicate that the ventromedial region of the prefrontal cortex appear to be involved in representing affect in absence of immediate elicitors whereas the dorsolateral region seems to play an important role in holding goals related to affective states (Davidson & Irwin, 1999). Moreover, the lateral prefrontal cortex has been implicated in the generation and strategic selection of control mechanisms used for regulation of emotions (Ochsner & Gross, 2004). Finally, the orbital and ventromedial regions of the frontal cortex seem important for coordinating emotional responses and information of what is appropriate according to the social context (Ochsner & Gross, 2004).

As discussed in an earlier section of the chapter, the ACC has been consistently involved in the online monitoring of relevant information and the control strategies used to regulate actions, thoughts and emotions. According to Bush et al. (2000), the ventral region of the ACC seems to be more directly involved in the control of emotionally-relevant information. Whalen and colleagues conducted an fMRI study wherein participants were asked to perform a counting Stroop task (e.g. counting the number of words presented on the computer screen) in which they used either neutral or negative words as stimuli. Their results showed activation of the rostral division of the anterior cingulate for negative as compared to neutral words (Whalen, Bush, McNally, Wilhelm, McInerney, Jenike & Rauch, 1998).

Attentional Capture by Emotionally-Relevant Information

Intuitively, we might think that an effective defensive system would be quickly activated without requiring much effort in order to provide immediate responses to threats. Cognitive studies seem to confirm such idea. Encoding of threatening information can be carried out in an automatic non-conscious way. For instance, Öhman and Soares (1993) observed conditioned skin conductance responses (SCR) elicited by masked pictures of snakes and spiders that had been previously paired to electrical shocks. A similar result was found using pictures of angry faces (Esteves, Dimberg & Öhman, 1994). Another piece of evidence shows that rapid detection of pictures of snakes and spiders among distracting pictures of mushrooms and flowers is unaffected by the position of the target pictures in the display or the amount of distracters (Öhman, Flykt & Esteves, 2001). Additionally, threatening faces, especially those displaying anger, are detected faster and more accurately among neutral distracters than happy faces (Öhman, Lundqvist & Esteves, 2001). All these data suggest that affective (threatening) information is processed immediately and has an automatic effortless influence on selective attention.

Imaging studies and reports of patients with brain damage indicate that encoding of threatening stimulation is mediated by the amygdala. Bechara and colleagues (1995) reported the case of a patient with bilateral lesions of the amygdala that was unable to show conditioned SCR despite being able to verbally inform about the conditioned-inconditioned stimuli contingencies. However, another patient with a bilateral lesion in the hippocampus showed the opposite pattern. A third patient with damage in both the amygdala and the hippocampus could neither inform about the associations between conditioned and inconditioned stimuli nor show conditioned SCR. In a PET study, Morris, Öhman & Dolan (1998) observed activation of the amygdala to masked as well as unmasked pictures of angry faces, though the pattern of activation was lateralized. The right amygdala was activated for masked pictures, whereas unmasked pictures activated the left amygdala. Further, the amygdala seems to respond preferentially to negative stimulation. Using fMRI, Whalen et al., (1998) showed greater activation of the amygdala for masked pictures of fearful faces than happy faces.

Different mechanisms have been suggested to mediate the influence of affective-relevant information on attentional selection. One such mechanism is the enhancement of processing in neural areas that represent the selected stimulus (Compton, 2003). Another mechanism consists of a transient change in attentional thresholds in the presence of emotional stimuli (Phelps, 2006). Thus, processing of the affective information appears to be enhanced by automatically facilitating the activation of brain regions involved in its encoding.

Automatic attentional capture has also been observed for appetitive stimulation. This evidence comes mainly from studies of people having substance abuse problems (see review by Robbins & Ehrman, 2004). In a study carried out with social consumers of alcohol and cannabis, Jones, Jones, Blundell and Bruce (2002) examined participants' ability to detect stimulation related to those substances. In their study, Jones et al. used the flicker paradigm. This paradigm consists of successively presenting two versions of the same visual scene, one original and a second one that has been slightly changed. Participants' task was to detect the change. Pictures depicting the scenes were presented during 250 ms and were followed by a mask displayed for 80 ms. In this particular study, scene changes could relate to either alcohol, cannabis or neutral objects. Results showed that participants who detected changes involving alcohol-related stimulation consumed more alcohol than those detecting neutral changes. A similar pattern was found for cannabis-related *vs.* neutral stimulation.

All this evidence indicates that the salience of different types of information is determined by motivational aspects related to people's personal experiences. Salience of stimulation cause in turn biases in the functioning of the brain systems leading to the automatic facilitation of the processing of that particular stimulation.

Modulation of Attention by Motivational Styles and Variables

The appetitive/approach and defensive/avoidance motivational systems seem to be expressed in particular behavioral styles which in turn appear to have an effect on self-regulation. In his regulatory focus theory, Higgins (1997) has proposed that people's strategic choices and ways of pursuing their goals are based in two different motivationally-based styles. The "Promotion-focused" style involves approaching situations with a concern for accomplishment and achievement of positive outcomes. On the other hand, the "Prevention-focused" style relates to concerns for safety, protection, and prevention of negative outcomes (Crowe & Higgins, 1997). These two styles can either be expressed in personality traits or have been temporarily induced by instructions or patterns of consequences associated to responses. Higgins and colleagues have shown that in both cases the motivational orientation style affect processes involved in decision making, such as generating alternative strategies for facing particular situations, estimating the probability of occurrence of events and displaying bias toward risky or conservative responses (Higgins & Spiegel, 2004). Thus, motivation-based styles appear to modulate cognitive aspects related to executive functions. This modulation might be mediated by the interaction between brain regions involved in processing emotional arousal and valence and those implicated in attentional modulation. Indeed, in a recent fMRI study conducted by Cunningham, Raye & Johnson (2005) participants showed activation in the amygdala and ACC while making judgments about the valence (good/bad) of concepts. Interestingly, greater activation in these regions was associated to positively-rated stimuli for individuals with promotion focus, whereas the activation was associated to negative stimuli for participants with prevention-focus. These results suggest that motivation plays an important role in determining which aspects of the stimulation are more likely to engage people's attention.

Another interesting example of how individual differences relate to motivation and hence affect self-regulatory abilities comes from studies about temperament and motivation for achievement. The concept of mastery motivation refers to a disposition to curiosity and interest, taking pleasure in mastering problems, and showing preference for more challenging tasks than for easier ones, and has been related to the positive emotionality system (Shiner, 1998). Individual differences in both dimensions of surgency/extraversion and effortful control have a positive relationship with achievement in social and academic settings during childhood (Shiner, 2000). In studies with early adolescents, we have found that both executive attention as measured with conflict tasks and temperamental effortful control are significant predictors of academic achievement and schooling abilities (Checa, Rodríguez-Bailón & Rueda, 2007). In addition, the temperamental dimension of surgency/extraversion has been related to sustained attention. Indeed, before systems for effortful control are developed in the preschool period, surgency/extraversion seems to be the key temperamental dimension contributing to interest and sustained involvement (Rothbart & Bates, 2006).

In our laboratory at the University of Granada, we have conducted a study to examine whether executive attention is modulated by motivational variables. In order to measure executive attention efficiency participants were required to perform a numeric version of the Stroop task. The task consisted on selecting the number with the highest value among two digits displayed on the screen. Value and size dimensions of the two digits could either be congruent (the larger number was the highest in value) or incongruent (highest number with smaller size). Motivation was manipulated by presenting a cue previous to the display of the target which indicated whether the participant would be gaining (if a correct response is made), loosing (if an error is made), or neither gaining nor loosing (neutral condition) points in each trial. At the end of the experiment, points could be exchanged for gifts or course credits. Results showed improved conflict resolution under conditions subject to consequences (either gaining or loosing points) as compared to the neutral condition. Patterns of brain activation were also registered with event-related potentials during task performance and we observed a modulation of the attentional effect by motivation. Under conditions subject to consequences the attentional effect observed over mid frontal channels appeared earlier and had a larger amplitude compared to the motivationally neutral condition (Rueda, Checa & Santonja, 2007). These results indicate that the efficiency of the executive attention network can be improved under conditions in which actions lead to consequences that are meaningful according to people's goals.

CONCLUDING REMARKS: ATTENTION AND MOTIVATION INTERDEPENDENCE ON REGULATING BEHAVIOR

After the well-known controversy about the primacy and/or independence of affect and cognition in the 1980s, centered in the work by Robert Zajonc and Richard Lazarus, behavioral and neuroimaging studies have considerably advanced our knowledge of the interactions between cognition and emotion. Two decades of research later, data seem to have strengthened the idea that motivationally-relevant information can be automatically processed, without accessing superior cognitive systems related to attentional control and consciousness. Complementarily, more recent information is showing that the processing of affective information and emotional states can be regulated by superior cognitive processes.

Within the recently emerging field of Cognitive Neuroscience, converging evidence is used to emphasize that affective and cognitive mechanisms seem to interact in all stages of processing to the point that it is difficult to disentangle them (Phelps, 2006). Under some circumstances, these interactions follow a *bottom-up* pathway, but they also appear to be implemented by *top-down* influences. Moreover, prevalence of control or top-down processes or stimulation-driven reactive responses seems to be subject to individual differences.

As argued by Compton (2003), the brain has evolved to perceive and respond to stimulation in the context of its biological, social and personal meaning. All cognitive processes are thus guided by personal, social and/or biological goals. From an evolutionary viewpoint, it seems reasonable to argue that the processing of affective, and hence motivationally-relevant, stimulation is favored in our biological system. During evolution our brain has been provided with structures and mechanisms that guaranty immediate responses to events that threat our basic goal for survival. Treatment of affects and basic motivational impulses by the brain clearly involves subcortical structures such as the amygdala and striatum. Also, the flexible adaptation to a complex environment requires interpreting the stimulation according to the specific context in which it takes place. Those same structures and mechanisms are complemented by cortical brain regions implicated in more elaborated sensorio-perceptual processes as well as control centers of the frontal lobe and ACC that play a part in regulating impulses into appropriate behavior according to specificities of particular situations. This regulatory system directly implicated in achieving our social and personal goals is more recent in the evolutionary history.

The human brain is the product of adaptive mechanisms coined during evolution with the purpose of responding to demands set by our complex environment. The frame of social and personal motivations is especially complex and dynamic in human relationships. Brain structures related to self-regulation have adapted to that environment, providing the mechanisms necessary for the continuous selection and monitoring of information according to situational (momentary) circumstances as well as more personal objectives based on values, cultural and social norms. Due to differences in both constitution and experience, individuals' skills to carry out such endeavor seem to vary largely.

ACKNOWLEDGEMENTS

We are grateful to Brian Phillips for assistance in preparation of the manuscript. This work was supported by grants from the Spanish Ministry of Education (code SEJ2005-01473) and the Regional Government of Andalucía (Programa de Retorno de Doctores a Universidades de Andalucía) to the first author.

REFERENCES

Anderson, S. W., Damasio, H., Tranel, D., & Damasio, A. R. (2000). Long-term sequelae of prefrontal cortex damage acquired in early childhood. *Developmental Neuropsychology*, 18(3): 281-296.

Beauregard, M., Levesque, J., & Bourgouin, P. (2001). Neural correlates of conscious self-regulation of emotion. *Journal of Neuroscience, 21,* RC 165.

Bechara, A., Tranel, D., Damasio, H., Adolphs, R., Rockland, C., y Damasio, A. (1995). Double dissociation of conditioning and declarative knowledge relative to the amygdala and hippocampus in humans. *Science*, 269: 1115-1118.

Botvinick, M. M., Braver, T. S., Barch, D. M., Carter, C. S., & Cohen, J. D. (2001). Conflict monitoring and cognitive control. *Psychological Review,* 108: 624-652.

Botvinick, M., Nystrom, L. E., Fissell, K., Carter, C. S. & Cohen, J. D. (1999). Conflict monitoring versus selection-for-action in anterior cingulated cortex. *Nature*, 402: 179-181.

Broadbent, D. E. (1958). *Perception and Communication*. London: Pergamon.

Bunge, S. A., Dudukovic, N. M., Thomason, M. E., Vidya, C. J. & Gabrieli, J. D. E. (2002) Immature frontal lobe contributions to cognitive control in children: Evidence from fMRI. *Neuron*, 33: 1-20.

Bush, G., Luu, P., & Posner, M. I. (2000). Cognitive and emotional influences in the anterior cingulate cortex. *Trends in Cognitive Science,* 4(6): 215-222.

Bush, G., Whalen, P. J., Rosen, B. R., Jenike, M. A., McInerney, S. C. y Rauch, S. L. (1998). The counting stroop: An interference task specialized for functional neuroimagen – Validation study with functional MRI. *Human Brain Mapping,* 6: 270-282.

Carlson, S. M., Moses, L. J., & Claxton, L. J. (2004). Individual differences in executive functioning and theory of mind: An investigation of inhibitory control and planning ability. *Journal of Experimental Child Psychology,* 8: 299-319

Carlson, S. T., & Moses, L. J. (2001). Individual differences in inhibitory control in children's theory of mind. *Child Development,* 72: 1032-1053.

Casey, B. J., Thomas, K. M., Welsh, T. F., Badgaiyan, R. D., Eccard, C. H., Jennings, J. R. & Crone, E. A. (2000). Dissociation of response conflict, attentional selection, and expectancy with functional magnetic resonance imaging. *PNAS*, 97(15): 8728-8733.

Casey, B. J., Trainor, R. J., Orendi, J. L., Schubert, A. B., Nystrom, L. E., Giedd, J. N., Castellanos, F. X., Haxby, J. V., Noll, D. C., Cohen, J. D., Forman, S. D., Dahl, R. E., & Rapoport, J. L. (1997). A developmental functional MRI study of prefrontal activation during performance of a go-no-go task. *Journal of Cognitive Neuroscience,* 9: 835-847.

Chang, F., & Burns, B. M., (2005). Attention in preschoolers: Associations with Effortful control and motivation. *Child Development,* 76: 247-263.

Checa, P., Rodríguez- Bailón, R., & Rueda, M. R. (2007) Measures of attentional control predict early-adolescents academic achievement and schooling skills. Manuscript in preparation.

Compton, R. C. (2003). The interface between emotion and attention: A review of evidence from psychology and neuroscience. *Behaviour and Cognitive Neuroscience Reviews,* 2(2): 115-129.

Compton, R. J., Banich, M. T., Mohanty, A., Milham, M. P., Herrington, J., Miller, G., Scalf, P. E., Web, A., & Heller, W. (2003). Paying attention to emotion: An fMRI investigation of cognitive and emotional Stroop task. *Cognitive, Affective, and Behavioral Neuroscience,* 3: 81-96.

Corbetta, M., & Shulman, G. L. (2002). Control of goal-directed and stimulus-driven attention in the brain. *Nature Neuroscience Reviews, 3:* 201-215.

Corbetta, M., Kincade, J. M., Ollinger, J. M., McAvoy, M. P.& Shulman, G. (2000) Voluntary orienting is dissociated from target detection in human posterior parietal cortex, *Nature Neuroscience* 3: 292-297.

Crowe, E., & Higgins, E. T. (1997). Regulatory focus and strategic inclinations: Promotion and prevention in· decision-· making. *Organizational Behaviour and Human Decision Processes,* 69: 117-132.

Cunningham, W. A., Raye, C. L., & Johnson, M. K. (2005). Neural correlates of evaluation associated with promotion and prevention regulatory focus. *Cognitive, Affective, & Behavioral Neuroscience.* 5(2): 202-211.

Damasio, A. (1994). *Descartes Error: Emotion, Reason and the Brain.* New York: G. P. Putnam.

Davidson, M. C. & Marrocco, R. (2000). Local infusion of scopolamine into intraparietal cortex slows covert orienting in rhesus monkeys. *Journal of Neurophysiology,* 83: 1536-1549.

Davidson, R. J., Irwin, W. (1999). The functional neuroanatomy of emotion and affective style. *Trends in Cognitive Sciences,* 3(1): 11-21.

Desimone, R., & Duncan, J. (1995). Neural mechanisms of selective visual attention. *Annual Review of Neuroscience,* 18: 193-222.

Duncan, J., Seitz, R. J., Kolodny, J., Bor, D., Herzog, H., Ahmed, A., Newell, F. N., & Emslie, H. (2000). A neural basis for general intelligence. *Science,* 289: 457-460.

Eisenberg, N., Fabes, R. A., Nyman, M., Bernzweig, J., & Pinulas, A. (1994). The relations of emotionality and regulation to children's anger-related reactions. *Child Development,* 65: 109-128.

Eisenberg, N., Smith, C. L., Sadovsky, A., & Spinrad, T. L. (2004). Effortful control: Relations with emotion regulation, adjustment, and socialization in childhood. In: R. F. Baumeister & K. D. Vohs (Eds.), *Handbook of self regulation: Research, theory, and applications.* New York: Guilford Press. pp. 259-282.

Eriksen, B. A., & Eriksen, C. W. (1974). Effects of noise letters upon the identification of a target letter in a nonsearch task. *Perception & Psychophysics,* 16: 143-149.

Esteves, F., Dimberg, U., y Öhman, A. (1994). Automatically elicited fear: conditioned skin conductance responses to masked facial expressions. *Cognition and Emotion,* 8: 393-413.

Everitt, B. J. & Robbins, T. W. (1997). Central cholinergic systems and cognition. *Annual Review of Psychology,* 48: 649-648.

Fan, J., Flombaum, J. I., McCandliss, B. D., Thomas, K. M., & Posner, M. I. (2003). Cognitive and brain consequences of conflict. *NeuroImage,* 18 : 42-57.

Fazzio, R. H. (2001). On the automatic activation of associated evaluations: An overview. *Cognition and Emotion,* 15: 115-141.

Fitzsimons, G. M. & Bargh, J. A. (2004). Automatic Self-Regulation. In R. Baumeister and K. Vohs (Eds.), *Handbook of self-regulation.* New York: Guilford Press. pp 151-170.

Fonagy, P., & Target, M. (2002). Early intervention and the development of self-regulation. *Psychoanalytic Quarterly,* 22: 307-335.

Gehring, W. J., Gross, B., Coles, M. G. H., Meyer, D. E., & Donchin, E. (1993). A neural system for error detection and compensation. *Psychological Science,* 4: 385-390.

Gerardi-Caulton, G. (2000). Sensitivity to spatial conflict and the development of self-regulation in children 24-36 months of age. *Developmental Science,* 3(4): 397-404.

González, C., Fuentes, L. J., Carranza, J. A., & Estévez, A. F. (2001). Temperament and attention in the self-regulation of 7-year- old children. *Personality and Individuals Differences,* 30: 131-946.

Hebb, D. O. (1949). *The organization of behaviour: A neuropsychological theory.* New York: Wiley.

Higgins, E. T. (1997). Beyond pleasure and pain. *American Psychologist,* 52: 1280-1300.

Higgins, E. T., and Spiegel, S. (2004). Promotion and prevention strategies for self-regulation: A motivated cognition perspective. In R. Baumeister and K. Vohs (Eds.), *Handbook of self-regulation.* New York: Guilford Press. pp 171-188.

Holroyd, C. B., & Coles, M. G. H. (2002). The neural basis of human error processing: Reinforcement learning, dopamine and the error related negativity. *Psychological Review,* 109: 679-709.

James, W. (1890). *The principles of psychology.* New York: H. Holt and Company.

Jones, B.C., Jones, B.T., Blundell, L. & Bruce, G. (2002) Social users of alcohol and cannabis who detect substance-related changes in a change blindness paradigm report higher levels of use than those detecting substance-neutral changes. *Psychopharmacology,* 165: 93-96.

Knutson, B., Adams, C. M., Fong, G. W., & Hommer, D. (2001). Anticipation of increasing monetary reward selectively recruits nucleus accumbens. *Journal of Neuroscience,* 21(16), RC159.

Kochanska, G. (1991). Socialization and temperament in the development of guilt and conscience. *Child Development,* 62: 1379-1392.

Kochanska, G. (1997). Multiple pathways to conscience for children with different temperaments from toddlerhood to age 5. *Developmental Psychology,* 3: 228-240.

Kochanska, G., Murray, K. T., & Harlan, E. T. (2000). Effortful control in early childhood: Continuity and change, antecedents, and implications for social development. *Developmental Psychology,* 36: 220-232.

Kochanska, G., Murray, K., Jacques, T. Y., Koenig, A. L., & Vandegeest, K. A. (1996). Inhibitory control in young children and its role in emerging internationalization. *Child Development, 67:* 490-507.

Kopp, C. B. (1992). Emotional distress and control in young childrens. In R. A. Fabes & N. Eisenberg (Eds.), *Emotion and its regulations in early development.* San Francisco, CA: Jossey-Bass. pp 41-56.

Lang, P. J., Bradley, M. M., & Cuthbert, B. N. (1997). Motivated attention: affect activation and action. In: *Attention and orienting: sensory and motivational processes.* (Lang, P. J., Simons, R. F., Balaban, M. T., eds.), Hillsdale, NJ: Lawrence Erlbaum. pp 119-137.

Lang, P. J., Davis, M., Öhman, A. (2000). Fear and anxiety: animal models and human cognitive psychology. *Journal of Affective Disorders, 61:* 137-159.

Losier, B. J. W., & Klein, R. (2001). A review of the evidence for a disengage deficit following parietal damage. *Neuroscience and Behavioural Reviews, 25:* 1-13.

MacDonald, A. W., Cohen, J. D., Stenger, V. A., Carter, C. S. (2000). Dissociating the role of the dorsolateral prefrontal and anterior cingulate cortex in cognitive control. *Science,* 288: 1835-1838.

Mandler, G. (1984). *Mind and body: Psychology of emotion and stress.* New York: Norton & Company.

Marrocco, R. T., & Davidson, M. C. (1998). Neurochemistry of attention. In R. Parasuraman (ed.), *The Attentive Brain.* Cambridge, Mass: MIT Press, pp. 35-50.

Morris, J. S., Öhman, A., y Dolan, R. (1998). Conscious and unconscious emotional learning in the human amygdala. *Nature,* 393: 467-470.

Norman, D. A., & Shallice, T. (1986). Attention to action: Willed and automatic control of behavior. In R. J. Davidson, C. E. Schwartz, & D. Shapiro (Eds.), *Consciousness and self-regulation.* New York: Plenum Press. pp. 1-18.

Oatley, K. y Jenkins, J. M. (1992). Human emotions: Function and dysfunction. *Annual Review of Psychology,* 43: 55-85.

Ochsner K. N., Gross, J. J. (2004). Thinking makes it so: a social cognitive neuroscience approach to emotion regulation. In: R.F Baumeister, and K.D. Vohs (Eds.) *Handbook of Self-Regulation: Research Theory, and Applications.* New York: Guilford Press. Pp: *229-255.*

Ochsner, K. N., Bunge, S. A., Gross, J. J., & Gabrieli, J. D. E. (2002). Rethinking feelings: An fMRI study of the cognitive regulation of emotion. *Journal of Cognitive Neuroscience,* 14: 1215-1229.

Ochsner, K. N., Gross, J. J. (2005). The Cognitive control of emotion. *Trends in Cognitive Sciences, 9:* 242-249.

Ochsner, K. N., Kossyln, S. M., Cosgrove, G. R., Cassem, E. H., Price, B. H., Nierenberg, A. A., & Rauch, S. L. (2001). Deficits in visual cognition and attention following bilateral anterior cingulotomy. *Neuropsychology,* 39: 219-230.

Öhman, A. (1997). As fast as the blink of an eye: Evolutionary preparedness for preattentive processing of threat. In P.J. Lang, R.F. Simons, & M.T. Balaban (Eds.), *Attention and orienting: Sensory and motivational processes.* Mahwah, NJ: Lawrence Erlbaum. pp. 165-184.

Öhman, A. (1999). Distinguishing unconscious from conscious emotional processes: methodological considerations and theorical implications. En T. Dagleish & M. Power (Eds), *Handbook of Cognition and Emotion.* Chichester: Wiley. pp.321-352

Öhman, A. y Soares, J. J. F. (1993). On the automatic nature of phobic fear: condiciones electrodermal responses to masked fear-relevant stimuli. *Journal Abnormal Psychology,* 102: 121-132.

Öhman, A. y Soares, J. J. F. (1994). 'Unconscious anxiety': phobic responses to masked stimuli. *Journal of Abnormal Psychology,* 103: 231-240.

Öhman, A., Flykt, A., y Esteves, F. (2001). Emotion drives attention: Detecting the snake in the grass. *Journal of Experimental Psychology: General,* 130: 466-478.

Öhman, A., Lundqvist, D., y Esteves, F. (2001). The face in the crowd revisited: A threat advantage with schematic stimuli. *Journal of Personality and Social Psychology,* 80: 381-396.

Phelps, E. (2006). Emotion and Cognition: Insights from Studies of Human Amygdala. *Annual Review Psychology,* 57: 27-53.

Posner, M. I., & Dehaene, S. (1994). Attentional networks. *Trends in Neuroscience,* 7: 75-79.

Posner, M. I., & DiGirolamo, G. J. (1998) Executive attention: Conflict, target detection, and cognitive control. In R. Parasuraman (Ed.), *The attentive brain.* Cambridge: MIT Press. pp. 401-423

Posner, M. I., & Petersen, S. E. (1990). The attention system of the human brain. *Annual Review of Neuroscience,* 13: 25-42.

Posner, M. I., & Raichle, M. E. (1994*). Images of mind.* Scientific American Books.

Posner, M. I., & Raichle, M. E. (Eds.) (1998). Overview: The neuroimaging of human brain function. *Proceedings of the National Academy of Sciences of the USA,* 95: 763-764.

Posner, M. I., Rueda, M. R. & Kanske P. (2007). Probing the mechanisms of attention. In: J.T. Cacioppo, J.G. Tassinary & G.G. Berntson (Eds.) *Handbook of Psychophysiology. 3er Edition.* Cambridge, UK: Cambridge University Press. pp: 410-432.

.Rainville, P., Duncan, G. H., Price, D. D., Carrier, B., & Bushnell, M. C. (1997). Pain affect encoded in human anterior cingulated but not somatosensory cortex. *Science,* 277: 968-970.

Robbins, S.J. & Ehrman, R.N. (2004). The role of attentional bias in substance abuse. *Behavioral and Cognitive Neurescience Reviews,* 3: 243-260.

Rolls, E. T. (2000). The orbitofrontal cortex and reward. *Cerebral cortex,* 10(3): 284-294.

Rothbart, M. K. & Bates J. E. (2006). Temperament in children's development. In W. Damon & L. Lerner (Series Eds.) & N. Eisenberg (Vol. Ed.). *Handbook of child psychology:* Vol. 3. *Social, emotional, and personality development* (6th ed.). New York: Wiley. pp 99-166.

Rothbart, M. K., & Rueda, M. R. (2005). The development of effortful control. In: U. Mayr, E. Awh and S.W. Keele (Eds.) *Developing individuality in the human brain: A tribute to Michael I. Posner.* Washington, DC: American Psychological Association. pp. 167-188

Rothbart, M. K., Ahadi, S. A., Hershey, K., & Fisher, P. (2001). Investigations of temperament at three to seven years: The Children's Behavior Questionnaire. *Child Development,* 72: 1394-1408.

Rothbart, M. K., Ellis, L. K., Rueda, M. R., & Posner, M. I. (2003). Developing mechanisms of conflict resolution. *Journal of Personality,* 71: 1113-1143.

Rueda, M. R. Checa, P. & Santonja, M., (2007). Does motivation modulate executive attention? A developmental ERP study. Poster presented at *2007 Biennial Meeting of the Society for Research on Child Development (SRCD).* Boston (USA), Mars 29th – April 1st 2007.

Rueda, M. R., Posner, M. I., & Rothbart, M. K. (2004). Attentional control and self regulation. In: R. F. Baumeister & K. D. Vohs (Eds.), *Handbook of self regulation: Research, theory, and applications.* New York: Guilford Press. pp. 283-300.

Rueda, M. R., Posner, M. I., & Rothbart, M. K. (2005). The development of executive attention: contributions to the emergence of self-regulation. *Developmental Neuropsychology,* 28 (2): 573-594.

Schaefer, S. M., Jackson, D. C., Davidson, R. J., Aguirre, G. K., Kimberg, D. I. & Thompson-Schill, S. L. (2002). Modulation of amygdalar activity by the conscious regulation of negative emotion. *Journal of Cognitive Neuroscience,* 14: 913–921.

Shiner, R. L. (1998) How shall we speak of children's personality in middle childhood? A preliminary taxonomy. *Psychological Bulletin,* 124: 308-332.

Shiner, R. L. (2000). Linking childhood personality with adaptation: Evidence for continuity and change across time into late adolescence. *Journal of Personality and Social Psychology,* 78: 310-325.

Stewart, C., Burke, S. & Marrocco, R. (2001). Cholinergic modulation of covert attention in the rat. *Psychopharmacology,* 155 (2): 210-218.

Thompson, R. A. (1994). Emotion regulation: A theme in search of definition. In N. A. Fox (Ed.), *The development of emotion regulation: Biological and behavioural considerations. Monographs of the Society for Research in Child Development,* 59, pp. 25-52.

Turken, A. U., & Swick, D. (1999). Response selection in the human anterior cingulate cortex. *Nature Neurosceince,* 2(10): 920-924.

van Veen, V., & Carter, C. S. (2002). The timing of action-monitoring processes in the anterior cingulate cortex. *Journal of Cognitive Neuroscience,* 14: 593-602.

Vohs, K. D., & Baumeister, R. F. (2004). *Handbook of self regulation: Research, theory, and applications.* New York: Guilford Press.

Whalen, P. J., Bush, G., McNally, R. J., Wilhelm, S., McInerney, S. C., Jenike, M A. ,& Rauch, S. I. (1998). The emotional counting stroop paradigm: A functional magnetic resonance imaging probe of the anterior cingulated affective division. *Biological Psychiatry,* 44: 1219-1228.

Whalen, P. J., Rauch, S. L., Etcoff, N. L., McInerney, S. C., Lee, M. B., y Jenike, M. A. (1998). Masked presentations of emotional facial expressions modulate amygdala activity without explicit knowledge. *The Journal of Neuroscience,* 18(1): 411–418.

In: Psychology of Motivation
Editor: Lois V. Brown, pp. 47-63

ISBN: 978-1-60021-598-8
© 2007 Nova Science Publishers, Inc.

Chapter 3

The Motivational Function of Emotions: A "Feeling is for Doing" Perspective

Rob M. A. Nelissen and Marcel Zeelenberg

Social and Economic Psychology, Tilburg University, The Netherlands

Abstract

In this chapter we outline a recently developed "Feeling-is-for-Doing" perspective for the influence of specific emotions on decision-making and behavior. This perspective holds that discrete emotions present functional psychological mechanism involved in orchestrating goal-directed behavior. Studies corroborating the basic premises of this perspective are presented, along with results indicating that investigating the impact of specific emotions on people's decisions is indeed illustrative of the fundamental motives underlying their behavior. The Feeling-is-for-Doing perspective is then related to and compared with other theories about emotional influences on decision-making.

Always view interactions with others through the dispassionate lens of game theory: [...] Successful game strategies are often counter-intuitive; once you accept that idea, emotions start to make a lot more sense.

The Mind Game. Hector MacDonald, 2000; p. 49

Introduction

The Affect Revolution

Emotions have reinvaded the social sciences as valid accounts of human behavior (see for overviews, Loewenstein & Lerner, 2003; Schwarz, 2000). Several developments have contributed to this renewed interest. In psychology, Zajonc's (1980; see for an overview, Zajonc, 1998) studies showed that evaluative responses occur automatically and out of conscious awareness, separating affective processes from cognitive operations and thus designating affective phenomena as an independent field of research. Additionally, Damasio's (1994) research on patients with brain damage to neural structures associated with affective functions, indisputably demonstrated the indispensable contribution of affective processing to proper individual functioning and optimal decision-making. Simultaneously, in the field of behavioral economics, consistent violations from the principles of rational self-interest required the development of behavioral models with improved descriptive validity (e.g., Camerer, 2003; Colman, 2003). Emotional variables are often assigned a prominent position in these renewed models (e.g., Mellers, Schwartz & Ritov, 1999; Zeelenberg, van den Bos, van Dijk, & Pieters, 2002).

Finally, current emotion research is characterized by a pragmatic rather than a conceptual stance. This holds that in order to qualify as a valid explanatory concept, emotions must prove their merits by associations with some external criterion. Naturally, in the social sciences observed behavior presents the prime candidate to testify for these pragmatic merits (see for an elaborate argumentation along these lines, Zeelenberg & Pieters, 2006). Hence, rather than trying to determine *what* exactly constitutes an emotional episode – a question that paralyzed progress in the past and is unlikely to be resolved in the near future (e.g., Kleinginna & Kleinginna, 1981), research focus has shifted to investigating *how* emotions affect behavioral decisions. Notably, the development of reliable verbal and non-verbal ways to measure the occurrence of emotions (e.g., Larsen & Fredrickson, 1999), enabled the rise of this approach. Just as Fiske (1992) used the phrase "Thinking is for doing" to illustrate her pragmatic stance with respect to social cognition, we use the phrase "Feeling is for doing" to denote our pragmatic position in studying emotional influences on decision-making.

Beyond Valence

Consequently, both psychologists and economists have come to share an increasing interest in the role of emotions in decision-making and behavior in general. In current decision research (as in many fields outside core emotion theory), however, emotions are often superficially treated as valenced feeling states. That is, emotions are often equated with affect and reduced to a value on a positive-negative dimension. As such, positive emotions are thought to add utility and negative emotions to subtract utility of decision outcomes. Decision-making then, boils down to "hedonic calculus", in which pain and pleasure are summed and the net best alternative is picked (see also, Bentham, 1871). For instance, Cabanac (1992) proposes to compare emotions in terms of pleasure, which he refers to as the "common currency". Similarly, in Mellers et al.'s (1999) "subjective expected pleasure theory", counterfactual emotions (e.g., regret, disappointment, elation, rejoicing, and surprise) are expressed on a single "pain-pleasure" dimension.

This one-dimensional valence based approach has several shortcomings (see for an extended discussion, Zeelenberg & Pieters, 2006). First, behavioral consequences can be very different, even for emotions with the same valence, as we will show later in this chapter. Second, some emotions are hard to unambiguously assign a positive or negative valence. For instance, are surprise, schadenfreude, and hope unequivocally positive or negative feelings? We thus argue that, especially when one is interested in decision-making, a focus on the mere valence of emotions is insufficient. Solomon and Stone (2002, p. 431) aptly summarize this conviction. These emotion philosophers recently reviewed the emotion literature and concluded that:

> The analysis of emotions in terms of "valence", while it recognizes something essential about emotions [...] is an idea that we should abandon and leave behind. It serves no purpose but confusion and perpetrates the worst old stereotypes about emotion, that these are simple phenomena unworthy of serious research an analysis.

Thus, when interested in how emotions influence behavioral decision making, a focus on specific emotions is clearly required.

Overview

We have recently proposed a Feeling-is-for-Doing (FifD) approach to study the influence of emotions on people's decisions (e.g., Zeelenberg, Nelissen & Pieters, 2007; Zeelenberg & Pieters, 2006). Central to this approach is a focus on the entire spectrum of human emotions and the appreciation that this variety of feelings exists for the sake of behavioral guidance. The FifD approach predicts differential behavioral effects for different emotions, even if they are of similar valence, such as regret and disappointment, shame and guilt, and fear and anger.

In the following, we will first elaborate on the basic propositions of the FifD approach. Subsequently, we will present several studies that show how adopting a FifD perspective may help to resolve long-standing issues in research on interdependence situations. Specifically, we will demonstrate how considering the emotional concomitants of ultimatum offers may reveal the extent to which Allocators' decisions in ultimatum bargaining are motivated by concerns for fairness. We will then address several studies that indicate how decisions in interdependence situations may shed light on the psychological processes by which emotions influence behavioral decisions. Several perspectives have been developed on how emotions affect our decisions. Up till now, however, studies have not compared these approaches empirically. We will conclude with several issues that need to be taken into account in future research on emotions and decision-making.

FEELING IS FOR DOING

In a nutshell, the FifD approach holds that emotions are the primary motivational system underlying goal-directed behavior. It considers emotions to be evolved psychological solutions to adaptive problems (Cosmides & Tooby, 2000). Each emotion (e.g., fear) signals the implications of the present situation (being chased by Satan, the neighbors' dog) to maintain or realize a particular goal (to avoid harm). During an emotional experience, psychological processes (e.g., directing attention, activating relevant knowledge from memory) are recruited and action (running away) is motivated to accomplish this goal.

Emotions and Goals

Hence, the FifD approach emphasizes the goal-related nature of emotions, both concerning their elicitation as well as pertaining their behavioral consequences. In accordance with the former, appraisal theories of emotion elicitation outline the cognitive processes by which situations or events are analyzed along a number of dimensions that ultimately determine their relevance for individual concerns or goals (e.g., Ellsworth & Scherer, 2003). Although people may differ in their appraisal of a specific event, similar appraisals always accompany the elicitation of the same emotions. Knowledge of the content of these appraisals, therefore, helps us understand the antecedent conditions of specific emotions. Smith and Ellsworth (1985) identified six basic dimensions (pleasantness, certainty, attention, control, anticipated effort, and responsibility) on which various emotions can be differentiated. Supposedly, environmental stimuli vary along these dimensions, which causes them to elicit different emotions. For example, anger will be aroused if an event is appraised as unpleasant, one is certain about what happened, and perceives the event as caused by someone else. (Note that not all dimensions need to be involved in the elicitation of a particular emotion.) Research indicating that various emotions can indeed be discerned with respect to these appraisal dimensions, shows that different perceptions of goal-relevance indeed cause different emotional responses (Smith & Ellsworth, 1985). Furthermore, experimental manipulation of appraisals on a particular dimension (e.g., responsibility), for instance by having participants attribute events either to themselves or to another person, causes different emotional responses to an ambiguously described event (Neumann, 2000, for similar findings see, van Dijk, Zeelenberg & van der Pligt, 1999). Whereas repeated attribution to oneself elicited guilt (which is characterized by appraisals of personal responsibility for a negative event), external attributions resulted in anger (characterized by appraisals of other people's responsibility for negative events). Appraisal theories nicely capture the informational value of emotions as signals of goal-concern.

According to the FifD approach, goal-relatedness is apparent both from the elicitation of particular emotions, as well as from the behavioral response that follows an emotional experience. Fear signals danger as much as it motivates escape. Several authors attributed a central place to these behavioral aspects, claiming them to be the defining elements of an emotional state (e.g., McDougall, 1908; Tomkins, 1962; Frijda, 1986). Different views have emanated from considerations about the relation between emotion and motivation (see for an overview, Frijda, 2000). Some conceive emotions as the *cause* of motivation (e.g., Johnson-Laird & Oatley, 1992). Others regard emotions as the consequence of instigated dispositions for actions. For instance, McDougall (1908) refers to emotions as the "actualizations of instinct". Similarly, Buck (1999) speaks of emotions as the "readouts of motivation". Some (e.g., Bindra, 1959) have argued to abandon the distinction altogether. These views, however, share the notion that behavior is causally linked to the arousal of emotional states (Frijda, 2000).

In support of the idea that emotions are associated with distinct behavioral goals, Roseman and colleagues demonstrated that specific emotions are accompanied by the experience of distinct action goals, or "emotivations", defined as the end-result towards which behavior is directed (Roseman, Wiest & Schwartz, 1994). Similarly, we have shown that the frequency with which people experience certain emotions is related to the importance they adhere to the particular goal that is associated with that emotion (Nelissen, Dijker & DeVries,

2006). Specifically, we assessed frequency ratings for each of 11 positive and negative emotions, and correlated those with importance ratings of 10 value-types listed in the Schwartz' Value Survey (Schwartz, 1994). Values are regarded as motivational constructs that specify abstract goals guiding people's actions across context and time. We expected and found correspondence between importance-ratings and frequency estimates for values and emotions sharing a similar underlying goal. For example, we found that fear was associated with security values. So, people who indicated to often feel afraid ascribed greater importance to security values than people who less frequently experienced fear. The overall pattern of correlations in our data attested for the proposed relation between emotions and behavioral goals.

Building on these findings, the FifD approach argues that emotional states are associated with implicitly activated goals for action. This motivational aspect needs to be put at the forefront of explanations for the behavioral consequences of specific emotional states.

A Functional Perspective

As briefly mentioned, the FifD perspective attributes adaptive significance to the link between emotions and goals. Assuming that emotions exist for the sake of behavioral guidance, and perceiving behavior in general as a mechanism by which organisms enhance their inclusive fitness, we take the elicitation and behavioral influences of experienced emotional states to constitute a psychological solution to specific adaptive problems (cf., Cosmides & Tooby, 2000; Tooby & Cosmides, 1990). Adaptive problems are defined as recurrent conditions that presented opportunities or obstacles for physical and social survival. Hence, adaptive problems encountered consistently for long periods during evolutionary development (such as the potential for mate promiscuity, threat from predators, or maintaining status in a social group), spurred the development of psychological mechanisms generating behavioral patterns aimed to overcome the problem or to seize the opportunities present. Emotions like jealousy, fear, and pride or shame, constitute those mechanisms. They orchestrate systems of perception, attention, and memory and prioritize goals for action, aimed to maximize fitness or avoid decreases thereof vis-à-vis general classes of adaptive problems.

For instance, feelings of jealousy usually follow signs of imminent adultery, such as one's partner showing a lot of interest in someone else. Jealousy may be a beneficial trait that evolved precisely because it prevents the negative consequences of promiscuity. This idea is supported by empirical studies that show how stimuli that elicit feelings of jealousy are tailored to sex-dependent adaptive problems associated with adultery (Buss, 1999, but see DeSteno, Bartlett, Braverman, & Salovey, 2002 for a different view). Whereas men report feeling more jealous after their (female) partner commits an act of sexual infidelity, women report more jealousy if their partner commits "emotional infidelity", for instance by an intimate friendship with another woman. This pattern in emotional responding to infidelity follows from sexual selection pressures. As the greatest cost to a female's fitness would be to raise children without the help of her partner, emotional ties of that partner with another female constitutes a substantial threat. On the other hand, a male's fitness is most severely compromised by raising offspring that is not his own. Hence, sexual promiscuity presents a greater threat to men than is does to women. Many researchers nowadays share the view that emotions present mechanisms that prioritize goals for individual behavior in a way that during the course of evolution has proven most successful in enhancing the inclusive fitness of individuals (e.g., Ekman, 1992; Plutchik, 1991; Tooby & Cosmides, 1990; Haselton & Ketelaar, 2005).

Emotions and Interdependence Situations

Interdependence situations present a special class of adaptive problems. Interdependence situations constitute multiple-person interactions in which an individual's outcomes are dependent upon the choices made by others (cf. Thibaut & Kelley, 1959). Interdependence situations are ubiquitous in everyday life and involve tradeoffs between personal and group interests, conflicts between fairness and selfishness, and issues of trust in sequential interactions. Consider instances of reciprocal altruism: repeated acts of cooperation between unrelated members of a social group (Trivers, 1971). The opportunity for reciprocal altruism presents a classic example of an interdependence situation and a common adaptive problem for individuals living in social groups. Helping individuals to whom one is not related is beneficial (in an evolutionary sense) only if others will reciprocate the favor. Although mutual cooperation would likely increase the fitness of both partners, it is even more profitable to accept yet not to return favors. Consequently, individuals face a strong impetus to behave selfishly in these situations, that is, to exploit the benevolence of others.

Economic games are designed to model various interdependence situations. The case of reciprocal altruism is modeled, for instance, by sequential prisoner dilemma (PD) games. In the sequential PD game, two players alternately have a choice to cooperate or to defect. Mutual cooperation has a higher payoff (say €5 to both players) than mutual defection (€2 to each). Yet, if one player cooperates whereas the other defects, the defecting party gains even more (e.g., €8) whereas the cooperator then received the "suckers' payoff" (of €0). As defection is the dominant strategy, assuming self-interest would lead one to predict the player who decides first to defect, for another self-interested player would exploit a cooperative move by defecting in turn. This is not, however, what is commonly observed. In the numerous studies in which people play this game, a substantial number of people choose to cooperate and reciprocate a cooperative first move (Dawes, 1980). Under certain conditions, people even play cooperatively when the other player has already defected (Batson & Ahmad, 2001). In general, humans appear to consistently violate principles of self-interest when playing economic games (see for an overview, Camerer, 2003). Why is it that people ignore prescriptions of apparent rationality when they are so obvious given the simple structure of this and other games? Have millions of years of psychological evolution then created a species of collectively stupid individuals? Of course not...

As soon as we realize the long-term consequences of ostensibly rational strategies, we come to understand the adaptive value of behavioral decisions that run counter to predictions based on rational self-interest. Consider, for instance, a sequential PD game like the one described before, but now one in which two players interact an unknown number of times. In such (infinitely) repeated games, mutual cooperation would be a more profitable strategy than mutual defection. Hence, if both players would defect all the time, reciprocal altruism would perish and all suffer a personal loss as outcomes are lower than in a system which allows instances of reciprocal altruism. Yet what makes people overcome their rational, self-interested tendencies for defection? Theorists from Adam Smith (1759) to Robert Trivers (1971) and more recently John Elster (2004), and Robert Frank (2004), have argued that emotions operate as mechanisms for sustaining commitments to strategies that run counter to deceptively attractive immediate rewards. Frank (1988, p. 82) summarized this argument as follows:

> The idea is that if the psychological reward mechanism is constrained to emphasize rewards in the present moment, the simplest counter to a specious reward from cheating is to have a current feeling that tugs in precisely the opposite direction [...] because [the emotion] coincides with the moment of choice [...] it can negate the spurious attraction of the imminent material reward.

Hence, it is argued that feelings (like guilt) have evolved as restraints from exploiting acts of cooperation. Similarly, feelings of gratitude induce tendencies to reciprocate favors, whereas threats to retaliate others' failures to reciprocate are rendered credibility as they are accompanied by feelings of anger. In this perspective, emotions act as safeguards to detrimental behavioral tendencies that would otherwise stop individually favorable, long-term strategies dead in their tracks.

Several emotions are assumed to have developed in response to the type of adaptive problems presented by interdependence situations. These emotions do not arise in response to imminent personal concerns, like fear or jealousy. Rather, they signal adverse implications – particularly of personal conduct – for other people's welfare. Therefore, these feelings are referred to as moral emotions (cf., Haidt, 2003). Moral emotions fall into two large categories (Haidt, 2003; Ketelaar, 2005). On the one hand, other-focused emotions, like anger, arise in response to someone else intentionally causing harm to another person. On the other hand, self-focused emotions like guilt arise in response to or anticipation of oneself being responsible for another person's misfortune. Recent empirical tests corroborate these assertions by demonstrating exactly these kinds of effects for a number of purportedly moral emotions. For instance, feelings of guilt have been shown to enhance cooperation in PD and other economic games (De Hooge, Breugelmans & Zeelenberg, 2007; Ketelaar & Au, 2003; Nelissen, Dijker & DeVries, 2007). Alternately, anger has been found to instigate punishment of norm-violations in several economic games (e.g., Nelissen & Zeelenberg, 2007; Pillutla & Murnighan, 1996).

Summary

The studies discussed in this section present initial support for the basic propositions of the FifD approach, which holds that emotions drive behavioral decisions in the direction of specific goals and that this impact constitutes a functional process. Furthermore, it seems that a certain class of emotions (like guilt, gratitude, moral anger, etcetera) developed especially for their merits in upholding reciprocal altruism by coordinating decision-making in interdependence situations. This makes economic games, which constitute the blueprints of various interdependence situations, a useful tool for studying the effects of these moral emotions. Reflecting the conditions to which the behavioral effects of moral emotions were tailored by evolution, economic games present the key paradigm to map the psychological processes by which these emotions exert their influence. We will show how emotion-induced decisions in interdependence situations favor certain perspectives about emotional influences on behavior over others. First, however, we will illustrate how the FifD perspective on emotions may contribute to clarifying some controversies pertaining people's decisions in interdependence situations.

EMOTIONS AS INDICATORS OF MOTIVES UNDERLYING DECISIONS IN ULTIMATUM BARGAINING

From the previous discussion and the results cited therein, it seems apparent that emotions do indeed play a crucial role in motivating behavior that runs counter to self-interest and instigate seemingly irrational acts of trust, reciprocity and fairness. Therefore, we thought it should also be possible to determine whether people are truly concerned with fairness when involved in negotiations by measuring the extend to which particular emotions affect their decisions in bargaining situations.

Fairness, Fear and Guilt in Ultimatum Bargains

Over the past decades, the question of whether people have a sincere concern for fairness has spurred much research, mainly focusing on ultimatum bargaining (see for overviews, Camerer & Thaler, 1995; Güth & Tietz, 1990; Roth, 1995). The ultimatum game (Güth, Schmittberger & Schwarze, 1982) models the final step of negotiations, in which one player (the allocator) offers a proportion of some commodity to another player (the responder), who subsequently decides to accept this offer or not. If accepted, the commodity (usually some amount of money) will be distributed as proposed. If the offer is rejected, both players receive nothing. Results from ultimatum bargains consistently violate assumptions of rational self-interest, which prescribe people should offer (and accept) the minimal amount (as this is more than nothing). On average, allocators offer 30 – 40 %, with a 50 -50 split being the mode. At first, this was understood to indicate that allocators "often rely on what they consider a fair result" (Güth et al., 1982, p. 243). Nevertheless, offers below 20% of the pie are also rejected half the time. Anticipating this, allocators may not propose equal amounts out of a concern for fairness, but rather out of strategic self-interest (SSI), that is, in order to avoid rejection. At present, researchers have yet to reach consensus on this matter. We will argue that examining the influence of fear and guilt on allocators' decisions in ultimatum bargains can be informative with respect to the relative importance of fairness and SSI.

As already stated, fear is associated with an implicit goal to avoid personal harm. In an ultimatum game, the focal threat is that of a rejected offer, which would comprise the most detrimental outcome to the allocator. We therefore predict that the extent to which SSI underlies offers is reflected by allocators' fear over rejection when proposing unequal offers. Guilt is associated with a goal to avoid or repair moral transgressions, particularly from acts that cause harm to another person. We therefore predict that feeling guilt over proposing an unequal offer reflects the extent to which allocators are motivated by concerns for fairness. We found support for the idea that these emotions are indeed viable indicators of allocators' motives (Nelissen, Leliveld & Zeelenberg, 2006). In three studies we showed that individual and situational differences in the importance of fairness and SSI motives are indeed related to experiences of guilt and fear respectively.

Three Studies

In the first study, we assessed levels of anticipated fear and guilt over proposing unequal offers for people who differ in the extent to which they consider fairness important. Hereto we compared individuals with different social value orientations. Social value orientations are defined as stable, individual preferences for outcome distributions between oneself and another person (McClintock, 1972). In general, two types of social value orientations are discerned, pro-selves and pro-socials. Pro-selves are motivated to maximize their own outcome, whereas pro-socials also strive for equality and try to maximize joint outcomes (e.g., Van Lange, 1999). This implies different motives to refrain from unequal offers for pro-social and pro-self allocators. The latter, being solely interested in maximizing their own payoff, merely try to avoid rejection. Pro-socials try to avoid rejection as well as they are also concerned with their personal outcome, yet they also strive to achieve a fair outcome for the other player. Previous research has indeed demonstrated that pro-socials are truly concerned with fairness as they, unlike pro-selves, are not inclined to trick responders by making an unfair offer look like an equal split when given an opportunity thereto (Van Dijk, De Cremer & Handgraaf, 2004). Corroborating this, we found that pro-social and pro-self allocators differ in the level of guilt (but not fear) they experience over unequal offers, supporting our assumption that feelings of guilt reflect the extent to which people are concerned with fairness.

In the second study, we compared situational differences in the importance of fairness and the need to avoid rejection. The need to avoid rejection was manipulated by varying the dependency of the allocators' payoff on the responders decision to accept or reject the offer. Hereto, we used a manipulation that altered the consequences of rejection by specifying a proportion of the proposed amount that players would still receive in case of rejection. Our manipulation included a high-dependency (rejection reduces the payoff substantially) and a low-dependency (rejection only slightly reduces the payoff) condition. Additionally, initial ownership was manipulated to vary the importance of fairness. Hereto, we adopted an elegant procedure, designed by Leliveld and co-workers, in which offers are compared between a give and a take-frame of the standard ultimatum game (Leliveld, van Dijk & van Beest, 2007). In the give-frame, allocators decided how much of their endowment to give to the responder. In the take-frame, allocators took a proportion of the endowment initially owned by the responder. As taking can be considered more inappropriate than giving the same amount, people are generally more reluctant to take than to give a certain proportion of the initial endowment. We investigated whether the effects of our manipulations of dependency and ownership varied for individuals with varying dispositions for fear and guilt.

Emotional dispositions capture individual variation in the tendency to experience particular emotional states. We predicted that, if guilt is indeed related to fairness concerns, the effects of initial ownership should be more pronounced for allocators high in dispositional guilt. Similarly, the impact of dependency should be stronger for individuals high in dispositional fear. Our results confirmed the first expectation, but the effects of dependency were the same irrespective of the level of dispositional fear. It thus seems that SSI motivates offers of allocators alike, whereas only a subset, those that are likely to experience guilt, are affected by fairness concerns. Note that in the first study, we also did not find differences in levels of anticipatory fear between pro-socials and pro-selves. We reasoned that because of the interdependent nature of the ultimatum bargaining situation, it may well have been that allocators' invariably consider the risk of rejection. Avoiding rejection then motivates allocators alike, while individual differences exist in the extent to which fairness influences offers.

Though preliminary, these results show that emotions can reveal the nature of motives underlying peoples behavior as was suggested by the FifD perspective. Moreover, they show how considering emotional influences may help resolve issues that three decades of designing experimental manipulations on ultimatum bargaining could not elucidate. From an emotional viewpoint then, people are motivated by fairness to the extent that they experience feelings reflecting fairness, in this case guilt. In the following section we will turn the table and use behavior in games to draw conclusions on the nature of emotional influences.

DECISIONS IN INTERDEPENDENCE SITUATIONS AS INDICATORS OF PROCESSES MEDIATING EMOTIONAL INFLUENCE

As outlined, the Feeling-is-For-Doing approach is a *goal-based account* of the influence of experienced emotions on people's decisions. Generally, emotions are predicted to guide decisions in the direction of the outcome that is (most) conducive to the attainment of the emotional goal. Hence, goal-based accounts focus on the goal setting and striving implications of emotional experiences.

Information or Motivation

Apart from the studies cited in the previous section, several others have explicitly adopted and supported a goal-based perspective, by demonstrating congruence between observed decisionals and the goals associated with particular emotional states (e.g., Fessler, Pillsworth & Flamson, 2004; de Hooge et al., 2007; Ketelaar & Au, 2003; Raghunathan & Pham, 1999). Nevertheless, these results do not conclusively attest for the idea that goal-activation associated with emotional arousal causes these effects. So far, only a single empirical study that we are aware of has indicated a goal-activation mechanism to be involved in the observed consequences of induced emotional states (Nelissen et al., 2007). This study reported fear to reduce and guilt to increase cooperation in a prisoner-dilemma interaction. These effects were qualified, however, by a significant interaction between the emotional state and an individual's social value orientation. Specifically, fear only decreased cooperation for pro-socials, whereas only guilty pro-selves showed increased levels of cooperation.

Social value orientations can be understood in terms of individual variation in the chronic accessibility of situation-relevant goals for action (De Cremer & Van Lange, 2001; Van Lange, 1999). Specifically, when confronted with a social dilemma, pro-selves only have their self-interest in mind and attempt to make as much as possible profit, whereas pro-socials also take the other players interest into account. Temporal goal-activation due to an induced emotional state only changes the behavior of individuals to whom this goal was not already chronically accessible (Higgins, 1996). Hence fear, inducing a goal to avoid personal risk, does not affect pro-socials, as they are already chronically motivated to avoid the risk of loosing to the other party. Guilt on the other hand, associated with an implicit goal to make-up for transgressions, inducing a tendency to cooperate, does not affect pro-socials, as they already have the other player's interest in mind. These interactions suggest that both emotions and individual dispositions operate through the same underlying mechanism of goal-accessibility, yet obviously present only an indirect indication thereof. Goal-based perspectives to account for the effects of emotions are recent and we are just beginning to understand how emotions work. Proceeding along this line, future studies should directly test whether emotional states are indeed related to increased goal-activity.

Still, apart from goal-based perspectives on emotional influences, other approaches have been proposed as well. Specifically, *information-based accounts* highlight the nature of inferences that people in a particular emotional state are likely to draw. Focusing on the cues that emotions give about past goal performance, information-based accounts zoom in on the feedback function of emotions. Generally, they predict emotional influences in case of commonality between the central appraisal dimensions associated with the emotion and the principal dimension of judgment involved in a particular choice situation.

For instance, the appraisal tendency hypothesis (e.g., Lerner & Keltner, 2000) conceives that each emotion activates a tendency to evaluate future events in line with the central dimensions of the appraisal that triggered the emotion. These *appraisal tendencies* thus are perceptual inclinations by which emotions color the cognitive interpretation of stimuli. Support comes from a series of studies in which dispositional and situationally induced differences in people's experiences of fear and anger were found to be associated with differences in risk-perception (Lerner & Keltner, 2000; 2001). Fear and anger differ in their appraisals of control and certainty, which are low in fear and high in anger. Perceptions of risk depend mainly on people's estimates of their abilities to exert personal control in a particular situation and a sense of predictability (i.e., certainty) over the outcome of that situation. When afraid, people make more pessimistic judgments of risk (i.e., estimating the number of casualties due to various events) than people who are angry. Moreover, fear was also associated with preferences for risk-averse options, whereas anger was associated with risk-seeking preferences.

Past and Future Oriented Approaches

It is important to note that the information-based accounts take a backward looking stance with respect to goal progress. That is, emotions provide information about how one is currently doing. This affective feedback informs about the extent of goal progress, but does not provide the decision maker with clear guidelines for how to attain these goals in the future. Goal-based perspectives are by definition future oriented as they emphasize the directives of emotional states for future goal pursuit. We therefore argue for the superior suitability of goal-based perspectives to account for the influence of specific emotions on behavioral decisions (see for a more detailed description of this argument, Zeelenberg,

Nelissen & Pieters, 2006). Closer inspection at a theoretical level reveals that information-based accounts are more apt at accounting for judgment effects than at decision-making effects, and related goal pursuits. That is, emotions clearly color or bias judgments. Such, almost automatic appraisal tendency effects of emotions are well documented. Yet, interestingly, in these studies the emotion is the "end" of a goal pursuit sequence, and this was followed by a moment were judgments were called for, and the latter were obviously colored by the former. Thus when goal pursuit ends (or did not yet initiate) and an emotion is still activated, it influences judgment in an appraisal consistent fashion. Yet, when the emotion is part of a sequence of ongoing goal pursuit, such "appraisal consistency" effects are much less obvious. Then, one needs to know the overarching goal of people and the activated emotion to predict future behavior, as we saw earlier. Motivational perspectives, by emphasizing the implicit goals associated with current feeling states instead of foregrounding inferential processes, provide this link.

Future research should compare both perspectives, preferably by a direct empirical investigation, for instance of the impact of emotions like guilt and regret on people's decisions about allocations in a trust game. Guilt and regret share virtually similar appraisals (cf. Smith & Ellsworth, 1985). Notably, both feelings are related to perceptions of personal responsibility for a negative event. Consequently, the Appraisal Tendency Framework would predict similar effects of both emotions on the size of the amount allocated to the trustee. Nevertheless, guilt and regret are associated with widely diverging goals for behavior. Specifically, guilt is associated with a goal to prevent or make up for a social transgression, whereas regret is related to the goal to repair (or prevent) a personal loss. Thus, from a goal-based perspective, guilt would be expected to increase amounts allocated to a trustee (compared to a control group, whereas regret would cause allocators to avoid negative personal outcomes, decreasing the amount transferred to the trustee. Results form studies like these would aid to resolve issues concerning the psychological processes by which emotions affect behavior.

Towards Integration?

Sometimes integration is advocated of the informational and motivational functions of emotions into a single model, arguing that "affective states convey not only situational appraisal information, but also motivational information" (Pham, 2004, p. 363). Similarly, in its original formulation, the Appraisal Tendency Approach is claimed to encompass not only cognitive-appraisal theories, but also functional views of emotions, delineating the regulating role of emotions in shaping behavioral responses (Lerner & Keltner, 2000). Yet both assertions overlook that inference (backward looking for meaning of past states) and motivation (forward looking for desirable end-states and ways to get there) are fundamentally distinct processes that require independent demonstration and that neither of both automatically implies the other. In other words, as we have tried to demonstrate activation of appraisal tendencies cannot simply be equated with the activation of goals for action. Hence, suggesting that emotions cause different situational inferences and *as a result* will induce different goals (Pham, 2004), constitutes too big a leap in the face of current data.

It is not our intention to contest the idea that emotions have at the same time an informational and a motivational component—they do. Nor do we contradict the assertion that both can be meaningfully related, as was already noted by Frijda (1988, 2006) when discussing the "Laws of Emotion." As such, we find ourselves supportive to (future) attempts at integrating motivational and informational effects of emotions into a single framework. In our opinion, however, such attempts are still premature, especially as both informational and motivational perspectives still await further validation themselves.

In sum, studies on emotional influences on behavior in interdependence situations not only show that certain findings contradict predictions from informational accounts, this perspectives also seem to lack sufficiency and capability to explain reported effects of emotional states on decision-making. Informational accounts seem to be better suited to explain the effect of emotion on cognitive processing. Goal-based accounts seem to be more appropriate for investigating the ways in which emotions impact the behavioral decisions we make.

CONCLUSION

We have proposed a Feeling-is-for-Doing perspective to understand emotional influences on decision-making and behavior. As outlined in the present chapter, this perspective maintains that specific emotions are the primary motivational system underlying goal-directed behavior. The behavioral consequences of emotional states are functional in negotiating interactions of people with their (social) environment. In support of the Feeling-is-for-Doing perspective, research has established the goal-related nature of discrete emotional states, both in terms of elicitation by situational cues of concern-relevance, and in terms of behavioral end-states. We have further illustrated that measuring moral emotions may reveal peoples motives in interdependent situations. Finally, we pursued the notion that goal-based accounts, like the Feeling-is-for-Doing perspective, provide a more suitable approach for understanding emotions-specific influences on behavior than other, mainly information-based accounts. Still, research emphasis has only just shifted to more detailed questions concerning the nature of psychological processes, and we are reluctant to provoke resistance on this point which would be detrimental to progress in this domain. Rather, we adhere to the view that the diversifications and deepening of research questions, illustrated by issues like these, testifies for the general appreciation of emotional influences in decision-making research. It seems that in spite of some dispute, there is abundant agreement that in order to comprehend what we *do* we need to consider what we *feel*.

REFERENCES

Batson, C. D., & Ahmad, N. (2001). Empathy induced altruism in a prisoner's dilemma II: What if the target of empathy has defected? *European Journal of Social Psychology, 31,* 25-26.

Bentham, J. (1789/1948). *An introduction to the principles of morals and legislation.* New York: Hafner.

Bindra, D. (1959). *Motivation: A systematic reinterpretation.* New York: Ronald Press.

Buss, D. M. (1999). The evolutionary psychology of human social strategies. In E. T. Higgins & A. W. Kruglanski (Eds.), *Social psychology: Handbook of basic principles* (Vol. 1, pp. 3-38). New York: Guilford Press.

Cabanac, M. (1992). Pleasure, the common currency. *Journal of Theoretical Biology,* 155, 173-200.

Camerer, C. F. (2003). Strategizing in the brain. *Science, 300,* 1673-1675.

Camerer, C., & Thaler, R. H. (1995). Anomalies: Ultimatums, dictators and manners. *Journal of Economic Perspectives, 9,* 209-219.

Colman, A. M. (2003). Cooperation, psychological game theory, and limitations of rationality in social interaction. *Behavioral and Brain Sciences, 26,* 139-198.

Cosmides, L., & Tooby, J. (2000). Evolutionary psychology and the emotions. In M. Lewis & J. M. Haviland-Jones (Eds.), *Handbook of Emotions* (pp. 91-115). New York: Guilford Press.

Damasio, A. R. (1994). *Descartes' error: Emotion, reason, and the human brain.* New York: Putnam.

Dawes, R. M. (1980). Social dilemmas. *Annual Review of Psychology, 31,* 169-193.

De Cremer, D., & Van Lange, P. A. M. (2001). Why prosocials exhibit greater cooperation than proselfs: the roles of social responsibility and reciprocity. *European Journal of Personality, 15:* 5-18.

DeSteno, D., Bartlett, M. Y., Braverman, J., & Salovey, P. (2002). Sex differences in jealousy: Evolutionary mechanism or artefact of measurement? *Journal of Personality and Social Psychology, 83,* 1103-1116.

Ekman, P. (1992). An Argument for Basic Emotions. *Cognition and Emotion, 6:* 169-200.

Ellsworth, P. C., & Scherer, K. R. (2003). Appraisal processes in emotion. In Davidson, R. J., Scherer, K. R., & Goldsmith, H. H. (Eds.) *Handbook of affective sciences.* New York, NY: Oxford University Press.

Elster, J. (2004). Emotions and rationality. In A. S. R. Manstead, N. Frijda & A. Fischer (Eds.), *Feelings and emotions: The Amsterdam symposium* (pp. 30-48). Cambridge: Cambridge University Press.

Fessler, D. M. T., Pillsworth, E. G., & Flamson, T. J. (2004). Angry men and disgusted women: An evolutionary approach to the influence of emotions on risk taking. *Organizational Behavior and Human Decision Processes, 95,* 107-123.

Fiske, S. T. (1992). Thinking is for doing: Portraits of social cognition from Daguerreotype to laserphoto. *Journal of Personality and Social Psychology, 63,* 877-889.

Frank, R. H. (2004). Introducing moral emotions into models of rational choice. In: A. S. R. Manstead, N. Frijda, & A. Fischer (Eds.), *Feelings and emotions: The Amsterdam symposium* (pp. 422 - 440). New York: Cambridge University Press.

Frijda, N. H. (2000). The psychologists' point of view. In M. Lewis & J. M. Haviland-Jones (Eds.), *Handbook of emotions* (pp. 59-74). New York: Guilford Press.

Frijda, N. H. (1988) The laws of emotion. *American Psychologist, 43,* 349-358.

Frijda, N. H. (1986). *The emotions.* Cambridge, England: Cambridge University Press.

Güth, W., Schmittberger, R., & Schwarze, B. (1982). An experimental analysis of ultimatum-bargaining. *Journal of Economic Behavior and Organization, 3,* 367-388.

Güth, W., & Tietz, R. (1990). Ultimatum bargaining behavior: A survey and comparison of experimental results. *Journal of Economic Psychology, 11,* 417-449.

Haidt, J. (2003). The moral emotions. In R. J. Davidson, K. R. Scherer & H. H. Goldsmith (Eds.), *Handbook of affective sciences* (pp. 852-870). NY: Oxford University Press.

Haselton M. G., & Ketelaar, T. (2007). Irrational emotions or emotional wisdom? The evolutionary psychology of affect and behavior. In J. P. Forgas (Ed.), *Hearts and minds: Affective influences on social cognition and behavior.* New York: Psychology Press.

Higgins, E. T. (1996). Knowledge activation: Accessibility, applicability, and salience. In E. T. Higgins & A. W. Kruglanski (Eds.), *Social psychology: Handbook of basic principles.* (pp. 133-168). New York: Guilford Press.

Hooge, I. E. de, Breugelmans, S. M., & Zeelenberg, M. (2007). Moral sentiments and cooperation: Differential influences of shame and guilt. *Cognition and Emotion*, in press.

Johnson-Laird, P. N., & Oatley, K. (1992). Basic Emotions, Rationality, and Folk Theory. *Cognition and Emotion,* 6: 201-223.

Ketelaar, T., & Au, W. T. (2003). The effects of feelings of guilt on the behavior of uncooperative individuals in repeated social bargaining games: An affect-as-information interpretation of the role of emotion in social interaction. *Cognition and Emotion,* 17, 429-453.

Kleinginna, P. R., & Kleinginna, A. M. (1981). A categorized list of emotion definitions, with suggestions for a consensual definition. *Motivation and Emotion*, 5, 345-379.

Leliveld, M. C., Van Dijk, E., & Van Beest, I. (2006). De rol van aanvankelijk bezit in ultimatum onderhandelingen. In R. W. Holland, J. Ouwerkerk, C. van Laar, R. Ruiter, & J. Ham (Eds.), *Jaarboek Sociale Psychologie* (pp. 301-310). Groningen, the Netherlands: ASPO Pers.

Lerner, J. S., & Keltner, D. (2001). Fear, anger, and risk. *Journal of Personality and Social Psychology,* 81: 146-159.

Lerner, J. S., & Keltner, D. (2000). Beyond valence: Toward a model of emotion specific influences on judgement and choice. *Cognition and Emotion,* 14: 473-493.

Loewenstein, G. & Lerner J. S. (2003). The role of affect in decision making. In R. Davidson, H. Goldsmith, & K. Scherer (Eds.), *Handbook of affective science* (pp. 619-642). Oxford: Oxford University Press.

MacDonald, H. (2000). *The mind game.* London, UK: Penguin Books.

McClintock, C. G. (1972). Social motivation – a set of propositions. *Behavioral Science,* 17, 438-454.

McDougall, W. (1908). *An introduction to social psychology.* London: Methuen.

Mellers, B. A., Schwartz, A., & Ritov, I., (1999). Emotion-based choice. *Journal of Experimental Psychology: General,* 128, 346-361.

Nelissen, R. M. A., Dijker, A. J., & De Vries, N. K. (2007). Emotions and goals: Assessing relations between values and emotions. *Cognition and Emotion*, in press.

Nelissen, R. M. A., Dijker, A. J., & de Vries, N. K. (2007). How to turn a hawk into a dove and vice versa: Interactions between emotions and goals in a give-some dilemma game. *Journal of Experimental Social Psychology,* 43, 280-286.

Nelissen, R. M. A., & Zeelenberg, M. (2007). Why we punish: Emotional determinants of altruistic punishment, manuscript under review.

Nelissen, R. M. A., Leliveld, M. C., & Zeelenberg, M. (2007). *Feeling fairness: Emotions as indicators of allocators' motives in ultimatum bargaining.* manuscript under review.

Neumann, R. (2000). The causal influence of attributions on emotions: A procedural priming approach. *Psychological Science,* 11: 179-182.

Pham, M. T. (2004). The logic of feeling. *Journal of Consumer Psychology,* 14, 360-369.

Pillutla, M. M., & Murnighan, J. K. (1996). Unfairness, anger, and spite: Emotional rejections of ultimatum offers. *Organizational Behavior and Human Decision Processes,* 68, 208-224.

Plutchik, R. (1991). Emotions and Evolution. In K. T. Strongman (Ed.), *International Review of Studies on Emotion* (Vol. 1). Sussex: Wiley, J. & Sons.

Raghunathan, R., & Pham, M. T. (1999). All negative moods are not equal: Motivational influences of anxiety and sadness on decision making. *Organizational Behavior and Human Decision Processes,* 79, 56–77.

Roseman, I. J., Wiest, C., & Swartz, T. S. (1994). Phenomenology, behaviors, and goals differentiate discrete emotions. *Journal of Personality and Social Psychology,* 67, 206-221.

Roth, A. E. (1995). Bargaining experiments. In J. H. Hagel, & A. E. Roth (Eds.), *The handbook of experimental economis* (pp. 253-348). Princeton, NJ: Princeton University Press.

Schwarz, N. (2000). Emotion, cognition, and decision making. *Cognition and Emotion,* 14: 433-440.

Schwartz, S. H. (1994). Are there universal aspects in the structure and contents of human values? *Journal of Social Issues,* 50, 19-45.

Solomon, R. C., & Stone, L. D. (2002). On "positive" and "negative" emotions. *Journal for the Theory of Social Behaviour,* 32, 417-443.

Smith, A. (1759/1976). *The theory of moral sentiments.* Oxford: Clarendon Press.

Smith, C. A., & Ellsworth, P. C. (1985). Patterns of cognitive appraisal in emotion. *Journal of Personality and Social Psychology,* 48, 813-838.

Thibaut, J. W., & Kelley, H. H. (1959). *The social psychology of groups.* Oxford, England: John Wiley.

Tomkins, S. S. (1962). The positive affects (Vol. 1): Affect, imagery, and consciousness. New York: Springer.

Tooby, J., & Cosmides, L. (1990). The past explains the present: Emotional adaptations and the sructure of ancestral environments. *Ethology and Sociobiology,* 11: 375-424.

Van Dijk, E., De Cremer, D., & Handgraaf, M. J. J. (2004). Social value orientations and the strategic use of fairness in ultimatum bargaining. *Journal of Experimental Social Psychology, 40,* 697-707.

Van Dijk, W. W., Zeelenberg, M., & van der Pligt, J. (1999). Not having what you want versus having what you not want: The impact of type of negative outcome on the experience of disappointment and related emotions. *Cognition and Emotion, 13,* 129-148.

Van Lange, P. A. M. (1999). The pursuit of joint outcomes and equality in outcomes: an integrative model of social value orientations. *Journal of Personality and Social Psychology,* 77, 337-349.

Zajonc, R. B. (1998). Emotions. In D. Gilbert, S. T. Fiske & G. Lindzey (Eds.), *The handbook of social psychology* (pp. 591-632). NY: Oxford University Press.

Zajonc, R. B. (1980). Feeling and thinking: Preferences need no inferences. *American Psychologist,* 35: 151-175.

Zeelenberg, M., van den Bos, K., van Dijk, E., & Pieters, R. (2002). The inaction effect in the psychology of regret. *Journal of Personality and Social Psychology, 82,* 314-327.

Zeelenberg, M., & Pieters, R. (2006). Feeling is for doing: A pragmatic approach to the study of emotions in economic behavior. In De Cremer, D., Zeelenberg, M., & Murnighan, K. (Eds.) *Social Psychology and Economics*. Mahwah, NJ: Erlbaum.

Zeelenberg, M., Nelissen, R. M. A., & Pieters, R. (2007) Emotion, motivation and decision making: A feeling-is-for-doing approach. In: Plessner, H., Betsch, C., & Betsch, T. (Eds.), *A new look on intuition in judgment and decision making*. Mahwah, NJ: Erlbaum.

In: Psychology of Motivation
Editor: Lois V. Brown, pp. 65-82

ISBN: 978-1-60021-598-8
© 2007 Nova Science Publishers, Inc.

Chapter 4

SOCIAL PSYCHOLOGICAL MOTIVATIONS AND FOUNDATIONS OF DIETARY PREFERENCE

Marc Stewart Wilson [*]
Victoria University, Wellington, New Zealand
Michael W. Allen [†]
Sydney University, Sydney, Australia

ABSTRACT

This chapter represents a summary of a programme of research conducted over the past ten years focusing on the motivations, explanations, and correlates of dietary preference and behaviour. While there is a significant body of literature attesting to the psychophysiological correlates and of different dietary practices, as well as a clinical literature on pathological dietary behaviours and avoidances, there is only a relatively small body of research investigating the psychological motivations for adopting different practices. In a number of studies we have sought to locate diet into existing theories of choice and behaviour in social psychology, focusing particularly on the motivational foundation of social values, materialism, and beliefs about hierarchy and tradition. In this chapter we bring together the findings of this range of studies to try to give an overall picture of how dietary behaviour can be fitted into the broad context of social psychology. As well as discussing the role that values, materialism, and other beliefs and attitudes account for a range of dietary behaviours we have as a specific interest the foundations of the 'decision' to consume or abstain from consuming meat, and animal-derived products. As well as acting as a microcosm for broader dietary behaviour, meat abstention also represents a social 'deviant' practice in many Western cultures, as it is adopted by a minority.

---

[*] Correspondence should be addressed to Dr. Marc Wilson. Senior Lecturer, School of Psychology, PO Box 600, Victoria University of Wellington, Wellington, New Zealand, Telephone 463-5225, Fax 463-5402, Email. marc.wilson@vuw.ac.nz

[†] Senior Lecturer, University of Sydney, Discipline of Marketing, School of Business, Economics and Business Building (H69), Sydney NSW 2006, Australia, Phone: +61 2 9351 6003, Fax: +61 2 9351 6732, Email: m.allen@econ.usyd.edu.au

That we eat because we have to, is such a truism that it seems almost silly to invite discussion about motivations towards eating. Clearly, there is great variation in whether, and how much, people in different places actually eat, but this is heavily influenced by situational and environmental features rather than simply individual choice. At the same time, what we choose to eat is much more open to variation and choice, and therefore should be an obvious source of interest to social scientists and psychological researchers (e.g., Allen & Ng, 2003; Allen, Wilson, Ng, & Dunne, 1999; Amato & Partridge, 1989; Beardsworth & Keil, 1997; Wiggins, 2001). Obvious also because so much of what we eat is governed not by deliberation but tradition (at the cultural level) and habit (at the individual level).

This chapter presents a review of an ongoing programme of research into psychological aspects of food-choice, with a particular focus on the practice of meat consumption (and avoidance). This focus partly reflects our individual preference (one of us is a proselytising vegetarian), but one need only go out for a meal with friends or colleagues to appreciate the symbolic, psychological, and physiological importance of meat in almost any cultural dietary scheme. In the event that someone we eat with indicates a non-normative preference either explicitly (by stating their preference outright) or implicitly (by what they order) the scene is set for discussion about the 'reasons' for their practice.

As well as the social importance associated with food and food rituals, meat consumption is a specific practice that has very real positive and negative consequences for the individual. We're not only talking here about the nutrition provided by meat, and meat substitutes, but also the negative consequences that are potentially beyond the control of the individual. For example, one need only look to Britain during the mid-1990s (during the 'Mad Cow' scare), and early 2000s ('Foot and Mouth') to see dramatic reaction to health-related fears arising from food. These scares co-occur around the same time as an alleged increase in the popularity of meat-free diets (Leech, 1996). Indeed, health-related arguments are commonly reported by those who reduce or remove meat from their diets, or engage in other dietary changes. Goode, Beardsworth, Haslam, Keil, and Sherratt (1995) reported that the majority of a British sample indicated dietary changes due to an increased awareness of healthy diets, while one third reported dietary change due to a food scare. Reduced meat consumption is recommended by some sources for a healthy diet. For example the World Health Organisation (1990) endorses increased consumption of vegetables and fruit and decreased meat as part of a healthy diet. At the same time, complete abstinence from meat and animal products may be problematic for health. Recently, a New Zealand couple have been convicted of failing to provide the necessities of life following the death of their infant child from a vitamin B deficiency attributed to their vegan lifestyle (Dominion Post, June 5, 2002).

What motivates people to reduce or eliminate meat and other animal products from their diet? One obvious next step is to simply ask them. While this is intuitive, reasonable, and necessary, we shall take as our start point not the characteristics of individuals, but the social meanings of meat. One of our starting points in this research programme was provided by Twigg (1983) who argued that "Meat is the most highly prized of food. It is the centre around which a meal is arranged. It stands in a sense of the very idea of food itself" (p. 22). In fact, the status of meat exceeds its potential nutritional importance, and extends into the realm of the meanings with which it has become associated. Some of this meaning is socially constructed, with meat symbolising individual-level values that themselves derive from cultural-level values. These meanings are reflected in the reasons why many individuals choose to eat or abstain from eating various foodstuffs. In fact, what is considered as food in the first place is clearly and culturally constituted, as indicated by the variation in what is considered appropriate or inappropriate to eat. Our early studies investigated the human values, attitudes, and personal traits of omnivores and vegetarians to explore the ways in which the social values of meat may be reflected in the personal characteristics of meat eaters and abstainers. We shall start by presenting some of the background to this investigation.

In general usage, the term 'vegetarian' implies a distinct social grouping (and that non-vegetarians are also a distinct group). However, numerous studies have tended to suggest that as well as important differences, the overlap between 'groups' is much greater than the difference. For example, Cooper, Wise and Mann (1985) reported that vegetarians display hypochondriasis more than the general population, and an analytical cognitive style in which relationships in the environment are isolated and intellectualised. Similarly, Back and Glasgow (1981) reported that vegetarians define themselves through opposition – not so much on who they are, but who they are not. At the same time, other psychological studies have found fewer and weaker differences between vegetarians and omnivores (the term we will use to describe people who do eat meat). Examples include West (1972) and Lester (1979) who reported that vegetarians show the same personality profiles as omnivores. Even Cooper, et al's (1985) finding of elevated symptomatology in vegetarians was for hypochondriasis, which could be explained as simple health concerns, consistent with the possibility that vegetarians are motivated more strongly by health concerns. Thus, when vegetarians are compared to health conscious omnivores very few alternativist, anti-social, or attitudinal differences are found (Hamilton, 1993).

Surveys on dietary motivation are equivocal as to the relative importance of health reasons as motivations of vegetarianism. Such a focus on health as a 'cause' is often reflected in the assumption that they are more healthy. Studies of health symptomatology show little difference between vegetarians and non-vegetarians (Cooper et al., 1985; Mooney & Walbourn, 2001). The reverse has also been suggested - that vegetarians are less healthy than meat eaters. An illustration of how the issue of concern with health issues might work both ways can be found in the research suggesting that, far from representing an healthy alternative, vegetarian eating styles might actually be an eating disorder by proxy. Rao, Gowers, and Crisp (1986) reported that a sample of vegetarian anorectics showed a markedly greater fear of "fatness" than non-vegetarian anorectics. Sullivan and Damani (2000) also argue that vegetarianism is disproportionately prevalent in eating-disordered individuals. In this way, focus on health can also be pathological, and it should not automatically be assumed that vegetarian equals healthy.

One reason some past psychological studies have found few differences between vegetarians and omnivores is that the studies were limited to psychopathological, clinical, or health-related areas and samples. This exclusive focus overlooks more deeply rooted symbolic meanings of meat, the social values contained in those meanings, and ways that meat consumers and abstainers attend to these meanings and values. Outside of psychology, two streams of research have attempted to consider and classify the symbolism and cultural values of meat and animal products. In one, the meanings associated with meat are abstracted from their cultural uses and contexts (Adams, 1990; Fiddes, 1989). For instance, Fiddes' (1989) examined historical texts, modern scientific analyses, meat merchandising and other sources, and found a consistent theme of meat representing the domination of humans over nature. Similarly, Adams (1990) argues that meat consumption represents masculinity, power, and domination also manifest in other subjugatory practices (e.g., slavery, sexism). Both

Adams (1990) and Fiddes (1989) argue that the specific symbolism of meat is part of a broader symbolism in which meat is associated with multiple manifestations of hierarchical domination, from males over females, to humans over animals and nature. The hierarchical domination that meat symbolises transcends the specific, and perhaps more relevant, human-to-animal relationship, to prescribe how human-to-human relationships should be organised. Or as Fiddes (1989) suggested, "what meat exemplifies, more than anything, is an attitude: the masculine world view that ubiquitously perceives, values, and legitimates hierarchical domination of nature, of women, and of other men and, as its corollary, devalues less domineering modes of interaction between humans and with the rest of nature"(p. 210).

In a second strand, symbolic meanings of meat are contrasted with those of other foodstuffs (Heisley, 1990; Twigg, 1983). Heisley's (1990) study, for example, found that (particularly red) meat was associated with masculinity and power whereas fruits, vegetables and grains were generally associated with femininity and weakness. Twigg (1983) outlines a hierarchy of food symbolism in which red meat occupies the second highest position (just short of the taboo items of human flesh, carnivores, and uncastrated animals) but more "powerful" than white meat, fish, vegetables and fruit. By "powerful", Twigg meant that "deeply embedded in dominant culture is the idea of animal food as containing certain qualities, a particular power. This power centres around the qualities of strength, aggression, passion, sexuality – all that culture has traditionally designated as humankind's animal nature" (p. 22) and, "men in particular are thought in some sense to need meat, especially red meat, and a series of masculine qualities are encapsulated in the ideal of redbloodedness." (p. 24)

THE MOTIVATIONAL IMPORTANCE OF HIERARCHY AND INEQUALITY

Our initial investigation (Allen, Wilson, Ng & Dunne, 2000) focused on this theme of hierarchical domination. If, as Adams (1990) and Fiddes (1989) claim, individuals evaluate and identify with the symbolic meanings of meat that represent hierarchy, then omnivores and vegetarians should differ in their endorsement of hierarchy – these 'groups' should differ in the extent to which they display hierarchy-relevant individual differences. We tested this by administering measures of Right-Wing Authoritarianism (RWA: Altemeyer, 1980, 1998) and Social Dominance Orientation (SDO: Sidanius & Pratto, 1999). RWA is defined as a covariation of three families of attitudes about authority (Altemeyer, 1980): authoritarian submission (belief that people should submit to the will of the authorities they perceive to be legitimate), authoritarian aggression (serious sanctions may be inflicted upon those who do not submit to legitimate authority), and conventionalism (a strongly traditional orientation towards contemporary issues). SDO measures an individual's level of endorsement of group-based hierarchy, and plays a central role in testing the hypotheses of Social Dominance theory (SDT: Sidanius & Pratto, 1999), a central argument of which is that post-industrialist societies have typically evolved hierarchical social systems that serve to maintain the position of those at the top of such hierarchies to the detriment of those at relatively lower levels. Both RWA and SDO have been found to strongly predict prejudice, as well as rightist/conservative political preference, preference for hierarchy-enhancing (e.g., military, police, prosecutorial) occupations, and support for the Iraq War (Altemeyer, 1981; Sidanius & Pratto, 1999; McFarland, 2005; Wilson & Evers, 2004).

We reasoned, if meat symbolises hierarchy and meat abstention symbolises a rejection of hierarchy, that strong omnivores should endorse RWA and SDO more than vegetarians and other weak omnivores. To this end, 158 householders resident in a large metropolitan area in New Zealand were sampled, completing measures of SDO and RWA, as well as a food consumption diary in which they indicated the number of servings of various food groups that they had consumed in the previous few days: participants indicated the total number of times in three days before responding to the survey they had eaten red and white meat, dairy products and seafood/fish. The three-day period was chosen as long enough to reduce floor effects but short enough for respondents to make accurate counts.

The average total number of servings (red meat, white meat, diary products, and fish/seafood combined) was 7.8 (SD=3.5), of which the average number of red meat servings was 1.7 (SD=1.3), white meat servings was 1.0 (SD=.9). The numbers of times each individual had eaten red and white meat was divided by his or her total number of servings to compensate for larger eaters and to shift the focus toward meat preference. Of the total number of servings, the average proportion of red meat servings was .23 (SD=.17), white meat servings was .14 (SD=.13). The vegetarians in the current sample (those who self-identified as such) along with those omnivores whose combined consumption of red and white meat was less than one standard deviation below the mean were placed into a "Vegetarians and Weak Omnivores" group (n=33). The "Vegetarians and Weak Omnivores" group was 31% male and 69% female. The remaining omnivores were divided at the mean consumption of red and white meat combined into Strong versus Moderate groups. The "Strong Omnivore" group (n=72) was 56% male and 44% female. The "Moderate Omnivore" group (n=51) was 57% male and 43%.

The mean RWA and SDO scores for the three consumption groups are illustrated in Figure 1. Given that strong omnivores were expected to endorse hierarchical domination more than vegetarians and weak omnivores, the two groups were compared using directional t-tests that showed strong omnivores endorsed RWA ($t=(82)=-2.4$, $p<.01$) and SDO ($t(79)=-1.9$, $p<.05$) more so than vegetarians and weak omnivores.

Vegetarians and weak omnivores were less authoritarian than moderate omnivores ($t(72)=-2.3$, $p<.05$), but moderate omnivores and strong omnivores were similar ($t(102)=-.2$, $p=.85$). SDO scores of moderate omnivores were similar to those of strong omnivores ($t(95)=-.4$, $p=.73$), and to that of vegetarians and weak omnivores ($t(68)=-1.3$, $p=.22$).

Overall, the results show that the groups differed in endorsement of RWA and SDO, with moderate omnivores and strong omnivores higher more authoritarian than vegetarians and weak omnivores, and strong omnivores more socially dominant than vegetarians and weak omnivores. This is a relative difference however - both vegetarian and omnivore means still fell into the "disagree" region of SDO. Moreover, the difference between the groups was inconsistent, particularly for moderate omnivores who did not differ in SDO from vegetarians and weak omnivores and strong omnivores, but who were more similar to strong omnivores than to vegetarians and weak omnivores in RWA. Thus, whereas strong omnivores differ from vegetarians and low omnivores in hierarchical domination, the standpoint of moderate omnivores is unclear.

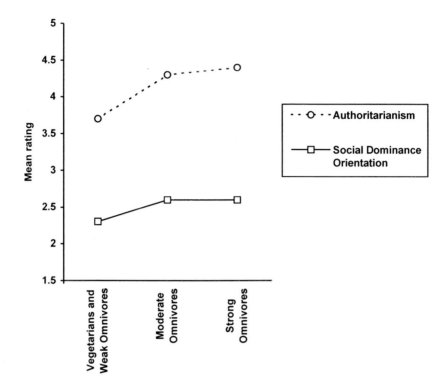

Figure 1. Mean SDO and RWA scores for the three consumption groups.

Importantly, the RWA and SDO measures used in this study did not ask respondents how humans should interact with animals, but specifically address human-to-human relationships. If one assumes, for illustrative purposes, that eating animals is a form of human over animal domination, then it follows that those individuals who most strongly endorsed hierarchical domination in human-to-human relations (strong omnivores) also enacted the greatest degree of human-to-animal domination (eating more animals), whereas the group that least preferred hierarchical domination (vegetarians and weak omnivores) enacted the least human-to-animal domination (eating fewer or no animals). Overall, the pattern of meat consumption, RWA and SDO is consistent with Adams' (1990) and Fiddes' (1989) suggestion that the symbolism of meat not only prescribes dominance in human-to-animal relationships but in human-to-human relationships as well.

The finding that strong omnivores were higher in RWA than vegetarians and weak omnivores supports the findings of Peterson, Doty and Winter (1993) in which high authoritarians were critical of environmental activism and were more likely to agree that "human beings have been given dominion over nature". The difference in RWA between omnivores and vegetarians is particularly striking given the lack of any salient threatening outgroup that characterised the attitudinal stimuli used by Peterson et al (1993). Likewise, SDO as conceived of by Sidanius and Pratto (1999) measures respondents' desire for domination for their social group, but this desire for dominance appears to go beyond the human sphere and into that of nature.

Although the present study shows that vegetarians and omnivores differ in RWA and SDO, whether hierarchical domination endorsement is the only, or even the most important, difference between vegetarians and omnivores cannot be certain. Moreover, authoritarianism comprises components other than power, such as aggression and conformity, and so conceivably, vegetarians and omnivores may differ in those dimensions as well. The limitation of comparing vegetarians and omnivores in RWA and SDO is that the measures are specific in two ways. The first is that RWA and SDO only measure hierarchical domination endorsement and related concerns, not more divergent forms of thinking about and relating to others, such as collectivism, universalism, and so on. A second way that authoritarianism and Social Dominance Orientation are specific is that the measures are at the same level of abstraction, that is, at the personality level. Vegetarians and omnivores could differ in more context-bound preferences such as attitudes toward particular objects or how they account for their behaviours, and some of those context-bound differences between omnivores and vegetarians could be manifestations of more general hierarchical domination differences. Therefore, a more comprehensive investigation is warranted in which vegetarians and omnivores are compared at multiple levels along the value-attitude-behaviour system to assess 1) how their preferences for hierarchical domination are associated with more context-bound preferences, 2) whether other, unforeseen differences exist between the groups, and 3) gauge the pre-eminence of hierarchical domination among the total differences.

The theme of hierarchy and inequality has continued in some of our subsequent studies, and the same basic relationships have emerged in five other student-based samples as well, with a range of other, related, constructs. For example more frequent meat consumption is associated with higher scores on group-based hierarchy measures like RWA ($r(176)=.32$, $p<.001$), SDO ($r(277)=.21$, $p<.001$; $r(508)=.14$, $p<.01$), Conservatism (Sidanius, 1976, 1991, reproduced in Knight, 1999; $r(268)=.13$, $P<.05$), , measures of interpersonal dominance such as Psychopathy (Levenson's Self-Report Psychopathy Scale: Levenson, Kiehl, & Fitzpatrick, 1995: $r(508)=.19$, $p<.001$), and measures of prejudice such as sexism (Swim, Aikin, Hall, & Hunter, 1995; $r(160)=.22$, $p<.01$), and traditional attitudes to women (Attitudes to Women Scale: Spence, Helmreich & Stapp, 1973; $r(160)=.27$, $p<.001$). Greater consumption is also associated with less pro-environmental attitudes (New Environmental Paradigm: Noe & Snow, 1990; $r(277)=-.15$, $p<.05$).

While these studies suggest that those people who feel relatively more positive towards hierarchy and authority also tend to greater meat consumption, people also perceive meat-eaters to be more supportive off inequality. Allen and Ng (2003) asked more than 200 adult Australians the question 'How much do you think that people who like [food type] a lot also believe in Equality (i.e. equal opportunity for all)?' with scores coded that a score of 7 indicated strong belief that inequality was associated with consumption. While all categories of consumer were rated as relatively unsupportive of inequality (all means were below the scale mid-point of 4), the means were ordered consistent with expectations, as shown in table 1.

That omnivores tend be less egalitarian, and are perceived as such, provides at least superficial support for Twigg (1983) and Adams' (1990) arguments that meat consumption (resulting as it does from domination over animals) reflects a worldview in which the meat-eater implicitly conceives of the world around them as structured hierarchically with humans at the top (and men above women) and animals and nature below.

**Table 1. Ratings of extent to which consumers of food types
are thought to endorse inequality**

	Mean (SE)
Red meat	3.89 (0.10)
White meat	3.57 (0.10)
Fish	3.56 (0.10)
Dairy	3.51 (0.10)
Cereals	3.37 (0.10)
Fruit	3.24 (0.10)
Vegetables	3.21 (0.10)

$F(6,230)=12.1$, $p<.001$.

THE IMPORTANCE OF HUMAN VALUES

In the second party of this initial report, we presented results from a second study looking more closely at the relationship between social values, consumption value, and dietary behaviour. Numerous studies have shown values to be foundational in attitudes towards products (not just dietary products) and purchasing behaviour (see Allen & Ng, 1999; Allen, Ng, & Wilson, 2002), as well as being important in almost all social attitudes and behaviours (see Rokeach, 1973; Schwartz, 1992). Perhaps The most frequently cited definition of what constitutes a human value (psychologically defined) is offered by Rokeach (1973) as an "enduring belief that a specific mode of conduct or end-state of existence is personally or socially preferable to an opposite or converse mode of conduct or end-state of existence" (p.5). Rokeach suggested that values form systems representing "an enduring organisation of beliefs concerning preferable modes of conduct or end-states of existence along a continuum of importance" (1973, p.5). The importance of different values should co-vary with the importance of others in the value system. Values are strongly prescriptive in nature and form the core around which other less enduring beliefs are organised. They are important in a range of other processes - the formation of specific attitudes is theoretically predicated upon more general values. Rokeach's conceptualisation of values, and the conceptualisation of a finite set of values as the foundation for an infinite set of attitudes continues to be a focus of research (e.g., Allen & Ng, 1999; Allen, Ng & Wilson, 2002; Braithwaite, 1997; Dickinson, 1991; Heaven, 1999; Schultz & Zelezny, 1998; Schwartz, 1992; Tetlock, 1986). Given the importance of values in other consumption, attitudinal, and behavioural domains, it made sense that meat-consumption and avoidance would also be founded (at the most basic level) on values.

The second study presented by Allen et al., (2000) involved 324 omnivore, and 54 vegetarian, participants who completed the Rockeach Values Survey (RVS: Rokeach, 1973), self-identified omnivorism-veganism, and the consumption diary described earlier. Consistent with the first study, omnivorism was associated with greater endorsement of hierarchical domination (endorsing values like power, relative rejection of equality, peace, social justice, etc). Additionally, and consistent with the notion that values co-vary as part of a values system, vegetarian participants placed more emphasis on experiential openness and the importance of emotion. The reason that this potentially expands on the hierarchy motivation component of dietary preference is that the values system coheres around two primary dimensions – self-enhancement (hierarchy) versus self-transcendence (egalitarianism) and conservation (tradition) versus openness to change (Schwartz, 1992). Specifically, Schwartz (1992) argued that individual values serve particular motivational functions, and that cross-cultural analysis of more than 60 different national samples suggest that there are ten or eleven basic motivational domains. These second-order motivations are organised in a circumplex around the two primary value domains of conservation-openness and self-transcendence/enhancement. This is illustrated in Figure 2.

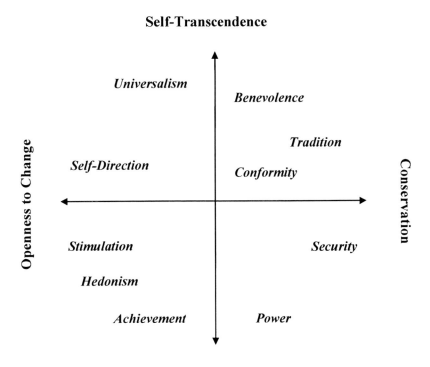

Figure 2. Two-dimensional value space showing second and   third order value domains.

That meat consumption seems to be associated not only with hierarchy-egalitarianism, but also with openness-tradition, suggests that food beliefs (broadly speaking) may map on to the two-dimensional value space proposed by Schwartz (1992). That is, if meat consumption and abstinence are reflective of endorsement of self-enhancment versus self-transcendence, might it also be the case that other dietary preferences might be associated with the relative importance given to change versus conservation? One possibility is that those people who endorse openness to change-type values might prefer (or at least be less ambivalent to) non-traditional food types than those who endorse conservation. We have made an initial step towards testing this proposition based on analysis of meal preferences provided by a sample of undergraduate students, who were asked to complete a range of survey measures based around dietary likes and dislikes. In particular, participants were asked to indicate how much they liked a list of 31 different meals. Unlike the food diary used in the earlier studies (and detailed already), the attitude objects weren't food categories (e.g., 'redmeat', 'cereals') but actual meals and named meal constituents. Where necessary, meal labels were qualified with a brief description. These included lentil dhal, navratan khorma (vegetable curry), spinach cannelloni, falafel kebabs, all examples of vegetarian and non-traditional meals for New Zealanders. Similarly, Macaroni cheese, cheesy potato bake, and baked beans are examples of traditional meat-free meals (and constituents). Meat-containing meals included roast chicken, lamb chops, and barbeque steak (traditional New Zealand meat-based meal types) and beef rendang, rogan josh, and mee goring (all non-traditional non-vegetarian meals). Broadly, the study was designed to evaluate the structure of meal preferences, but with the expectation that food preferences should map onto a two-dimensional solution, around primary dimensions that might be conceptually similar to the primary value domains of tradition-openness and hierarchy-egalitarianism.

Figure 3 shows the result of multidimensional scaling of the liking data for 106 student participants, including two hypothetical guidelines that we have placed to attempt to separate the map into approximately equal quadrants. Meals within the quadrants appear to share a family resemblance consistent with the rationale described above, suggesting that general food preferences might reflect the basic two-dimensional model of values proposed by Schwartz (1992). Of course, a more detailed test of this proposition will necessitate assessing whether preferences for the four food families shown above are statistically associated with actual value endorsement.

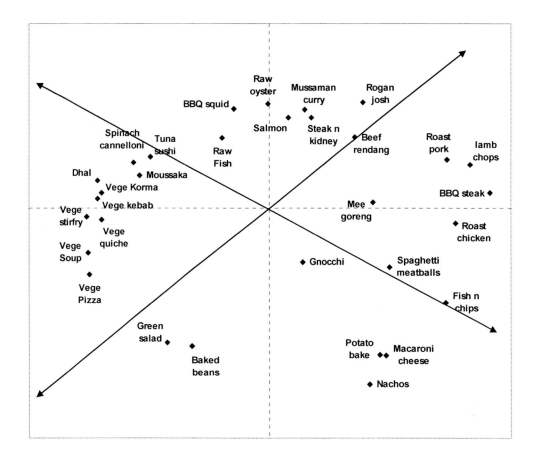

Figure 3. Perceptual map of meal-type preference data.

MATERIALISM AND DIETARY PREFERENCE

The relationship between values and dietary preference described already are based on analysis of values broadly defined. By this we mean that the measure of values, and the approach taken to their conceptualisation, is based on operatonalisation of values as a finite, but universal, set. At the same time, particular subsets or alternate conceptualisations of values have been offered by other authors. For example, Inglehart has argued that the values of materialism and postmaterialism are particularly important in relation to political attitudes, opinions, and preference (1990). Materialist values describes the need for physical or economic security, while Postmaterialist values transcend these immediate physical or economic needs (e.g., concerns for greater democratisation and involvement of people in the political process). Inglehart has accumulated a significant international body of findings suggesting that Western societies have become increasingly Postmaterialist since World War II (Abramson & Inglehart, 1995; Inglehart, 1990). Improvements in the standard of living since this time have lead to decreased anxiety over basic survival needs (shelter and clothing, for example) and, therefore, people who have never experienced material scarcity have turned towards more postmaterialist concerns. This Postmaterialist shift has been suggested as a possible explanation for the increased salience of environmental concerns, and popularity of pro-environment political parties towards the end of the 20th century (Vowles, Aimer, Catt, Lamare, & Miller, 1995). Since the turn of the millennium, however, there has been increased concern in the West over military and terrorist conflict and the insecurities that come with it. In terms of the values system proposed by Schwartz (1992), materialism has been shown to be most strongly associated with power and security motivations, and postmaterialism with universalism (Wilson, 2005). In this section, we summarise three studies investigating the hypothesised association between materialism and dietary behaviour (Allen & Wilson, 2005).

Inglehart maintains that survival insecurity characterises modern Western culture and stems from fear of military conflict and concerns about economic self-sufficiency. Survival insecurity fosters a syndrome of attitudes, norms, and beliefs in various domains such as politics (i.e., desiring strong leaders, social order), religion (i.e., belief in a higher power, absolute rules, predictability), and economics (i.e., striving for economic growth). While the supply of food has become more stable and secure over time (e.g., Mennell, Murcott & van Otterloo, 1992), within developed nations, food is still unequally distributed and does not reach all members. Those with a relative lack of access to reliable food supply might be referred to as food insecure, and simply stated, do not have steady access to enough food. The food insecure tend to occupy lower socio-economic positions, and spend less money on food (e.g., Nord, Andrews, & Carlson, 2003). Food insecurity may arise with or without hunger (e.g., Olson, 1999). Food insecure individuals who are not hungry have found other ways to cope with the insecurity, such as eating foods that are less expensive (but less varied)(e.g., Nord et al., 2003). Thus, whether the food insecure are hungry or not, their dietary intake of essential nutrients are often below recommended daily allowances (e.g., Dixon, Winkleby, & Radimer, 2001). Consequently, food insecurity contributes to poorer well-being, and increases the risk of chronic diseases such as cancer and heart disease (e.g., Pheley, Holben, Graham, & Simpson, 2002).

As Inglehart's (1990) research indicates, individuals vary in terms of their levels of survival security, and those individuals with an above-average drive for survival security have deep concerns for personal safety and access to products that serve basic needs (e.g., food, water, shelter, clothing, etc.). Survival security motivation underpins Inglehart's (1990) notion of materialism because he argues that survival insecurity during the formative years of human development can bring about materialism later in life (while survival security engenders post-materialism). Essentially, material deprivation in childhood should foster materialism in adulthood, and indeed, research has shown that childhood poverty is associated with adult materialism (e.g., Abramson & Inglehart, 1995; Cohen & Cohen, 1996). We suggest that survival insecurity leads to excessive concerns about products that satisfy basic necessities, even for materialists who no longer have genuine threats to their physical security.

Materialists likely strive for survival security, leading them to set the life goals of ensuring that they are safe and have access to products that satisfy basic needs. Of these products, food is central. Human survival requires it. In sum, we suggest materialism is one response to childhood survival insecurity, including food insecurity, and that adult materialists make food security a top life goal. Whether having the life goal of food security is sufficient for adult materialists to overcome the food insecurity of their childhood was difficult to predict, given that food insecurity stems from many factors outside of one's control (Nord et al., 2003). Although we expected that materialists would assign greater importance to the goal of food security and would report a higher incidence of food insecurity during childhood, we did not predict that food security (or insecurity for that matter) represents materialists' present-day experience. To test these expectations, we conducted a series of three studies.

Participants in the first study were 95 people who responded to a mailout of 350 surveys, sent to a random sample drawn from the telephone directory of a moderately-sized Australian city. Besides demographic characteristics, the questionnaire also included a reliable six-item materialism scale (Inglehart, 1977), Bickel, Nord, Price, Hamilton and Cook's (2000) measure of Food Insecurity, a set of questions inquiring about childhood food insecurity, and the extent to which "ensuring that you have enough food to eat" was of importance to them personally.

When Food security as goal, childhood food insecurity, and present-day food insecurity were regressed onto materialism, the three variables robustly predicted materialism. The Multiple-R (.64) indicates that the variables account for 40 percent of materialism variance, and all three variables were significant predictors of materialism. Food security as a goal was the strongest (positive) predictor of materialism (Beta=.54, $p<.001$) followed by childhood food insecurity (Beta=.41, $p<.001$), while present-day food insecurity was negatively predictive (Beta=-.19, $p<.05$). Therefore, a higher goal of food security, a greater incidence of childhood food insecurity, and a lack of present-day food insecurity characterize materialism. Though there was no sex difference in endorsement of materialism (male mean = 5.7, female mean = 5.6), increasing age was associated with greater materialism ($r(90)=.44$, $p<.001$).

While the results of this initial study were consistent with the view that materialism may stem from an individual's attempt to cope with childhood survival insecurity they also showed that, while materialists emphasized food security as a life goal and reported childhood food insecurity, they did not report present-day food insecurity.

In a second study, we investigated whether materialists' striving for food security affected their weight and food access behaviour (for example, whether they kept plentiful food stores), using a similar methodology to the first study. A postal questionnaire was distributed to a random sample of 460 Australian urban residents. One hundred forty were returned (30%), of which 115 were useable. Once again, we used Inglehart's (1977) six-item materialism measure, this time to divide the sample into high and low materialism groups based on a median split. To gauge food hording/storing behaviour, participants indicated the total number of servings they had in their kitchen (refrigerator, freezer, pantry, etc) of red meat, white meat, fish/seafood, dairy, fruit, vegetables, and cereals. Participants were instructed to go to their kitchen to make the best estimate possible. The survey also asked the number of adults and children in the household. Consequently, a Food Hording index was calculated for each participant by summing the total number of servings stored in the household, divided by the number of household members. Participants also provided information to calculate Body Mass Index (calculated as weight in kg divided by height in meters squared). Participants were divided into a Low/ Normal Weight group (those participants with BMI under 30, n=79), and an Obese group (those with BMI above 30, n=34).

Analyses indicated that high materialists stored more food than low materialists (t(102)= -2.0, p<.05), storing around 39 servings per household member compared to around 25 servings. Obese participants (with BMI above 30) also scored higher on materialism than Low/Normal Weight participants (t(113)=-1.9, p<.05). BMI was positively correlated with the Food Hording index (r(110)=.21, p<.05).

Adult materialists' strive to ensure that they overcome the survival insecurity of childhood may be successful, given that materialists hoard more food at home and tend to be obese, and do not report suffering from present day food insecurity. It follows that when food (or other physical) insecurity becomes salient, people should become more materialistic. To test this, we employed a standard mortality salience manipulation (Greenberg, Pyszczynski & Solomon, 1986) to prime survival insecurity by instructing them to think about their own death. We suggest that a grim concern of those motivated by survival security is their own death. As defined, individuals with an above-average drive for survival security have deep concerns about their safety and access to products that satisfy basic needs (food, shelter, etc). These products are salient ways of averting the ultimate end, which is death.

Additionally, if survival insecurity leads materialists to have an elevated concern about food security, then individuals who increase their endorsement of materialism due to a mortality salience manipulation should also increase the importance of food security as a goal. The emotional significance of food may also increase when materialists feel insecure.

Participants in this study were 124 people invited to participate by a group of second-year university students, who also acted as facilitators and a point of contact for participants. Half of the participants received a copy of the survey that included the mortality salience instructions (the experimental condition) while the other half did not. All participants completed the same measures. For a manipulation check, post-test ratings of survival security as state will be compared between the experimental and control groups. We predicted that participants for whom the Mortality Salience manipulation leads to feelings of insecurity would endorse materialism after the Mortality Salience manipulation (more than the control group) and should also assign more importance to food security as a life goal, and using food for emotional comfort. All participants supplied demographic characteristics, and completed a shortened version of the Marlowe-Crowne Scale of Social Desirability (Strahan & Gerbasi, 1972), Inglehart's (1977) six-item materialism scale, a measure of State-based General Survival Security as State (example items include "The amount of money I have makes me feel secure" and "I feel safe and secure"), and an expanded five-item measure of Food

Security as a Goal loosely based on Bickel et al's (2000) Food Insecurity scale. Participants also indicated their use of food for emotional comfort, by responding to five items (examples include "Eating gives me emotional satisfaction" and "I tend to get in a good mood after eating")

Participants first completed the Social Desirability scale and other distracter items, followed by the mortality salience manipulation (for the experimental participants) that involved completing two open-ended questions (i.e., "In the space below, write about what will happen to you as you physically die", and "In the space below, write about the emotions that the thought of your own death arouses in you"). All participants then completed the General Survival Security as State items, the Inglehart (1977) Materialism scale, food security as goal items, and use of food for emotional comfort, before debriefing.

The manipulation check indicated that participants in the experimental condition reported feeling less secure after the Mortality Salience manipulation than control participants. We divided participants into two groups based on high or low post-test feelings of security (the midpoint of the General Survival Security as State scale). A 2 (insecure vs. secure) by 2 (experimental vs. control) between-subjects ANOVA was performed on individuals' endorsement of materialism, indicating a significant main effect for security feeling ($F(1,123)=4.0$, $p<.05$), as well as a significant 2-way interaction between security feeling and experimental condition ($F(1,123)=10.6$, $p<.001$). As expected, when the Mortality Salience manipulation made participants feel insecure, they showed greater endorsement of materialism. Next, we divided participants at the median of the materialism scale. A 2 (insecure vs. secure) by 2 (experimental vs. control) by 2 (low materialism vs. high materialism) between-subjects ANOVA was carried out on the importance of food security as a life goal. Besides a significant main effect for materialism group ($F(1,111)=4.0$, $p<.05$), the ANOVA achieved a significant 3-way interaction between feelings of security, materialism, and experimental condition ($F(1,111)=3.3$, $p<.05$). Post-hoc tests found that the 2-way interaction between materialism and experimental condition was significant for participants who felt insecure ($F(1,52)=2.3$, $p<.05$), but not significant for participants who felt secure. participants who responded to the Mortality Salience manipulation by feeling insecure and supporting materialism assigned more importance to food security as a life goal. Finally, a 2 (insecure vs. secure) by 2 (experimental vs. control) by 2 (low materialism vs. high materialism) between-subjects ANOVA for participants' Use of Food for Emotional Comfort, yielded a significant 2-way interaction between feelings of security and materialism ($F(1,115)=8.5$, $p<.01$) and a 3-way interaction ($F(1,115)=3.8$, $p<.05$). Regarding the latter, post-hoc tests found that the 2-way interaction between materialism and experimental condition was significant for participants who felt insecure ($F(1,55)=6.6$, $p<.01$) but not for participants who felt secure. When the mortality salience manipulation made individuals feel insecure and increased their support for materialism, they also increased their use of food for emotional comfort.

These studies showed that materialists reported greater childhood food insecurity and made food security a top goal in adulthood, and that experimentally priming participants' feelings of survival insecurity led to greater materialism (and the associated materialist goal of food security). Additionally, the first study found that materialists do not currently experience food insecurity, and the second that materialists have a relative abundance of food at home and greater tendency to be obese. Materialism may be an individual's way of coping with childhood survival insecurity, by setting the goals in (early) adulthood to improve one's socio-economic status, satisfy basic needs, and surround oneself with possessions. Consequently, materialists make food security at top life goal, apparently with some success.

To conclude, the studies summarised in this chapter indicate a number of important conclusions about dietary preference in general, and meat consumption/abstinence in particular. Firstly, meat consumption is associated with a hierarchical worldview that may also be implicated in other, negative, attitudinal and behavioural domains (such as discrimination and oppression). Our foray into broader food likes may suggest that a second value dimension (conservation versus openness) is also an important plank upon which likes are based. Finally, we have extended Inglehart's (1990) consideration of the importance of materialism into the realm of dietary behaviour, showing that those who report childhood deprivation are motivated towards materialism in adulthood, and that this materialism manifests in food hoarding.

REFERENCES

Abramson, P.R., & Inglehart, R. (1995). *Value change in global perspective*. Ann Arbor: University of Michigan Press.

Adams, C.J. (1990). *The sexual politics of meat: A feminist-vegetarian critical theory*. New York: Continuum.

Allen, M.W., & Ng, S.H. (1999). The direct and indirect influences of human values on product ownership. *Journal of Economic Psychology, 20(1)*, 5-39.

Allen, M.W., Ng, S.H., & Wilson, M.S. (2002). The functional approach to instrumental and terminal values and the value-attitude-behaviour system. *European Journal of Marketing, 36*, 111-135.

Allen, M.W. & Ng, S.H. (2003). Human values, utilitarian benefits and identification: The case of meat. *European Journal of Social Psychology, 33*, 37-56.

Allen, M.W., & Wilson, M.S. (2005). Materialism and food security. *Appetite, 45*, 314-323.

Allen, M.W., Wilson, M.S., Ng, S.H., & Dunne, M. (2000). Values, beliefs and meat consumption: The values of omnivores and vegetarians. *Journal of Social Psychology, 140(4)*, 405-422.

Altemeyer, B. (1981). *Right-wing authoritarianism*. Winnipeg: University of Manitoba Press.

Amato, P.R., & Partridge, S.A. (1989*)*. *The new vegetarians: Promoting health and protecting life*. New York: Plenum Press.

Back, K.W., & Glagow, M. (1981). Social networks and psychological conditions in diet preferences: Gourmets and vegetarians. *Basic and Applied Social Psychology, 2(1)*, 1-9.

Beardsworth, A.D., & Keil, E.T. (1997). *Sociology on the menu: An invitation to the study of food and society*. London: Routledge.

Bickel, G., Nord, M., Price, C., Hamilton, W., & Cook J.(2000). *Guide to measuring household security revised*. Alexandria VA: United States Department of Agriculture, Food and Nutrition Service.

Braithwaite, V. (1997). Harmony and security value orientations in political evaluation. *Personality and Social Psychology Bulletin, 23*, 401-414.

Catt, H., Harris, P., & Roberts, N.S. (1992). *Voter's choice: Electoral change in New Zealand?* Palmerston North, NZ: Dunmore Press.

Cohen, P. & Cohen, J. (1996). *Life values and adolescent mental health*. Mahwah, NJ: Erlbaum.

Cooper, C.K., Wise, T.N., & Mann, L.S. (1985), Psychological and cognitive characteristics of vegetarians. *Psychosomatics, 26*, 521-527.

Dickinson, J. (1991). Values and judgements of wage differentials. *British Journal of Social Psychology, 30*, 267-270.

Dixon, L.B., Winkleby, M., & Radimer, K. (2001). Dietary intakes and serum nutrients differ between adults from food-insufficient and food-sufficient families: Third National Health and Nutrition Examination Survey, 1988-1994. *Journal of Nutrition, 131*, 1232-1246.

Fiddes, N. (1989). *Meat: A natural symbol*. New York: Routledge.

Goode, J., Beardsworth, A., Haslam, C., Keil, T., & Sherratt, E. (1995). Dietary dilemmas: Nutritional concerns of the 1990s. *British Food Journal, 97*, 3-12.

Greenberg, J., Pyszczynski, T., & Solomon, S. (1986). The causes and consequences of the need for self-esteem: A terror management theory. In R.F. Baumeister (Ed.), *Public Self and Private Self* (pp 189-212). New York: Springer-Verlag.

Hamilton, M.B. (1993). Wholefoods and healthfoods: Beliefs and attitudes. *Appetite, 20*, 223-228.

Heaven, P.C.L. (1999). Group identities and human values. *Journal of Social Psychology, 139*, 590-595.

Heisley, D.D. (1990). *Gender symbolism in food*. Unpublished doctoral dissertation. Northwestern University, Evanston, IL.

Inglehart, R. (1977). *Silent revolution: Changing values and political styles among Western publics*. Princeton, NJ: Princeton University Press.

Inglehart, R. (1990). *Culture shift in advanced industrialist society*. Princeton: Princeton University Press.

Knight, K. (1999). Liberalism and conservatism. In J.P.Robinson, P.R.Shaver, & L.S.Wrightsman (Eds.), *Measures of political attitudes* (pp. 59-158). San Diego, CA: Academic Press.

Leech, C. (1996). Mad cows shake up British agriculture. *Alternatives Journal, 22*, 4-5.

Lester, D. (1979). Food fads and psychological health. *Psychological Reports, 44*, 222.

Levenson, M. R., Kiehl, K. A., & Fitzpatrick, C. M. (1995). Assessing psychopathic attributes in noninstitutionalized population. *Journal of Personality and Social Psychology, 68*(1), 151-158.

McFarland, S.G. (2005). On the eve of war: Authoritarianism, Social Dominance Orientation, and American students' attitudes toward attacking Iraq. *Personality and Social Psychology Bulletin, 31*, 360-367.

Mennell, S., Murcott, A., & van Otterloo, A.H. (1992). *The sociology of food: Eating, diet and culture*. London: Sage Publications.

Mooney, K.M., & Walbourn, L. (2001). When college students reject food: Not just a matter of taste. *Appetite, 36*, 41-50.

Noe, F.P., & Snow, R. (1990). The new environmental paradigm and further scale analysis. *Journal of Environmental Education, 21*, 20-26.

Nord, M., Andrews, M., & Carlson, S. (2003). *Household food security in the United States. Food and Rural Economics Division*, Economic Research Service, U. S. Department of Agriculture. Alexandria, VA.

Olson, C.M. (1999). Nutrition and health outcomes associated with food insecurity and hunger. *Journal of Nutrition, 129*, 521S-524S.

Peterson, B.E., Doty, R.M., & Winter, D.G. (1993). Authoritarianism and attitudes toward contemporary social issues. *Personality and Social Psychology Bulletin, 19*, 174-184.

Pheley, A.M., Holben, D.H., Graham, A.S., & Simpson, C. (2002). Food security and perceptions of health status: A preliminary study in rural Appalachia. *Journal of Rural Health, 18*, 447-454.

Rao, K., Gowers, S., & Crisp, A. (1986). Some correlates of vegetarianism in anorexia nervosa. *International Journal of Eating Disorders, 5*, 539-544.

Ray, J.J. (1989). Authoritarianism research is alive and well in Australia: A review. *The Psychological Record, 39*, 555-561.

Rokeach, M. (1973). *The Nature of Human Values*. New York: Free Press.

Schultz, P.W., & Zelezny, L.C. (1998). Values and Pro-environmental behaviour. *Journal of Cross-Cultural Psychology, 29*, 540-558.Schwartz, S.H. (1992). Universals in the content and structure of values: Theoretical advances and empirical tests in 20 countries. *Advances in Experimental Social Psychology, 25*, 1-65.

Schwartz, S.H. (1992). Universals in the content and structure of values: Theoretical advances and empirical tests in 20 countries. *Advances in Experimental Social Psychology, 25*, 1-65.

Sidanius, J., & Pratto, F. (1999). *Social Dominance: An intergroup theory of social hierarchy and oppression*. Cambridge, UK: Cambridge University Press.

Spence, J., Helmreich, R., & Stapp, J. (1973). A short version of the Attitudes Toward Women Scale (AWS). *Bulletin of the Psychonomic Society, 2*, 219-220.

Strahan, R., & Gerbasi, K.C. (1972). Short, homogeneous versions of the Marlowe-Crowne Social Desirability Scale. *Journal of Clinical Psychology, 28(2)*, 191-193.

Sullivan, V., & Damani, S. (2000). Vegetarianism and eating disorders - Partners in crime? *European Eating Disorders Review, 8*, 263-266.

Swim, J.K., Aikin, K.J., Hall, W.S., & Hunter, B.A. (1995). Sexism and Raciwsm: Old fashioned and modern prejudices. *Journal of Personality and Social Psychology, 68*, 199-214.

Tetlock, P.E. (1986). A value pluralism model of ideological reasoning. *Journal of Personality and Social Psychology, 50*, 819-827.

Twigg, J. (1979). Vegetarianism and the meanings of meat. In A.Murcott (Ed.), *The sociology of food and eating*. Aldershot: Gower.

Vowles, J., Aimer, P., Catt, H., Lamare, J., & Miller, R. (1995). *Towards consensus ? The 1993 election in New Zealand and the transition to proportional representation*. Auckland, NZ: Auckland University Press.

West, E.D. (1972). The psychological health of vegans compared to two other groups. *Plant Foods Human Nutrition, 2*, 147.

World Health Organisation (1990). Diet, nutrition and the prevention of chronic diseases. *WHO, Geneva*.

Wiggins, S. (2001). Construction and action in food evaluation: Conversational data. *Journal of Language and Social Psychology, 20*, 445-463.

Wilson, M.S. (2005). A social value analysis of Postmaterialism. *Journal of Social Psychology, 145*, 209-224.

Wilson, M.S., & Evers, C. (2004). Student attitudes to the 2003 War in Iraq. 33rd Annual Meeting of the Society of Australasian Social Psychology, April 2004. Auckland, New Zealand.

In: Psychology of Motivation
Editor: Lois V. Brown, pp. 83-98

ISBN: 978-1-60021-598-8
© 2007 Nova Science Publishers, Inc.

Chapter 5

SELF-DETERMINATION THEORY AND THE THEORY OF PLANNED BEHAVIOR: AN INTEGRATIVE APPROACH TOWARD A MORE COMPLETE MODEL OF MOTIVATION

Martin S. Hagger[*]
University of Nottingham, Nottingham, United Kingdom
Nikos L. D. Chatzisarantis[†]
University of Plymouth, Devon, United Kingdom

ABSTRACT

The aim of this chapter is to provide an overview of recent research that integrates two key theories of motivation: the theory of planned behavior and self-determination theory. The chapter will adopt an evidence-based approach to evaluate how the integration of these theories provides a more complete model of motivation. After an overview of the component theories, two theoretical premises for theoretical integration will be discussed: (1) self-determination theory provides a formative explanation for the origin of the antedecents of intentional behavior and (2) self-determination theory constructs operate at a generalized contextual level and reflect the origin or *locus of causality* of an action while theory of planned behavior constructs are situational and reflect expectations regarding engagement in a specific future behavior. Empirical evidence for the integration of these theories is then presented in the form of a meta-analysis of 13 published studies. The meta-analytically derived correlations corrected for sampling and measurement error will then be used as a basis for a path analysis examining the pattern of relations among the variables from the integrated theory. The implications of the integrated models for future research and interventions are discussed.

[*] Correspondence concerning this chapter should be addressed to Martin S. Hagger, School of Psychology, University of Nottingham, University Park, Nottingham, NG7 2RD, United Kingdom, email: martin.hagger@nottingham.ac.uk

[†] Nikos L.D. Chatzisarantis, School of Psychology, University of Plymouth, Portland Square, Drake Circus, Plymouth, Devon, PL4 8AA, United Kingdom, email: nikos.chatzisarantis@plymouth.ac.uk

INTRODUCTION

Research into the antecedent factors and processes that underpin human motivation in social contexts has been conducted from an array of different perspectives. Motivation is often viewed as an outcome construct that is indicative of behavioral engagement or an antecedent construct that results in social behavior (Kehr, 2004). In the present chapter, we will examine motivation as both an outcome and a predictor of volitional behavior. In particular, we aim to examine the psychological antecedents that influence motivation and how motivation influences behavior from two theoretical approaches from the social cognitive (Ajzen & Fishbein, 1977) and organismic (Deci & Ryan, 1985) traditions. The overall aim is to provide support for the integration of these theories with the premise that they provide complimentary explanations for motivated behavior.

One leading theoretical perspective on motivation is the social cognitive tradition that aims to outline the processes leading from socially-based perceptions such as attitudes, expectancies, beliefs, judgements, norms, and expectations to intentional behavior (Ajzen & Fishbein, 1980). Prominent among these theories is the theory of planned behavior(Ajzen, 1985, 1991), which was developed as a systematic explanation of volitional behavioral engagement based on overt or deliberative decisions to form intentions and enact them. This approach has been shown to account for behavioral influences across a variety of social behaviors (Armitage & Conner, 2001; Conner & Armitage, 1998). In contrast, humanistic, or, more accurately, *organismic* approaches to motivation have focused on the contexts and dispositional orientations that give rise to motivational states. One such model of motivation is presented by self-determination theory(Deci & Ryan, 1985, 2000), a leading theory of human motivation that has been shown to be efficacious in identifying the influences and contingencies that affect motivation and persistence in a number of behavioral domains (Deci & Ryan, 1985, 2000; Deci & Ryan, 2002).

While independent meta-analyses have shown both theories as having promise in accounting for variation in a large cross-section of social behaviors and in a wide variety of contexts (e.g., Armitage & Conner, 2001; Chatzisarantis, Hagger, Biddle, Smith, & Wang, 2003; Deci, Koestner, & Ryan, 1999; Hagger, Chatzisarantis, & Biddle, 2002b), both have shortcomings in terms of their predictive utility. Self-determination theory does not chart the exact process by which motivation is converted into behavior and the theory of planned behavior has provided an adequate basis for the explanation of variance in intentions and social behavior without identifying the exact origins of the antecedents of the behavior (Hagger & Chatzisarantis, 2007).

This chapter proposes that both theories can serve to assist in overcoming these shortcomings by integrating constructs from these two prominent social psychological theories in a unified model of motivation to explain intentions and behavior. The chapter will review research conducted using both theories as a framework and evaluate whether the theories are complimentary and offer new and effective explanations of social behavior. The basis for integration is premises offered by Deci and Ryan (1985) and Vallerand (1997) that motivational theories can offer explanations for the origins of social cognitive beliefs and expectations outlined in models of intention. Specifically, the role of autonomous motivation, that is, motivation to pursue behaviors that serve to fulfil personally-relevant goals, in influencing intentions and behavior in a number of behavioral domains will be reviewed on the basis evidence from a number of recent investigations (e.g., Chatzisarantis, Hagger, Biddle, & Karageorghis, 2002; Edmunds, Ntoumanis, & Duda, 2006; Hagger & Armitage, 2004; Hagger, Chatzisarantis, & Harris, 2006a, 2006b; Phillips, Abraham, & Bond, 2003; Standage, Duda, & Ntoumanis, 2003; Wilson & Rodgers, 2004). It is proposed that autonomous motivation results in a tendency to form attitudes and perceptions of control, two key determinants of intention from the theory of planned behavior, in line with personally-relevant goals (e.g., Vansteenkiste, Simons, Lens, & Sheldon, 2004). In addition, it is proposed that the immediate antecedents of intentions mediate the effects of autonomous forms of motivation on intention in a motivational sequence i.e., autonomous motivation→attitudes/perceived control→ intentions→behavior (e.g., Chatzisarantis et al., 2002; Chatzisarantis, Hagger, Smith, & Sage, 2006; Hagger & Armitage, 2004; Hagger, Chatzisarantis, Barkoukis, Wang, & Baranowski, 2005; Hagger, Chatzisarantis, Culverhouse, & Biddle, 2003; Hagger et al., 2006). A meta-analysis of the extant research examining the effect size of autonomous forms of motivation on intentions and the antecedents of intentions will be reported. The analysis will illustrate the pattern of effects from these types of motivation on the specific antecedents of intentional behavior across behavioral domains. Findings are discussed with reference to the importance of theoretical integration in providing complete yet parsimonious explanations of behavior.

THE THEORY OF PLANNED BEHAVIOR

The theory of planned behavior has been a useful social cognitive framework to understand the antecedents of intentional behavior in a number of health behavior contexts (e.g., Armitage & Conner, 2001; Hagger et al., 2002b). Central to the theory is the construct of intention. Stated intentions to engage in social behavior is envisaged as the most proximal predictor of behavioral engagement. Intention is considered to be motivational in nature and reflects the level of deliberative planning an individual invests in pursuing a given behavior (see Meiland, 1970). Intention is viewed as a function of three sets of belief-based perceptions with respect to behavioral engagement: personal, normative, and control (Ajzen, 1985). Personal beliefs are an individual's expectation that the target behavior will result in outcomes and whether such outcomes are salient to the individual. These beliefs are summarised by direct measures of a person's *attitude*, which represent an individual's overall evaluation of the behavior (Ajzen, 2003). Normative beliefs are expectations that significant others will exert pressure or cajole the individual to engage in the target behavior and the individual's motivation to comply with those significant others. These beliefs are typically measured by direct measures of a person's *subjective norm* towards the behavior. Control-related beliefs reflect beliefs regarding the level of personal control an individual has over the target behavior, the presence of perceived or real barriers, and the perceived power attributable to each control belief. This is summarised in a direct measure of *perceived behavioral control* (PBC). In the theory, attitude, subjective norm, and PBC are considered *formative* variables in predicting intentions and predict behavior via the complete mediation of intentions (Hagger & Chatzisarantis, 2005). Considerable research has supported these hypothesized relationships and meta-analyses have supported the effects of the theory of planned behavior across a variety of social contexts (Armitage & Conner, 2001; Conner & Armitage, 1998; Hagger et al., 2002b).

SELF-DETERMINATION THEORY

Self-determination theory takes a different approach to understanding social behavior. While the theory of planned behavior examines the immediate belief-based constructs thought to determine behavioral engagement, self-determination theory focuses on the *quality* of an individual's motivation in a given context and the environmental factors that affect motivation in that context (Deci & Ryan, 1985; Ryan & Connell, 1989). Central to the theory is the distinction between autonomous versus controlled types of motivation (Deci & Ryan, 2000). Individuals that are autonomously motivated experience a sense of personal choice when behaving while those that are non-autonomously motivated feel controlled, pressured, or coerced into behaving by external forces. The relative degree of autonomy perceived by an individual in a given behavioral context is often viewed along a continuum of motivation known as the perceived locus of causality (PLOC, Ryan & Connell, 1989). The continuum is outlined by organismic integration theory (Deci, Eghrari, Patrick, & Leone, 1994), a sub-theory of self-determination theory, that specifies a taxonomy of the forms of motivation experienced by individuals in life contexts. This taxonomy represents the qualitative differences in the types of motivation and outlines the behavioral experiences and outcomes associated with each form of motivation. The continuum is characterised by two relatively autonomous forms of motivation: *intrinsic motivation* and *identified regulation*, and two relatively controlling forms of motivation: *external regulation* and *introjected regulation* (Ryan & Connell, 1989).

Intrinsic motivation represents the prototypical form of autonomous motivation and reflects engaging in a behavior for the intrinsic satisfaction of the behavior itself and for no external contingency. *Identified regulation* is also an autonomous form of motivation but is, strictly speaking, extrinsic in nature because behavior is motivated by the pursuit of personally-valued outcomes rather than for the behavior itself. Pursuing behaviors for external contingencies such gaining extrinsic rewards or avoiding punishment characterises *external regulation*. *Introjected regulation* refers to an extrinsic form of motivation in which behavioral control arises from contingencies administered by the self such as the pursuit of contingent self-worth or the avoidance of affective states such as guilt or shame. Intrinsic motivation and identified regulation lie adjacent to each other at the autonomous pole of the PLOC continuum while external regulation and introjected regulation are located alongside each other at the controlling end of the continuum (Ryan & Connell, 1989). Research adopting the PLOC to has shown that autonomous motives positively affect behavioral engagement (Chatzisarantis, Biddle, & Meek, 1997; Chatzisarantis et al., 2003; Pelletier, Dion, Slovinec-D'Angelo, & Reid, 2004; Vansteenkiste, Simons, Soenens, & Lens, 2004).

THEORETICAL INTEGRATION

Recently, researchers have sought to integrate self-determination theory and the theory of planned behavior because these approaches are deemed to provide complimentary explanations of the processes that underlie motivated behavior. Several researchers have integrated these approaches in mediational models to illustrate the processes that lead to decisions to engage in social behavior. For example, autonomous motives from the PLOC have been shown to directly predict behavioral intentions (Chatzisarantis et al., 2002; Hagger, Chatzisarantis, & Biddle, 2002a; Standage et al., 2003; Wilson & Rodgers, 2004). However, some researchers have tested a more complete model in which the styles of autonomous motivation from organismic integration theory predict intentions via the mediation of attitudes and PBC. This motivational sequence has been supported in a number of studies (Chatzisarantis et al., 2002; Hagger et al., 2002a; Hagger, Chatzisarantis, Barkoukis et al., 2005; Hagger et al., 2003; Hagger et al., 2006; Phillips et al., 2003).

The proposition that self-determination theory can augment social cognitive theories such as the theory of planned behavior has been suggested previously, but has only recently received empirical support. Numerous authors have proposed that motivational, organismic theories such as self-determination theory could potentially offer explanations for the origins of constructs in social cognitive theories. As Andersen, Chen, and Carter (2000) state, "most information processing [social cognitive] models are silent on matters central to self-determination theory" (p. 272). Deci and Ryan (1985) have suggested that social cognitive theories identify the immediate antecedents of behavior, but neglect the origins of the antecedents: "Cognitive theories begin their analysis with what Kagan (1972) called a motive, which is a cognitive representation of some future desired state. What is missing, of course, is the consideration of the conditions of the organism that makes these future states desired" (p. 228). Constructs such as attitudes, PBC, and intentions from social cognitive theories like the theory of planned behavior are measured as explicitly-stated expectancies regarding future behavioral engagement. Therefore the integration of these theories may offer more information as to the mechanisms that underlie intentional social and health behavior.

The integration of the theory of planned behavior and self-determination theory is based on two key premises. The first premise is based on the hypothesis that the relationship between autonomous motives from self-determination theory and the constructs from the theory of planned behavior is a *formative* one. People who have high levels of autonomous motivation in a given domain are likely to experience their behavior in that domain as personally relevant and valued in that it is concordant with their psychological needs (Sheldon, 2002). As a consequence, autonomously-motivated people will have a greater tendency to critically examine the importance and value of the outcomes of engaging in any future target behavior. In the case of exercise and dieting, autonomous people will be likely to find information that points to the importance of these health behaviors and thus form a positive attitude towards future participation in that behavior. In contrast, people who report high levels of controlling forms of motivation will tend to focus on external contingencies of the future engagement in a target behavior, which are likely to have little to do with the valued consequences of the behavior.

In addition, individuals with high levels of relative autonomous motivation are likely to feel more confident in reaching their goals and engaging in subsequent behavior to satisfy these goals because they quench their need for competence. Links between autonomous motivation and perceived competence have been found in previous research (e.g., Williams, Gagne, Ryan, & Deci, 2002; Williams, McGregor, Zeldman, & Freedman, 2004).

The second premise relates to the relative degree of generality reflected by the constructs from the two theories. As previously stated, the PLOC reflects an individual's dispositional motivational orientation in a particular context and is therefore expected to predict his/her behavioral engagement across a variety of specific behaviors in that context. Vallerand (2000) labels this form of motivation, *contextual-level motivation*, as it reflects motivational orientations that affect all forms of behavior in a given context. However, the constructs from the theory of planned behavior are *expectations* for engaging in the behavior in future and measures of these constructs therefore specify explicitly the behavior and time frame of that bout of behavior. These constructs are therefore akin to the "cognitive representation of some future desired state" as cited by Deci and Ryan (1985). Vallerand suggested that contextual level motivation, such as the PLOC, affects motivational orientations at the situational level in a top-down fashion (see also Guay, Mageau, & Vallerand, 2003). Intentions in the theory of planned behavior are hypothesized to be located at this level because they reflect expectations for engaging in a specific target behavior at as specific future point in time. They are therefore conceptualized as orientations to engage in a behavior at the situational level. In addition, Vallerand also hypothesized that contextual level motivation would also influence cognitions at the situational level. It is therefore expected that motivation at the contextual level would influence the beliefs that underlie engagement in specific bouts of a behavior in the future, which, according to the theory of planned behavior, are constructs like attitudes and PBC. In accordance with this theory, it would be expected that contextual level motives would predict the performance of behavior at the situational level and its antecedents.

EMPIRICAL SUPPORT FOR THE THEORETICAL INTEGRATION

There is a growing body of research that has supported the integration of the theory of planned behavior and self-determination theory. The development of research in this area began with Chatzisarantis, Biddle, and Meek (1997) who found that intentions based on self-determination theory (autonomous intentions) were a better predictor of behavior than 'traditional' forms of intentions. Similarly, Sheeran, Norman, and Orbell (1999) found that intentions based on attitudes were more likely to predict behavior than intentions based on subjective norms, and suggested that intentions based on attitudes reflected pursuing behaviors for personally valued outcomes (akin to an identified regulation), and therefore for more autonomous reasons compared with intentions based on subjective norms which reflected more controlling aspects of motivation such as external or introjected regulations. Together these results paved the way for more comprehensive studies in which the effects of self-determined forms of motivation influenced behavior.

Following these pioneering studies, researchers have been committed to comprehensive tests integrating the theories adopting hypotheses from both component theories to address hypotheses relating to social behavior in numerous contexts. Prominent among these studies are those that outline a clear motivational sequence in which the generalised motivational orientations from self-determination theory influence constructs from the theory of planned behavior (e.g., Chatzisarantis et al., 2002; Hagger et al., 2002a). In such studies, the theory of planned behavior acts as a conduit for the effects of autonomous forms of motivation on motivated behavior. The decision-making constructs from the theory of planned behavior reflect the formation of plans to engage in the behavior in the future and represent situational motivational orientations toward the target behavior. The self-determination theory motives serve to indicate a source of information that influences the decision-making process. For example, autonomous forms of motivation from self-determination theory are hypothesised to influence attitudes from the theory of planned behavior as an autonomous motivational disposition in a particular domain is likely to be an impetus to the formation of attitudes oriented towards servicing personally-valued goals and mediate the effects of autonomous motivation on intention.

Hagger, Chatzisarantis, and Biddle (2002a) found that self-determined forms of motivation affected intentions to engage in physical activity behavior, but only via the mediation of attitudes and perceived behavioral control. This provided support for the hypothesis that autonomous forms of motivation bias individuals' decision making in favour of forming attitudes congruent with their personal goals (attitudes) and perceptions that the behavior will lead to competence-related outcomes (perceived behavioral control). This was corroborated in a subsequent study which furthered these findings to actual behavior – autonomous motives affected behavior via a motivational sequence beginning with autonomous forms of motivation and ending with behavioral engagement mediated by attitudes, perceived behavioral control, intentions, and effort (Chatzisarantis et al., 2002). Since these studies, the indirect effect of autonomous motives from self-determination theory on intentions and behavior as stipulated by the proposed motivational sequence has been corroborated in other contexts including dieting behavior (Hagger et al., 2003; Hagger et al., 2006a, 2006b; Hagger, Chatzisarantis, Hein et al., 2005), while other researchers have supported direct links between autonomous forms of regulation and intentions in exercise (Wilson & Rodgers, 2004) and physical education (Standage et al., 2003) settings. The latter findings did not measure the immediate antecedents of intentions according to the theory of planned behavior (attitudes, subjective norms, and perceived behavioral control) and therefore render these findings as partial tests of the proposed motivational sequence[1].

A META-ANALYSIS

Given the growing body of research in the field has resulted in a reasonably-sized literature testing the proposed motivational sequence resulting from the integration of self-

---

[1] It is important to note that some studies have found direct effects of autonomous forms of regulation on intentions independent of the effects mediated by the attitudes, subjective norm, and perceived behavioral control constructs. Research has suggested that this direct effects accounts for variance shared between autonomous motives that·are not accounted for by the attitude and perceived behevaioural control constucts. One possible reason for this is that the mediated route may take into account forms of autonomous motivation that are not entirely intrinsic (i.e., performing the behavior for salient outcomes rather than the behavior itself). Chatzisarantis, Hagger, Smith, and Sage (2006) have argued that traditional self-report measures of autonomous motivation do not eliminate expectancies for extrinsic (albeit identified) motives as a basis for estimating motivation. Therefore direct effects of autonomous forms of motivation from self-determination theory on intentions unmediated by attitudes and perceived behavioral control may reflect methodological artifacts rather than true effects.

determination theory and the theory of planned behavior, we aimed to test whether there was consistency in the pattern of the proposed relationships across studies. This is important as we have noted some variations in the size of the effects across samples as well as some variations in the patterns of effects, such as the direct influence of autonomous forms of motivation on intentions (e.g., Hagger, Chatzisarantis, Barkoukis et al., 2005; Hagger et al., 2006b). Other than conceptual reasons, one possible explanation for these inconsistencies may be variation due to methodological artefacts. While researchers have generally taken care to measure the self-determination theory and theory of planned behavior constructs with some degree of precision, variation in the measures used (see Chatzisarantis et al., 2006) and also in the size of the samples used (e.g., Hagger, Chatzisarantis, Hein et al., 2005) has been noted.

A useful statistical method to establish whether the set of results are consistent across studies whist simultaneously eliminating the potential bias due to sample size is meta-analysis (Hedges & Olkin, 1985; Hunter & Schmidt, 1990; Rosenthal & Rubin, 1982). Meta-analysis is a quantitative research synthesis technique which aims to "objectively assimilate and quantify the size of effects across a number of independent empirical studies while simultaneously eliminating inherent biases in the research" (Hagger, 2006, p. 103). In a meta-analysis, effect sizes (e.g., zero-order correlations) between constructs of interest in a study are weighted for their sample size, such that studies with larger, ostensibly more-representative samples are given greater weight, and then averaged across studies. The technique also permits the correction for measurement error using alpha reliability coefficients or test-retest data to correct the measures for any bias in measurement due to lack of precision in measurement. In addition, measures of spread of the effect size across the studies, usually in the form of corrected standard deviations, is also given and are used to calculate *credibility intervals* (see Hagger et al., 2002b; Hagger & Orbell, 2003) These enable the researcher to test the hypothesis that the effect is significantly different from zero and whether the majority of the variation in the statistic across the studies is due to the artefact of sampling error or measurement error.

Criteria for inclusion in the meta-analysis included studies that had at least one effect size from the integration of the theory of planned behavior and self-determination theory. Such an effect size, for example, could be gleaned from a measure of one form of regulation from the perceived locus of causality continuum (e.g., intrinsic motivation) and one measure from the theory of planned behavior (e.g., intention). In addition, the differentiation between autonomous and controlled forms of motivational orientation from the perceived locus of causality would result in multiple effect sizes with the theory of planned behavior variables and with measures of behavior. Some researchers have resolved this by collapsing the perceived locus of causality constructs into a single measure of autonomous regulation using weighted scores of the component motivational constructs. This single scale is known as the relative autonomy index or self-determination index (e.g., Grolnick & Ryan, 1987; Guay et al., 2003). Studies that have adopted the relative autonomy index in integrative models using these theories have yielded clear, unambiguous relationships with the theory of planned behavior constructs which were easily assimilated into the meta-analysis. Those that used differentiated constructs were aggregated by collapsing effect sizes for the intrinsic and identified forms of regulation with a given theory of planned behavior constructs into effect size based on the mean average. Such effect sizes were considered equivalent to those using the relative autonomy index as the measure of autonomous forms of motivation.

We conducted a review of salient electronic databases (e.g., Embase, Medline, PsychINFO, Psyarticles, and Web of Science), journals published by the *American Psychological Association* and *British Psychological Association* as well as pertinent journals in the field of social psychology (e.g., *Basic and Applied Social Psychology, British Journal of Social Psychology, European Journal of Personality, European Journal of Social Psychology, Journal of Applied Social Psychology, Journal of Personality, Journal of Personality and Social Psychology, Journal of Social Psychology*, and *Personality and Social Psychology Bulletin*). We also contacted key authors in the field and consulted the publication data base of the *self-determination theory faculty* as to whether they had additional data sets including effects sizes from the integrated models.

Results of the literature search yielded 13 studies that met the search criteria. A substantial number of the studies that fell into the category of testing a single effect size, such as measuring behavioral intention alongside measures of intrinsic or identified regulation (Biddle, Soos, & Chatzisarantis, 1999; Ntoumanis, 2005; Sarrazin, Vallerand, Guillet, Pelletier, & Cury, 2002; Standage et al., 2003; Wilson & Rodgers, 2004). Other studies included correlations among all of the constructs from the theory of planned behavior with some or all of the regulation styles from the perceived locus of causality (Chatzisarantis et al., 2002; Chatzisarantis et al., 2006; Hagger et al., 2002a; Hagger, Chatzisarantis, Barkoukis et al., 2005; Hagger et al., 2003; Hagger et al., 2006a; Hagger, Chatzisarantis, Hein et al., 2007; Phillips et al., 2003). Some studies yielded multiple effect sizes as they included tests of the effect across different samples (Hagger, Chatzisarantis, Barkoukis et al., 2005; Hagger et al., 2006; Hagger, Chatzisarantis, Hein et al., 2005). Together, these studies yielded 18 possible effect sizes. While this is a relatively small number, Hunter and Schmidt (1990) suggest that meta-analysis should not only be confined to cumulating studies across an entire body of literature after an exhaustive literature search, but is also "valid for 'convenience' samples of studies that just happen to lie at hand" (p. 83). However, since the sample of studies was small we used the random effects meta-analysis model proposed by Hunter and Schmidt since this has been shown to provide more precise estimates of true effect sizes in simulation studies (Field, 2001, 2003).

Table 1. Corrected Zero-order Correlations Among the Theory of Planned Behavior and Self-Determination Theory Components Derived from the Meta-Analysis

Variable	1	2	3	4	5	6
1. Autonomous motivation	—					
2. Attitudes	.63(13)	—				
3. Subjective norm	.25(12)	.34(12)	—			
4. Perceived behavioral control	.54(13)	.53(13)	.37(12)	—		
5. Intention	.59(18)	.74(14)	.38(13)	.68(14)	—	
6. Behavior	.37(13)	.43(12)	.20(11)	.37(13)	.64(15)	—

Note. Number of effect sizes contributing to averaged corrected correlation from the meta-analysis given in parentheses; All coefficients significantly different from zero ($p < .01$).

The averaged weighted correlations corrected for artifacts of sampling and measurement error for the relationships among the theory of planned behavior and self-determination theory constructs from this sample of studies are given in Table 1. The correlations were all significantly different from unity. However, credibility intervals indicated that the variation in the effect sizes across studies that could be attributed to the corrected artifacts was relatively low in all cases and the percentage variation due to artifacts did not exceed the 75% criterion advocated by Hunter and Schmidt (1990) for a homogenous case. This suggested that all of the relationships may have been affected by other extraneous or 'moderator' variables. However, the relatively small sample of studies precluded a search for moderators.

While the zero-order correlations among these constructs yielded useful information as to the strength of the effects among constructs from these two theories, it was important to establish the pattern of relationships as stipulated by the motivational sequence in integrated models adopting these theories. In order to test this, the correlation matrix was used as input for a path analytic model that tested the proposed pattern of relationships from the motivational sequence across the sample of studies (e.g., Chatzisarantis & Biddle, 1998; Hagger et al., 2002a). The path model was estimated by simultaneous process using the EQS computer program and a maximum likelihood method (Bentler, 2004).

The model tested was identical to that proposed in the studies of Hagger and coworkers (see Hagger et al., 2006b). Autonomous forms of motivation were hypothesised to predict attitude, subjective norms, and perceived behavioral control from the theory of planned behavior, in accordance with the previously stated premises for integrating the theories. In keeping with the theory of planned behavior, attitude, subjective norms, and perceived behavioral control were also hypothesised to influence intentions and intentions were set to influence behavior. We also hypothesised a direct influence of autonomous forms of motivation on intention. The direct effect of autonomous motivation on intention unmediated by the attitude, subjective norms, and perceived behavioral control constructs has been found in some integrated models (e.g., Chatzisarantis et al., 2002; Hagger, Chatzisarantis, Barkoukis et al., 2005; Hagger, Chatzisarantis, Hein et al., 2005) but not in others (e.g., Hagger et al., 2002a; Hagger et al., 2006) and the test of this relationship in this cumulative synthesis of research on the integration of these theories may resolve the inconsistent findings for this relationship in the extant literature. A direct effect of autonomous forms of motivation on behavior was included for completion, although its effect was expected to be small and non-significant because the significant average reweighted correlation for this relationship ($r = .37, p < .01$; Table 1) was expected to be mediated by the motivational sequence comprising the theory of planned behavior constructs.

The resulting path model exceeded Hu and Bentler's (1999) recommended .95 cut off criterion for incremental fit indexes in path analysis (Comparative Fit Index = .99; Normed Fit Index = .99; Incremental Fit Index = .99) with small standardized root mean square residuals (SRMSR = .019) indicating adequate fit of the model with the data. Beta coefficients from the meta-analytic path analysis are provided in Figure 1.

In terms of specific effects in the model, there was a statistically significant effect of autonomous motivation on attitudes ($\beta = .62, p < .01$), subjective norms ($\beta = .25, p < .01$), and perceived behavioral control ($\beta = .54, p < .01$) in accordance with the hypothesised integrated mediational model. Attitudes ($\beta = .47, p < .01$), subjective norms ($\beta = .07, p < .01$), and perceived behavioral control ($\beta = .36, p < .01$) significantly predicted intentions and intentions significantly predicted behavior ($\beta = .65, p < .01$) in accordance with the theory of planned behavior. There was a significant direct effect for autonomous motivation on intention ($\beta = .07, p < .01$), but the size of the effect was small relative to the indirect effect of autonomous motivation in intention (β = .50, p < .01). The direct effect of autonomous motivation on behavior was not significant even though the average weighted correlation between autonomous motivation and behavior was statistically significant (r = .37, p < .01). Importantly, the significant total effect of autonomous motivation on behavior via the motivational sequence (β = .37, p < .01) mirrored this correlation. This confirms that there was complete mediation of this effect in the proposed motivational sequence, which is in keeping with hypotheses.

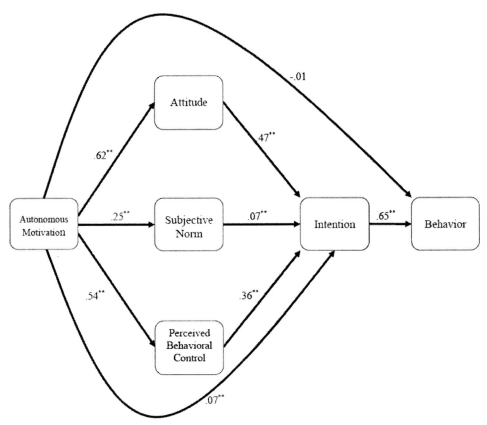

Note. Coefficients are standardized regression coefficients.
* p < .05. ** p < .01.

Figure 1. Meta analytic path analysis of the proposed motivational sequence arising from the integration of the Theory of Planned Behavior and Self-Determination Theory.

Overall, the model accounted for 67.1% and 41.0% of the variance in intentions and behavior respectively. In sum, the results of this multivariate path analysis based on the synthesis of results across studies integrating the theory of planned behavior with constructs from self-determination theory provided support for the proposed motivational sequence. These findings corroborate the hypothesized mechanisms involved such as the mediation of the effect of autonomous motivation on intention by the attitude, subjective norm, and perceived behavioral control constructs and the mediation of the effect of autonomous motives on behavior via the motivational sequence.

SUMMARY AND SUGGESTIONS FOR FUTURE INVESTIGATIONS

The present review of theory and research with a meta-analytic cummulation of current findings indicate considerable support for the integration of the theory of planned behavior and self-determination theory in determining motivated intentional action. The proposed model helps to resolve some of the limitations or boundary conditions of the two component theories. The proposed motivational sequence maps the complimentary components of the two theories. In the sequence, constructs from self-determination theory provide some impetus in terms of the formation of attitudes and perceptions of control that are in line with motives to engage in behavior for autonomous reasons. Attitudes and perceived behavioral control to engage in behaviors that are consistent with personally-valued goals and psychological needs to derive a sense of competence as implied by self-determination theory compel the individual to form plans or intentions to engage in similar behaviors in the future. Finally, intentions are converted into behavior. Importantly, it seems that within the proposed motivational sequence, attitudes and perceived behavioral control are necessary to convert autonomous forms of motivation into behavior and mediate the influence of autonomous motives on intentions and behavior.

Much of the research integrating these theories has been conducted using surveys with cross-sectional and prospective designs. These studies have supported the proposed motivational sequence, as indicated by the meta-analytically derived path analysis presented in this review. However, further research needs to be conducted to resolve any existing causality-related and conceptual issues. Current studies using this integrative approach have adopted valid and reliable measurement instruments (e.g., Hagger, Chatzisarantis, Hein et al., in press; Markland & Tobin, 2004) with large, representative samples and appropriate prospective designs to avoid confounding artifacts like common method variance (e.g., Hagger et al., 2003). However, the data are still correlational in nature which limits inferences of causality. We are already conducting research to further bolster support for the integrative approach advocated here by experimentally manipulating self-determination theory constructs and examining their influence of attitudes, perceived behavioral control, and intentions from the theory of planned behavior (Chatzisarantis & Hagger, 2006). Future research on this approach will adopt intervention and experimental designs to lend further support for the findings reported here.

In addition, it is also important to extend the proposed sequence to examine how global influences determine the adoption of autonomous motivational orientations. Such global influences are likely to arise from global motivational orientations such as basic psychological needs (Sheldon, Elliot, Kim, & Kasser, 2001), the organismic traits that predispose individuals to seek out novel tasks that satisfy innate needs for autonomy, competence, and relatedness (Deci & Ryan, 2000). We have already begun this line of research in a prospective study on health behaviors that includes basic psychological needs in the proposed motivational sequence (Hagger et al., 2006a). In addition, future research may examine other mechanisms by which individual differences in psychological need satisfaction might affect the constructs in the theory of planned behavior. For example, preliminary evidence has suggested that psychological needs for autonomy, comopetence and relatedness my moderate associations between attitudes, subjective norms, and perceived behavioral control and intentions (Harris & Hagger, in press). Further investigations to extend the effects of psychological needs from self-determination theory within the theory of planned behavior are advocated to promote a more complete model of human motivation.

REFERENCES

Ajzen, I. (1985). From intentions to actions: A theory of planned behavior. In J. Kuhl & J. Beckmann (Eds.), *Action-control: From cognition to behavior* (pp. 11-39). Heidelberg: Springer.

Ajzen, I. (1991). The Theory of Planned Behavior. *Organizational Behavior and Human Decision Processes, 50*, 179-211.

Ajzen, I. (2003). *Constructing a TPB questionnaire: Conceptual and methodological considerations.* Retrieved April 14, 2003, from University of Massachusetts, Department of Psychology Web site: http://www-unix.oit.umass.edu/~aizen: University of Massachusetts.

Ajzen, I., & Fishbein, M. (1977). Attitudes-behavior relations: A theoretical analysis and review of empirical research. *Psychological Bulletin, 84*, 888-918.

Ajzen, I., & Fishbein, M. (1980). *Understanding attitudes and predicting social behavior.* New Jersey: Prentice Hall.

Andersen, S. M., Chen, S., & Carter, C. (2000). Fundamental human needs: Making social cognition relevant. *Psychological Inquiry, 4*, 269-275.

Armitage, C. J., & Conner, M. (2001). Efficacy of the theory of planned behaviour: A meta-analytic review. *British Journal of Social Psychology, 40*, 471-499.

Bentler, P. M. (2004). *EQS structural equations modeling software* (Version 6.1) [Computer software]. Encino, CA: Multivariate Software.

*Biddle, S. J. H., Soos, I., & Chatzisarantis, N. (1999). Predicting physical activity intentions using goal perspectives and self-determination theory approaches. *European Psychologist, 4*, 83-89.

Chatzisarantis, N. L. D., & Biddle, S. J. H. (1998). Functional significance of psychological variables that are included in the theory of planned behaviour: A self-determination theory approach to the study of attitudes, subjective norms, perceptions of control and intentions. *European Journal of Social Psychology, 28*, 303-322.

Chatzisarantis, N. L. D., Biddle, S. J. H., & Meek, G. A. (1997). A self-determination theory approach to the study of intentions and the intention-behaviour relationship in children's physical activity. *British Journal of Health Psychology, 2*, 343-360.

Chatzisarantis, N. L. D., & Hagger, M. S. (2006). *Effects of a brief intervention based on the trans-contextual model on leisure time physical activity participation.* Unpublished manuscript, University of Plymouth, Plymouth, UK.

*Chatzisarantis, N. L. D., Hagger, M. S., Biddle, S. J. H., & Karageorghis, C. (2002). The cognitive processes by which perceived locus of causality predicts participation in physical activity. *Journal of Health Psychology, 7*, 685-699.

Chatzisarantis, N. L. D., Hagger, M. S., Biddle, S. J. H., Smith, B., & Wang, J. C. K. (2003). A meta-analysis of perceived locus of causality in exercise, sport, and physical education contexts. *Journal of Sport and Exercise Psychology, 25*, 284-306.

*Chatzisarantis, N. L. D., Hagger, M. S., Smith, B., & Sage, L. D. (2006). The influences of intrinsic motivation on execution of social behaviour within the theory of planned behaviour. *European Journal of Social Psychology, 36*, 229-237.

Conner, M., & Armitage, C. J. (1998). Extending the Theory of Planned Behavior: A review and avenues for further research. *Journal of Applied Social Psychology, 28*, 1429-1464.

Deci, E. L., Eghrari, H., Patrick, B. C., & Leone, D. R. (1994). Facilitating internalization: The self-determination theory perspective. *Journal of Personality, 62*, 119-142.

Deci, E. L., Koestner, R., & Ryan, R. M. (1999). A meta-analytic review of experiments examining the effects of extrinsic rewards on intrinsic motivation. *Psychological Bulletin, 125*, 627-668.

Deci, E. L., & Ryan, R. M. (1985). *Intrinsic motivation and self-determination in human behavior.* New York: Plenum Press.

Deci, E. L., & Ryan, R. M. (2000). The "What" and "Why" of goal pursuits: Human needs and the self-determination of behavior. *Psychological Inquiry, 11*, 227-268.

Deci, E. L., & Ryan, R. M. (2002). Self-determination research: Reflections and future directions. In E. L. Deci & R. M. Ryan (Eds.), *Handbook of self-determination research* (pp. 431-441). Rochester, NY: University of Rochester Press.

Edmunds, J. K., Ntoumanis, N., & Duda, J. L. (2006). A test of self-determination theory in the exercise domain. *Journal of Applied Social Psychology, 36*, 2240-2265

Field, A. P. (2001). Meta-analysis of correlation coefficients: A Monte Carlo comparison of fixed- and random- effects methods. *Psychological Methods, 6*, 161-180.

Field, A. P. (2003). The problems using fixed-effects models of meta-analysis on real-world data. *Understanding Statistics, 2*, 77-96.

Grolnick, W. S., & Ryan, R. M. (1987). Autonomy in children's learning: An experimental and individual difference investigation. *Journal of Personality and Social Psychology, 52*, 890-898.

Guay, F., Mageau, G. A., & Vallerand, R. J. (2003). On the hierarchical structure of self-determined motivation: A test of top-down, bottom-up, reciprocal, and horizontal effects. *Personality and Social Psychology Bulletin, 29*, 992-1004.

Hagger, M. S. (2006). Meta-analysis in sport and exercise research: Review, recent developments, and recommendations. *European Journal of Sport Science, 6*, 103-115.

Hagger, M. S., & Armitage, C. (2004). The influence of perceived loci of control and causality in the theory of planned behavior in a leisure-time exercise context. *Journal of Applied Biobehavioral Research, 9*, 45-64.

*Hagger, M. S., Chatzisarantis, N., & Biddle, S. J. H. (2002a). The influence of autonomous and controlling motives on physical activity intentions within the Theory of Planned Behaviour. *British Journal of Health Psychology, 7*, 283-297.

Hagger, M. S., Chatzisarantis, N., & Biddle, S. J. H. (2002b). A meta-analytic review of the theories of reasoned action and planned behavior in physical activity: Predictive validity and the contribution of additional variables. *Journal of Sport and Exercise Psychology, 24*, 3-32.

Hagger, M. S., & Chatzisarantis, N. L. D. (2005). *The social psychology of exercise and sport.* Buckingham, UK: Open University Press.

Hagger, M. S., & Chatzisarantis, N. L. D. (2007). The trans-contextual model of motivation. In M. S. Hagger & N. L. D. Chatzisarantis (Eds.), *Intrinsic motivation and self-determination in exercise and sport* (pp. 35-52). Champaign, Il: Human Kinetics.

*Hagger, M. S., Chatzisarantis, N. L. D., Barkoukis, V., Wang, C. K. J., & Baranowski, J. (2005). Perceived autonomy support in physical education and leisure-time physical activity: A cross-cultural evaluation of the trans-contextual model. *Journal of Educational Psychology, 97,* 376-390.

*Hagger, M. S., Chatzisarantis, N. L. D., Culverhouse, T., & Biddle, S. J. H. (2003). The processes by which perceived autonomy support in physical education promotes leisure-time physical activity intentions and behavior: A trans-contextual model. *Journal of Educational Psychology, 95,* 784–795.

*Hagger, M. S., Chatzisarantis, N. L. D., & Harris, J. (2006a). From psychological need satisfaction to intentional behavior: Testing a motivational sequence in two behavioral contexts. *Personality and Social Psychology Bulletin, 32,* 131-138.

Hagger, M. S., Chatzisarantis, N. L. D., & Harris, J. (2006b). The process by which relative autonomous motivation affects intentional behavior: Comparing effects across dieting and exercise behaviors. *Motivation and Emotion, 30,* 306-320.

*Hagger, M. S., Chatzisarantis, N. L. D., Hein, V., Pihu, M., Soós, I., & Karsai, I. (2007). *Teacher, peer, and parent autonomy support in physical education and leisure-time physical activity: A trans-contextual model of motivation in three cultures.* Unpublished manuscript, University of Nottingham, Nottingham, UK.

Hagger, M. S., Chatzisarantis, N. L. D., Hein, V., Pihu, M., Soós, I., & Karsai, I. (in press). The perceived autonomy support scale for exercise settings (PASSES): Development, validity, and cross-cultural invariance in young people. *Psychology of Sport and Exercise.*

Hagger, M. S., & Orbell, S. (2003). A meta-analytic review of the common-sense model of illness representations. *Psychology and Health, 18,* 141-184.

Harris, J., & Hagger, M. S. (in press). Do basic psychological needs moderate relationships within the theory of planned behavior? *Journal of Applied Biobehavioral Research.*

Hedges, L. V., & Olkin, I. (1985). *Statistical Methods for Meta-Analysis.* Orlando, FL: Academic Press.

Hu, L., & Bentler, P. M. (1999). Cutoff criteria for fit indexes in covariance structure analysis: Conventional criteria versus new alternatives. *Structural Equation Modeling, 6,* 1-55.

Hunter, J. E., & Schmidt, F. (1990). *Methods of meta-analysis: Correcting error and bias in research findings.* Newbury Park, CA: Sage.

Kehr, H. M. (2004). Implicit/explicit motive discrepancies and volitional depletion among managers. *Personality and Social Psychology Bulletin, 30,* 315-327.

Markland, D., & Tobin, V. (2004). A modification to the Behavioural Regulation in Exercise Questionnaire to include an assessment of amotivation. *Journal of Sport and Exercise Psychology, 26,* 191-196.

Meiland, J. W. (1970). *The nature of intention.* London: Methuen.

*Ntoumanis, N. (2005). A prospective study of participation in optional school physical education based on self-determination theory. *Journal of Educational Psychology, 97,* 444-453.

Pelletier, L. G., Dion, S. C., Slovinec-D'Angelo, M., & Reid, R. (2004). Why do you regulate what you eat? Relationships between forms of regulation, eating behaviors, sustained dietary behavior change, and psychological adjustment. *Motivation and Emotion, 28,* 245-277.

*Phillips, P., Abraham, C., & Bond, R. (2003). Personality, cognition, and university students' examination performance. *European Journal of Personality, 17*, 435-448.

Rosenthal, R., & Rubin, D. (1982). Comparing effect sizes of independent studies. *Psychological Bulletin, 92*, 500-504.

Ryan, R. M., & Connell, J. P. (1989). Perceived locus of causality and internalization: Examining reasons for acting in two domains. *Journal of Personality and Social Psychology, 57*, 749-761.

*Sarrazin, P., Vallerand, R. J., Guillet, E., Pelletier, L. G., & Cury, F. (2002). Motivation and dropout in female handballers: A 21-month prospective study. *European Journal of Social Psychology, 32*, 395-418.

Sheeran, P., Norman, P., & Orbell, S. (1999). Evidence that intentions based on attitudes better predict behaviour than intentions based on subjective norms. *European Journal of Social Psychology, 29*, 403-406.

Sheldon, K. M. (2002). The self-concordance model of health goal striving: When personal goals correctly represent the person. In E. L. Deci & R. M. Ryan (Eds.), *Handbook of self-determination research* (pp. 65-86). Rochester, NY: University of Rochester Press.

Sheldon, K. M., Elliot, A. J., Kim, Y., & Kasser, T. (2001). What is satisfying about satisfying events? Testing 10 candidate psychological needs. *Journal of Personality and Social Psychology, 80*, 325-339.

*Standage, M., Duda, J. L., & Ntoumanis, N. (2003). A model of contextual motivation in physical education: Using constructs from self-determination and achievement goal theories to predict physical activity intentions. *Journal of Educational Psychology, 95*, 97-110.

Vallerand, R. J. (1997). Towards a hierarchical model of intrinsic and extrinsic motivation. In M. P. Zanna (Ed.), *Advances in experimental social psychology* (pp. 271-359). New York: Academic Press.

Vallerand, R. J. (2000). Deci and Ryan's Self-Determination Theory: A view from the hierarchical model of intrinsic and extrinsic motivation. *Psychological Inquiry, 11*, 312-318.

Vansteenkiste, M., Simons, J., Lens, W., & Sheldon, K. M. (2004). Motivating learning, performance, and persistence: The synergistic effects of intrinsic goal contents and autonomy-supportive contexts. *Journal of Personality and Social Psychology, 87*, 246-260.

Vansteenkiste, M., Simons, J., Soenens, B., & Lens, W. (2004). How to become a persevering exerciser? Providing a clear, future intrinsic goal in an autonomy-supportive way. *Journal of Sport and Exercise Psychology, 26*, 232-249.

Williams, G. C., Gagne, M., Ryan, R. M., & Deci, E. L. (2002). Facilitating autonomous motivation for smoking cessation. *Health Psychology, 21*, 40-50.

Williams, G. C., McGregor, H. A., Zeldman, A., & Freedman, Z. R. (2004). Testing a self-determination theory process model for promoting glycemic control through diabetes self-management. *Health Psychology, 23*, 58-66.

*Wilson, P. M., & Rodgers, W. M. (2004). The relationship between perceived autonomy support, exercise regulations and behavioral intentions in women. *Psychology of Sport and Exercise, 5*, 229-242.

*Denotes study included in meta-analysis

In: Psychology of Motivation
Editor: Lois V. Brown, pp. 99-113

ISBN: 978-1-60021-598-8
© 2007 Nova Science Publishers, Inc.

Chapter 6

MOTIVATION AND RISK BEHAVIORS: A SELF-DETERMINATION PERSPECTIVE

Clayton Neighbors, Melissa A. Lewis, Nicole Fossos and Joel R. Grossbard*

University of Washington, WA, USA

ABSTRACT

Motivation lies at the root of many risk-related behaviors, including alcohol abuse, problem gambling, risky sex, and disordered eating behaviors. This chapter provides a review of empirical work examining risk-related behaviors from the perspective of Self-Determination Theory. Theoretical implications for incorporating self-determination in prevention and treatment of risk-related behavior are also considered.

Self-Determination Theory presents a humanistic perspective on motivation, assuming that individuals intrinsically strive to fulfill basic needs for competence, relatedness, and autonomy. In negotiating the environment, externally regulated behaviors are internalized and integrated into the self. Individual differences in motivational orientations emerge as a function of exposure to different environments with some individuals tending to operate more autonomously and others generally more oriented toward extrinsically controlling factors. A considerable volume of basic research has supported the main tenets of Self-Determination Theory and a growing body of literature has begun to explore its application to risk-related behaviors.

A large proportion of the chapter focuses on etiology, reviewing multiple connections between self-determination and risk behaviors with emphasis on social motivations and influences. Research related to alcohol abuse, problem gambling, risky sexual behavior, and disordered eating behaviors are reviewed in turn. Discussion and review of prevention and treatment implications focus primarily on correction of

---

* Please send correspondence to Clayton Neighbors, University of Washington, Department of Psychiatry and Behavioral Sciences, 4225 Roosevelt Way NE, Box 354794, Seattle, WA, 98195-6099; Phone (206) 685-8704; E-mail *claytonn@u.washington.edu*. Preparation of this chapter was supported in part by National Institute on Alcohol Abuse and Alcoholism Grants R01AA014576 and T32AA07455.

normative misperceptions, mandated treatment, and motivational interviewing. Finally, theoretical discussion is presented regarding the conceptualization of self-determination and intrinsic motivation related to potentially "addictive" healthy and unhealthy behaviors.

INTRODUCTION

Overview of Self-Determination Theory

Self-Determination Theory (SDT; Deci & Ryan, 1985b; Deci & Ryan, 2002) is a broad theory of human motivation focusing on basic psychological needs, integration of external regulations within the self, as well as environmental and individual differences in motivation. SDT has been applied extensively in the domains of work (Baard, Deci, & Ryan, 2004; Deci, Connell, & Ryan, 1989; Gagne & Deci, 2005; Gagne, Koestner, & Zuckerman, 2000), education (Grolnick & Ryan, 1989; Grolnick, Ryan, & Deci, 1991), and health (Williams, Deci, & Ryan, 1995; Williams, Cox, Hedberg, & Deci, 2000; Williams et al., 2002; Williams, Rodin, Ryan, Grolnick, & Deci, 1998), among others. The purpose of this chapter is to provide an overview of SDT as it relates to etiology, prevention, and treatment of risk-related behaviors, with emphasis on social influences in adolescence and young adulthood. Specific risk behaviors to be considered include heavy drinking, gambling, risky sex, and disordered eating.

Self-determination can be defined as the experience of freedom and choice in ones thoughts and actions; to do what one truly wants to do in contrast to doing what one feels compelled to do. From this perspective, there are at least three ways in which self-determination is directly applicable to risk behaviors. First, and most directly applicable to risky behaviors in adolescence and young adulthood, are the influences of social norms, "peer pressure", impression management, and expectations of others in the onset and maintenance of risky behaviors. Second, is the use of risky behaviors as a means of affect regulation, coping, and/or need substitution. A third, and perhaps less directly related application of SDT, is the consideration that in order for behavior to be truly self-determined, it must be conducive with fundamental psychological needs of autonomy, competence, and relatedness (Deci & Ryan, 2000; Ryan, 1995).

SDT can be thought of as a meta-theory of human motivation and consists of several inter-related mini-theories regarding *psychological needs, organismic integration, individual differences, and environmental influences*. Several excellent overviews of the overarching theory and its constituent mini-theories have been published (Deci & Ryan, 1985a; Deci & Ryan, 2002; Deci & Ryan, 1987; Ryan & Deci, 2002; Ryan & Deci, 2000) and are briefly summarized here.

Psychological Needs

SDT assumes that individuals have three basic fundamental psychological needs: autonomy, competence, and relatedness (Deci & Ryan, 2000; Ryan & Deci, 2000).

Satisfaction of these needs is presumed to result in optimal functioning and psychological well-being and has been associated with increased life satisfaction across cultures (Deci et al., 2001; Sheldon & Elliot, 1999; Sheldon, Elliot, Kim, & Kasser, 2001). To some extent, engaging in risk behaviors can be seen as more or less maladaptive strategies for satisfying these needs. For example, in the transition to adulthood, autonomy may manifest in experimentation with alcohol and other substances, gambling, sex, and other risk-related behaviors (Schulenberg & Maggs, 2002). Competence striving may manifest in attempts to achieve and/or maintain the "ideal" body image. Achieving acceptance by peers, avoiding rejection by peers, and sexual relationships can be considered means of pursuing relatedness needs.

Organismic Integration

SDT's perspective on organismic integration considers how environmental constraints and regulations are internalized and integrated into the self (Ryan & Deci, 2000). Regulations proceed in order from being external, to introjected, to identified, and finally become integrated. Socialization occurs whereby external regulations in the environment, which may take the form of rules, laws, or social norms, are initially regulated externally based on contingencies (i.e., rewards and punishments for following or not following regulations). Awareness of contingencies is internalized and behavioral regulations are manifested as what one "should" or "should not" do in a particular context (introjection). Subsequently, introjected regulations become valued in their own right (identification). For example, fear of getting caught doing something one is not "supposed" to do shifts to personal value of abstinence or moderation versus excess or illegal activity. Finally, identified regulations become integrated with other internalized regulations as inconsistencies are resolved to form an overall coherent and cohesive self concept. It is important to note that varying degrees of internalization and integration may be expressed as ambivalence about a particular behavior (Neighbors, Walker, Edleson, Roffman, Mbilinyi, in press).

Individual Differences and Environmental Influences

Other mini-theories comprising SDT include Cognitive Evaluation Theory and Causality Orientations Theory (Ryan & Deci, 2002; Ryan & Deci, 2000; Deci & Ryan, 2002). In essence Cognitive Evaluation Theory describes the process whereby, in the presence of salient contingencies (e.g., rewards for performance or task completion), behaviors which are intrinsically motivated can become extrinsically motivated (Deci, Koestner, & Ryan, 1999). Causality Orientations Theory describes the development of individual differences in global motivational orientations. Thus, individuals vary in the extent to which they are autonomous, controlled, and amotivated. The autonomy orientation is associated with more identified and integrated behavior regulation, intrinsic motivation, feelings of choicefulness, and generally doing what one does because it is consistent with what he or she truly wants to do. In contrast, the controlled orientation is associated with a tendency to engage in behaviors out of a sense of obligation and due to others' expectations and pressures in the environment. The impersonal orientation represents the relative absence of motivation, either autonomous or controlled, and is conceptually associated with learned helplessness and depression and feelings of incompetence.

In the following sections, literature is reviewed emphasizing the relationships between SDT and four specific risk-related behaviors: alcohol use, gambling, risky sexual behavior, and body image/eating disorders.

ALCOHOL USE

SDT has previously been applied to understanding the etiology, prevention and treatment of heavy alcohol use among adolescents (Williams et al., 2000), college students (Knee & Neighbors, 2002; Neighbors, Larimer, Geisner, & Knee, 2004; Neighbors, Lewis, Bergstrom, & Larimer, 2006; Neighbors, Walker, & Larimer, 2003; Rockafellow & Saules, 2006), and clinical populations (Ryan, Plant, & O'Malley, 1995; Wild, Cunningham, & Ryan, 2006). As noted above, individuals with more controlled global motivational orientations tend to report external and introjected forms of extrinsic motivation for engaging in behaviors. Previous research has suggested a link between self-determination and susceptibility to peer influence, such that those higher in controlled orientation may be more influenced by perceptions of normative behavior or social pressures from relevant peer groups. As detailed below, when applied to heavy alcohol use specifically, research suggests that controlled orientation is associated with reporting heavier alcohol consumption and more extrinsic reasons for using alcohol.

A number of studies have examined controlled orientation in relation to peer influences on drinking (Knee & Neighbors, 2002; Neighbors et al., 2003; Neighbors et al., 2004; Neighbors et al., 2006; Rockafellow & Saules, 2006). Knee and Neighbors (2002) examined controlled orientation, extrinsic motivation for drinking, and perceptions of peer pressure as predictors of alcohol use in samples of college students and fraternity members. In the college sample, controlled orientation moderated the relation between peer pressure and alcohol use, but only for men. However, this relationship was not significant in a fraternity sample.

Similarly, Rockafellow and Saules (2006) examined the role of extrinsic motivation for athletic participation in the relationship between athletic involvement and substance use using the rationale that those who report engaging in athletics for extrinsic reasons (reasons other than pure enjoyment of the activities) would also be more likely to be susceptible to peer influences for engaging in substance use. Results revealed that athletes and exercisers who reported extrinsic reasons for athletic involvement indeed reported higher rates of alcohol use than those who were involved for intrinsic reasons.

Neighbors, Lewis, Bergstrom, and Larimer (2006) specifically examined the role of controlled orientation in the efficacy of a personalized normative feedback intervention on reducing drinking in a sample of college students. Normative feedback alcohol interventions aim to reduce alcohol use and normative misperceptions regarding drinking by providing accurate information about the typical drinking practices of a relevant reference group. SDT would posit that individuals who drink primarily for the extrinsic reasons of wanting to fit in with a social group should be more influenced by an intervention that aims to reduce misperceptions (overestimations) regarding the drinking practices of the relevant social group. Results revealed that controlled orientation did not moderate the influence of the intervention on reducing alcohol use or perceived norms, but indicated that controlled orientation did moderate the effect of the intervention on changes in negative consequences associated with alcohol use, such that students higher in controlled orientation who received normative feedback reduced their consequences relative to other students. Many negative consequences are more salient to others, such as getting sick or passing out, compared to the actual number of drinks one has. Students higher in controlled orientation may have been extrinsically motivated to reduce these salient, visible indicators of concern (i.e., alcohol-related problems). This study provided partial support for targeting normative feedback alcohol interventions towards more control-oriented college students.

In addition to research examining global forms of motivation (intrinsic vs. extrinsic), research has also begun to examine more specific reasons for drinking (affect enhancement, coping, social, conformity) in line with SDT. Neighbors et al. (2004) found that control oriented students tend to use alcohol as means of affect regulation (affect enhancement and coping) and gaining social approval, and this relationship was partly due to basing one's self-esteem more heavily on contingencies (e.g., others' expectations). In a related study, Neighbors, Walker, and Larimer (2003) examined the moderating influences of self-determination (i.e., autonomous and controlled orientations) on the relationship between alcohol expectancies and alcohol-related behaviors (use and problems) and between subjective evaluations of alcohol effects and alcohol-related behaviors. Results revealed that positive alcohol expectancies were more strongly associated with alcohol use and problems among lower autonomy individuals, and among male students higher in controlled orientation. For subjective evaluations of alcohol effects, more positive evaluations of alcohol effects were associated with higher alcohol use among students lower in autonomy orientation and higher in controlled orientation (particularly men).

SDT has also been applied to substance abuse treatment adherence and outcome. Ryan, Plant, and O'Malley (1995) applied SDT (external vs. internal motivations for entering treatment) to treatment adherence in an outpatient alcohol treatment program. Findings indicated that internal motivation was positively associated with treatment outcomes. Results also indicated that those who were both internally *and* externally motivated were the most likely to continue their treatment, but external motivation was only related to treatment outcome when in the presence of internal motivation.

Wild, Cunningham, and Ryan (2006) reported similar findings in examining the relationships between participants' motivations for treatment (e.g., external, introjected, identified) and both objective measures and participants' perceptions of external pressures to enter treatment (e.g., legal, formal or social) in relation to treatment outcomes. Results indicated that external treatment motivation was associated with being legally mandated into treatment, perceiving social pressure to enter treatment, and experiencing less severe problems associated with use. Conversely, identified motivation for entering treatment was associated with self-referral and more severe problems associated with use, and was negatively associated with perceptions of coercion into treatment. Identified motivation for entering treatment also predicted higher levels of engagement in treatment.

With respect to treatment strategies, approaches which support autonomy (i.e., Motivational Interviewing; MI; Miller & Rollnick, 2002) have become among the most popular treatments for alcohol abuse and dependence, especially among individuals who may not initially want to change and/or express ambivalence about change. MI is a client-centered approach for helping clients resolve ambivalence about change by expressing empathy, supporting client autonomy and competence, and enhancing intrinsic motivation to change. Moreover, connections between MI and SDT have been described in detail (Markland, Ryan, Tobin, & Rollnick, 2005; Neighbors et al., in press; Vansteenkiste & Sheldon, 2006).

In sum, applications of SDT to alcohol use and treatment have provided several insights. First, peer influences, arguably the strongest influence on alcohol use among adolescents and young adults, are moderated by individual differences in self-determination. Similarly, perceived contingencies of drinking are more strongly related to drinking among individuals who tend to be less self-determined. In both cases, these effects appear to be stronger among men than women. SDT also has implications for treatment engagement and suggests that entering treatment programs for intrinsic reasons regardless of the presence of other extrinsic pressures appears to be a crucial factor for clients engaging in the treatment and having more positive treatment outcomes. Finally, treatment approaches which are consistent with the tenets of SDT appear to be particularly effective.

GAMBLING

Relative to research directly related to self-determination and drinking behavior and treatment, considerably less research has examined connections between self-determination and gambling. The first study to examine relationships between self-determination and gambling found that more self-determined reasons for gambling such as monetary gain were associated with less gambling involvement in comparison to more self-determined reasons for gambling such as enjoyment and interest (Chantal, Vallerand, & Vallieres, 1995). In a related study, Chantal and Vallerand (1996) found that involvement in gambling activities that require some degree of knowledge and skill (i.e., horse racing) were associated with more self-determined reasons for gambling whereas gambling activities that rely entirely on chance and require no skill (i.e., lottery) were associated with less self-determined reasons for gambling. The latter study suggests that gambling activities which can satisfy competence needs may be associated with more enjoyment, at least with respect to non-problematic gambling. Neither of these studies considered how self-determination might be associated with more problematic gambling. Neighbors and Larimer (2004) examined relationships between autonomy and controlled orientations and problem gambling among college students in two studies and found that controlled orientation was consistently associated with problem gambling. They also reported mixed evidence suggesting that autonomy orientation was associated with less problem gambling. In addition, the relationships between causality orientations and problem gambling were mediated by gambling more frequently and spending more money gambling.

The apparent inconsistencies among the studies described in the previous paragraph suggest that recreational gambling, for fun and enjoyment, can be a self-determined activity. However, at the point in which gambling becomes problematic/addictive, it is less likely to be self-determined. Other studies underlying this point have considered two different types of "passion" toward gambling. Rousseau, Vallerand, Ratelle, Mageau, and Provencher (2002) distinguished harmonious passion for gambling from obsessive passion for gambling. Whereas harmonious passion is characterized by interest and enjoyment, obsessive passion involves preoccupation and compulsion. Subsequently, Ratelle, Vallerand, Mageau,

Rousseau, and Provencher (2004) found that obsessive passion for gambling was associated with less vitality and concentration in daily tasks, rumination, negative affect, and problem gambling. Similar relationships with harmonious passion were not evident. In examining the consequences of gambling as a function of passion more specifically, Mageau, Vallerand, Rousseau, Ratelle, and Provencher (2005) found that harmonious passion was associated with more positive affective and cognitive outcomes after gambling and obsessive passion was associated with more negative affective and cognitive outcomes. Thus, harmonious passion was associated with amusement, fun, and perceptions of challenge whereas obsessive passion was negatively associated with these outcomes and positively associated with feelings of guilt and being judged by others. In addition to highlighting a potential key to understanding the tipping point between non-problematic and problematic gambling, this line of research also has implications for organismic integration. The relationship between obsessive passion, feelings of guilt, and problematic gambling is consistent with the notion that problematic behavior may be more difficult to integrate, perhaps because they necessarily result in consequences that are inconsistent with personal values.

As with alcohol, treatment approaches for problem and pathological gambling which incorporate principles consistent with SDT (i.e., MI; Miller & Rollnick, 2002) by supporting autonomy and competence have begun to show considerable promise (Larimer et al., under review; Hodgins, Currie, & el-Guebaly, 2001; Takushi et al., 2004; Wulfert, Blanchard, Freidenberg, & Martell, 2006). Also consistent with the alcohol literature, overestimates of others' gambling frequency and expenditure is associated with more problematic gambling (Larimer & Neighbors, 2003) and correction of these misperceptions is associated with reduced gambling behavior (Larimer et al., under review). To the extent that self-determination is associated with susceptibility to peer influences on gambling, as it is with alcohol use, prevention and intervention approaches which incorporate social norms might be more effective among students who are more controlled (Neighbors et al., 2006).

In sum, with some exceptions, research findings related to self-determination and gambling largely mirror research related to self-determination and alcohol use. Whereas self-determined reasons for alcohol use have not been identified, some evidence suggests that gambling can be intrinsically motivated and promote competence, but only to the extent that gambling is non-problematic and not accompanied by preoccupation and/or compulsion.

SEXUAL BEHAVIOR

Individuals differ in their external motivations to adhere to social norms related to sexual behavior (Oliver & Hyde, 1993) or gender roles (Wood, Christensen, Hebl, & Rothgerber, 1997). Social norms related to the expectation and approval of sexual behavior differ for men and women and have historically prescribed greater acceptance of sexual activity outside of marriage for men than women (Crawford & Popp, 2003; Marks & Fraley, 2005; Milhausen & Herold, 2001; Sprecher, McKinney, & Orbuch, 1987). With regard to gender roles, women are expected to be subservient and cater to partner needs (Impett & Peplau, 2003; Sanchez, Kiefer, & Ybarra, 2006). SDT provides a theoretical framework for who is more likely to be driven to conform to these norms and how this relates to sexual behavior. Recent research has demonstrated relationships between causality orientations and sexual behavior, such that less self-determined individuals show a sensitivity to, valuing of, and/or compliance with social norms or gender roles and that this in turn relates to risky sexual behavior, initiation of sexual behavior, sexual submission, and sexual satisfaction.

Lewis, Neighbors, and Malheim (2006) examined the relationships among controlled orientation, erotophilia (i.e., strong positive attitudes towards sexual cues), and risky sexual behavior in a sample of college students. Consistent with previous research demonstrating the relationship between controlled orientation and other risk-related behaviors, such as problem drinking and gambling (Neighbors et al., 2004; Neighbors & Larimer, 2004), findings demonstrated a positive association between controlled orientation and risky sexual behavior. Moreover, the relationship between risky sexual behavior and erotophilia was evident among male participants who were more controlled. Results suggested that being higher in controlled orientation and erotophilia interactively contributed to engaging in sexual risk taking among men. Diverging sexual behavior norms for men and women concerning the approval of risky sexual behavior were likely moderators of the stronger erotophilic-risk link among more controlled individuals. Previous research has demonstrated that social approval is a stronger motivator for individuals who are more controlled (Knee & Neighbors, 2002; Neighbors et al., 2004). Males higher in controlled orientation who had stronger responses to sexual cues were more influenced by social norms for involvement in risky sexual behavior. However, for erotophilic women, the desire and impulse to engage in sexual behavior is inconsistent with social norms for female sexual behavior, thus not being associated with more risky sexual behavior.

Additional research by Turner, Irwin, Tschann, and Millstein (1993) found that adolescents who received autonomous support from their parents were less likely to initiate sexual intercourse. While there is little research evaluating the associations among causality orientations and sexual behavior, initial findings indicate that controlled orientation is associated with engaging in risky sexual behavior whereas autonomy orientation is associated with a delay in initiating sexual activity. As found with the other high-risk behaviors discussed herein, it may be effective to target controlled individuals who engage in risky sex with interventions containing components that challenge perceptions of normative behavior for genders or enhance intrinsic reasons for engaging in behaviors.

In addition to engaging in sexual behavior, SDT also relates to sexual submissiveness and satisfaction. Sanchez, Crocker, and Boike (2005) explored the relationships among conforming to gender roles, self-esteem based on others' approval, sexual autonomy, and sexual pleasure in a sample of college students. For women and men, valuing gender conformity (i.e., placing importance on being feminine for females and masculine for males) was associated with experiencing less sexual pleasure. This relationship was mediated by higher self-esteem contingent on others' approval and lower sexual autonomy. In addition, Sanchez, Kiefer, and Ybarra (2006) examined the relationships among sexual submissiveness, arousal, and autonomy in a sample of female college students. Women who adopted a submissive role reported being less sexually aroused. Sexual autonomy mediated this relationship suggesting that submissive individuals are less autonomous and are thus less likely to be satisfied sexually. Together, these studies suggest that conforming to societal norms can be detrimental, especially for less autonomous individuals. Being externally motivated or focusing efforts on achieving traditional gender roles may undermine autonomy. Sanchez et al. (2005) suggested that this view is consistent with research examining the negative impact of self-worth based on external contingencies on autonomy (Crocker & Park, 2004; Deci, Eghrari, Patrick, & Leone, 1994).

To conclude, initial research on self-determination and sexual behavior indicates that being less self-determined or externally motivated by social norms, as with other behaviors, is associated with greater engagement in risky behaviors. Additionally, being less self-determined is associated with sexual submission and less sexual satisfaction. Research is needed to evaluate how this can be utilized in prevention and treatment efforts. As found with high-risk drinking and gambling behavior, overestimates of risky sexual behavior are associated with engaging in more risky sexual behavior (Lewis, Lee, Patrick, & Fossos, in press). However, research has yet to examine if correction of these misperceptions will relate to reduced sexual risk taking among more controlled individuals.

BODY IMAGE AND EATING DISORDERS

Etiological models of body dissatisfaction and eating pathology focus on the influence of sociocultural pressures on females to be thin and more recently, males to adopt a mesomorphic build. Motivations to conform to societal standards of physical appearance contribute to the development of maladaptive behavioral patterns, including dieting, excessive exercise, and eating disorders (Pelletier, Dion, & Levesque, 2004; Thompson & Stice, 2001). Given the role of motivational factors driving these deleterious behaviors, SDT can serve as a theoretical framework for understanding the development of body image concerns and eating disorders.

The little research that has considered SDT in the context of body dissatisfaction and eating pathology suggests greater levels of self-determination as a protective factor for the development of body dissatisfaction and eating disorders. Pelletier and colleagues (2004) examined the relationship between self-determination and symptoms associated with bulimia in a sample of female college students. More self-determined women indicated fewer tendencies to perceive sociocultural pressures about body image and were less likely to endorse society's positive beliefs about thinness, and reported fewer bulimic symptoms. Conversely, those adopting more extrinsic forms of motivation (i.e., less self-determined individuals) were more likely to internalize societal pressures to be thin, report greater body dissatisfaction, as well as more symptoms associated with bulimia. These results suggest the importance of considering self-determination as a protective factor for females confronted with potentially harmful sociocultural messages about body image and eating behaviors.

Though little research has utilized direct measures of self-determination in etiological models of body image concerns and eating pathology, social-cognitive factors associated with lower levels of self-determination have been indicated as contributing to such psychopathology. Individuals exposed to controlling environmental factors who perceive pressured evaluations are likely to be motivated by extrinsic goals, and this controlled orientation is associated with a contingency-based sense of self-worth (Deci & Ryan, 1985a, 2000). As applied to self-perceptions of physical appearance, females who perceive pressure and criticism from family members and peers about their appearance are at risk for experiencing body image concerns (Carlson Jones, 2004). Additionally, research has indicated an association between a fear of negative evaluation and attitudes related to restrictive eating and bulimic symptoms (Gilbert & Meyer, 2005). Bergstrom, Neighbors, and Lewis (2004) found that women who overestimated men's preference for thinness were more likely to have negative eating attitudes, especially those whose self-worth was more externally based on appearance. Such appearance-related concerns reported by females high in contingent self-esteem would seemingly increase their risk for engaging in appearance-related social comparisons, a process whereby individuals gather information that they use for self-evaluation.

In an experimental study, Patrick, Neighbors, and Knee (2004) examined female college students' tendencies to make appearance-related social comparisons as a function of contingent self-esteem. Results indicated that women higher in contingent self-esteem and lower in their self-perceptions of attractiveness, after viewing an advertisement, were more likely to make appearance-related comparisons with the models appearing in the advertisement. Additionally, utilizing an event-recording diary procedure, Patrick and colleagues (2004) found that women higher in contingent self-esteem felt worse after making social comparisons in their daily lives, and this association was mediated by their tendency to make upward social comparisons. Thus, higher levels of contingent self-esteem appear to increase the likelihood that individuals will compare themselves to extrinsic, and often times, unrealistic standards of physical appearance. Consequently, those with lower self-perceptions of appearance often experience negative affect associated with their increased body image dissatisfaction.

In terms of research focusing on treatments for eating disorder, SDT has been suggested as a framework for enhancing patients' intrinsic motivation to change their eating behaviors (Vansteenkiste, Soenens, & Vandereycken, 2005). Vansteenkiste and colleagues (2005) suggest that rather than simply enhancing patients' intrinsic motivation, it is important to support the gradual internalization of a seemingly non-enjoyable behavior (healthy eating behavior), so that patients accept the personal importance of such behaviors. The authors discriminate between two forms of internalized motivation, namely identified and introjected. As described by Deci and Ryan (1985a, 2000) identified motivation is associated with personal values and commitment, and introjected motivation is related to more controlling environments, often resulting in guilt, shame, and anxiety. Within the context of eating disorders, it is important to promote identified motivation such that patients' behaviors are supported by their own goals and values, rather than based on their internalization of what others prescribe to them as improving their health.

CONCLUSION

A key to preventing and treating risk-related behaviors and their consequences is understanding why individuals engage in those behaviors. SDT is a theory that has been useful in understanding why individuals engage in risk-related behaviors and in considering how to best reduce the incidence and consequences of those behaviors. In general, individuals who tend to be more extrinsically motivated and susceptible to social influences appear to engage in more problematic behaviors. Individuals experiencing problems related to risk behaviors also appear to express ambivalence about their behavior and about changing their behavior. Approaches which attempt to resolve this ambivalence in a way that supports autonomy and competence and builds intrinsic motivation for change are most likely to be effective.

REFERENCES

Baard, P. P., Deci, E. L., & Ryan, R. M. (2004). Intrinsic need satisfaction: A motivational basis of performance and well-being in two work settings. *Journal of Applied Social Psychology, 34,* 2045-2068.

Bergstrom, R. L., Neighbors, C., & Lewis, M. A. (2004). Do men find "bony" women attractive?: Consequences of misperceiving opposite sex perceptions of attractive body image. *Body Image, 1,* 183-191.

Carlson Jones, D. (2004). Body image among adolescent girls and boys: A longitudinal study. *Developmental Psychology, 40,* 823-835.

Chantal, Y. & Vallerand, R. J. (1996). Skill versus luck: A motivational analysis of gambling involvement. *Journal of Gambling Studies, 12,* 407-418.

Chantal, Y., Vallerand, R. J., & Vallieres, E. F. (1995). Motivation and gambling involvement. *Journal of Social Psychology, 135,* 755-763.

Crawford, M. & Popp, D. (2003). Sexual double standards: A review and methodological critique of two decades of research. *Journal of Sex Research, 40,* 13-26.

Crocker, J. & Park, L. E. (2004). The costly pursuit of self-esteem. *Psychological Bulletin, 130,* 392-414.

Deci, E. L., Connell, J. P., & Ryan, R. M. (1989). Self-determination in a work organization. *Journal of Applied Psychology, 74,* 580-590.

Deci, E. L., Eghrari, H., Patrick, B. C., & Leone, D. R. (1994). Facilitating internalization: the self-determination theory perspective. *Journal of Personality, 62,* 119-142.

Deci, E. L., Koestner, R., & Ryan, R. M. (1999). A meta-analytic review of experiments examining the effects of extrinsic rewards on intrinsic motivation. *Psychological Bulletin, 125,* 627-668.

Deci, E. L. & Ryan, R. M. (1985a). *Intrinsic motivation and self-determination in human behavior.* New York: Plenum.

Deci, E. L. & Ryan, R. M. (1985b). The General Causality Orientations Scale - Self-Determination in Personality. *Journal of Research in Personality, 19,* 109-134.

Deci, E. L. & Ryan, R. M. (1987). The Support of Autonomy and the Control of Behavior. *Journal of Personality and Social Psychology, 53,* 1024-1037.

Deci, E. L. & Ryan, R. M. (2000). The "what" and "why" of goal pursuits: Human needs and the self-determination of behavior. *Psychological Inquiry, 11,* 227-268.

Deci, E. L. & Ryan, R. M. (2002). Overview of self-determination theory: An organismic dialectical perspecitve. In E.L.Deci & R. M. Ryan (Eds.), *Handbook of self-determination research* (pp. 3-36). University of Rochester Press.

Deci, E: L., Ryan, R. M., Gagne, M., Leone, D. R., Usunov, J., & Kornazheva, B. P. (2001). Need satisfaction, motivation, and well-being in the work organizations of a former Eastern bloc country: A cross-cultural study of self-determination. *Personality and Social Psychology Bulletin, 27,* 930-942.

Gagne, M. & Deci, E. L. (2005). Self-determination theory and work motivation. *Journal of Organizational Behavior, 26,* 331-362.

Gagne, M., Koestner, R., & Zuckerman, M. (2000). Facilitating acceptance of organizational change: The importance of self-determination. *Journal of Applied Social Psychology, 30,* 1843-1852.

Gilbert, N. & Meyer, C. (2005). Fear of negative evaluation and the development of eating pathology: A longitudinal study of nonclinical women. *International Journal of Eating Disorders, 37,* 307-312.

Grolnick, W. S. & Ryan, R. M. (1989). Parent styles associated with childrens self-regulation and competence in school. *Journal of Educational Psychology, 81,* 143-154.

Grolnick, W. S., Ryan, R. M., & Deci, E. L. (1991). Inner resources for school-achievement - motivational mediators of childrens perceptions of their parents. *Journal of Educational Psychology, 83,* 508-517.

Hodgins, D. C., Currie, S. R., & el-Guebaly, N. (2001). Motivational enhancement and self-help treatments for problem gambling. *Journal of Consulting and Clinical Psychology, 69,* 50-57.

Impett, E. A. & Peplau, L. A. (2003). Sexual compliance: Gender, motivational, and relationship perspectives. *Journal of Sex Research, 40,* 87-100.

Knee, C. R. & Neighbors, C. (2002). Self-determination, perception of peer pressure, and drinking among college students. *Journal of Applied Social Psychology, 32,* 522-543.

Larimer, M. E. & Neighbors, C. (2003). Normative misperception and the impact of descriptive and injunctive norms on college student gambling. *Psychology of Addictive Behaviors, 17,* 235-243.

Larimer, M. E., Neighbors, C., Lostutter, T. W., Whiteside, U., Cronce, J. M., Kaysen, D., & Walker, D. D. (2006). Brief motivational feedback vs. cognitive behavioral therapy for disordered gambling: A randomized clinical trial. Manuscript under review.

Lewis, M. A., Lee, C. M., Patrick, M. E., & Fossos, N. (in press). Gender-specific normative misperceptions of risky sexual behavior and alcohol-related risky sexual behavior. *Sex Roles.*

Lewis, M. A., Neighbors, C., & Malheim, J. (2006). Indulgence or restraint? Gender differences in the relationship between controlled orientation and the erotophilia-risky sex link. *Personality and Individual differences, 40,* 985-995.

Mageau, G. A., Vallerand, R. J., Rousseau, F. L., Ratelle, C. F., & Provencher, P. J. (2005). Passion and gambling: Investigating the divergent affective and cognitive consequences of gambling. *Journal of Applied Social Psychology, 35,* 100-118.

Markland, D., Ryan, R. M., Tobin, V. J., & Rollnick, S. (2005). Motivational interviewing and self-determination theory. *Journal of Social & Clinical Psychology, 24,* 811-831.

Marks, M. J. & Fraley, R. C. (2005). The sexual double standard: Fact or fiction? *Sex Roles, 52,* 175-186.

Milhausen, R. R. & Herold, E. S. (2001). Reconceptualizing the sexual double standard. *Journal of Psychology & Human Sexuality, 13,* 63-83.

Miller, W. R. & Rollnick, S. (2002). *Motivational interviewing: Preparing people for change.* (2 ed.) New York: Guilford Press.

Neighbors, C., Larimer, M. E., Geisner, I. M., & Knee, C. R. (2004). Feeling controlled and drinking motives among college students: Contingent self-esteem as a mediator. *Self and Identity, 3,* 207-224.

Neighbors, C., Walker, D. D., Edleson, J. L., Roffman, R. A., & Mbilinyi, L. F. (in press). Self determination theory and motivational interviewing: Complementary models to elicit voluntary engagement by partner-abusive men. *American Journal of Family Therapy.*

Neighbors, C., Walker, D. D., & Larimer, M. E. (2003). Expectancies and evaluations of alcohol effects among college students: self-determination as a moderator. *Journal of Studies on Alcohol, 64,* 292-300.

Neighbors, C. & Larimer, M. E. (2004). Self-determination and problem gambling among college students. *Journal of Social & Clinical Psychology, 23,* 565-583.

Neighbors, C., Lewis, M. A., Bergstrom, R. L., & Larimer, M. E. (2006). Being controlled by normative Influences: Self-determination as a moderator of a normative feedback alcohol intervention. *Health Psychology, 25,* 571-579.

Oliver, M. B. & Hyde, J. S. (1993). Gender differences in sexuality: A meta-analysis. *Psychological Bulletin, 114,* 29-51.

Patrick, H., Neighbors, C., & Knee, C. R. (2004). Appearance-related social comparisons: the role of contingent self-esteem and self-perceptions of attractiveness. *Personality and Social Psychology Bulletin, 30,* 501-514.

Pelletier, L. G., Dion, S., & Levesque, C. (2004). Can self-determination help protect women against sociocultural influences about body image and reduce their risk of experiencing bulimic symptoms? *Journal of Social & Clinical Psychology, 23,* 61-88.

Ratelle, C. F., Vallerand, R. J., Mageau, G. A., Rousseau, F. L., & Provencher, P. (2004). When passion leads to problematic outcomes: A look at gambling. *Journal of Gambling Studies, 20,* 105-119.

Rockafellow, B. D. & Saules, K. K. (2006). Substance use by college students: The role of intrinsic versus extrinsic motivation for athletic involvement. *Psychology of Addictive Behaviors, 20,* 279-287.

Rousseau, F., Vallerand, R. J., Ratelle, C. F., Mageau, G., & Provencher, P. J. (2002). Passion and gambling: On the validation of the Gambling Passion Scale (GPS). *Journal of Gambling Studies, 18,* 45-66.

Ryan, R. M. (1995). Psychological needs and the facilitation of integrative processes. *Journal of Personality, 63,* 397-427.

Ryan, R. M. & Deci, E. L. (2000). Self-determination theory and the facilitation of intrinsic motivation, social development, and well-being. *American Psychologist, 55,* 68-78.

Ryan, R. M. & Deci, E. L. (2002). Overview of self-determination theory: An organismic-dialectical perspective. In E.Deci & R. M. Ryan (Eds.), *Handbook of self-determination research* (pp. 3-33). Rochester: Rochester Press.

Ryan, R. M., Plant, R. W., & O'Malley, S. (1995). Initial motivations for alcohol treatment: Relations with patient characteristics, treatment involvement, and dropout. *Addictive Behaviors, 20,* 279-297.

Sanchez, D. T., Crocker, J., & Boike, K. R. (2005). Doing gender in the bedroom: Investing in gender norms and the sexual experience. *Personality and Social Psychology Bulletin, 31,* 1445-1455.

Sanchez, D. T., Kiefer, A. K., & Ybarra, O. (2006). Sexual submissiveness in women: Costs for sexual autonomy and arousal. *Personality and Social Psychology Bulletin, 32,* 512-524.

Schulenberg, J. E. & Maggs, J. L. (2002). A developmental perspective on alcohol use and heavy drinking during adolescence and the transition to young adulthood. *Journal of Studies on Alcohol, Suppl. 14*, 54-70.

Sheldon, K. M. & Elliot, A. J. (1999). Goal striving, need satisfaction, and longitudinal well-being: The self-concordance model. *Journal of Personality and Social Psychology, 76*, 482-497.

Sheldon, K. M., Elliot, A. J., Kim, Y., & Kasser, T. (2001). What is satisfying about satisfying events? Testing 10 candidate psychological needs. *Journal of Personality and Social Psychology, 80*, 325-339.

Sprecher, S., McKinney, K., & Orbuch, T. L. (1987). Has the double standard disappeared? An experimental test. *Social Psychology Quarterly, 50*, 24-31.

Takushi, R. Y., Neighbors, C., Larimer, M. E., Lostutter, T. W., Cronce, J. M., & Marlatt, G. A. (2004). Indicated prevention of problem gambling among college students. *Journal of Gambling Studies, 20*, 83-93.

Thompson, J. K. & Stice, E. (2001). Thin-ideal internalization: Mounting evidencce for a new risk factor for body-image disturbance and eating pathology. *Current Directions in Psychological Science, 10*, 181-183.

Turner, R. A., Irwin, C. E., Tschann, J. M., & Millstein, S. G. (1993). Autonomy, relatedness, and the initiation of health risk behaviors in early adolescence. *Health Psychology, 12*, 200-208.

Vansteenkiste, M. & Sheldon, K. M. (2006). There's nothing more practical than a good theory: Integrating motivational interviewing and self-determination theory. *British Journal of Clinical Psychology, 45*, 63-82.

Vansteenkiste, M., Soenens, B., & Vandereycken, W. (2005). Motivation to change in eating disorder patients: A conceptual clarification on the basis of self-determination theory. *International Journal of Eating Disorders, 37*, 207-219.

Wild, T. C., Cunningham, J. A., & Ryan, R. M. (2006). Social pressure, coercion, and client engagement at treatment entry: A self-determination theory perspective. *Addictive Behaviors, 31*, 1858-1872.

Williams, G. C., Deci, E. L., & Ryan, R. M. (1995). Building health-care partnerships by supporting autonomy: Promoting maintained behavior change and positive health outcomes. In P.Hinton-Walker, A. L. Suchman, & R. Botehlo (Eds.), *Partnerships, power, and process: Transforming health care delivery*. Rochester: University of Rochester Press.

Williams, G. C., Cox, E. M., Hedberg, V. A., & Deci, E. L. (2000). Extrinsic life goals and health-risk behaviors in adolescents. *Journal of Applied Social Psychology, 30*, 1756-1771.

Williams, G. C., Minicucci, D. S., Kouides, R. W., Levesque, C. S., Chirkov, V. I., Ryan, R. M. et al. (2002). Self-determination, smoking, diet and health. *Health Education Research, 17*, 512-521.

Williams, G. C., Rodin, G. C., Ryan, R. M., Grolnick, W. S., & Deci, E. L. (1998). Autonomous regulation and long-term medication adherence in adult outpatients. *Health Psychology, 17*, 269-276.

Wood, W., Christensen, P. N., Hebl, M. R., & Rothgerber, H. (1997). Conformity to sex-typed norms, affect, and the self-concept. *Journal of Personality and Social Psychology, 73*, 523-535.

Wulfert, E., Blanchard, E. B., Freidenberg, B. M., & Martell, R. S. (2006). Retaining pathological gamblers in cognitive behavior therapy through motivational enhancement: A pilot study. *Behavior Modification, 30*, 315-340.

In: Psychology of Motivation
Editor: Lois V. Brown, pp. 115-128

ISBN: 978-1-60021-598-8
© 2007 Nova Science Publishers, Inc.

Chapter 7

A MOTIVATIONAL-COGNITIVE MODEL OF PROSPECTIVE MEMORY: THE INFLUENCE OF GOAL RELEVANCE

Suzanna L. Penningroth and Walter D. Scott
Department of Psychology, University of Wyoming, Laramie, Wyoming, USA

ABSTRACT

Prospective memory is defined as memory for actions to be performed in the future, such as remembering to take a medication or remembering to mail a bill. A cognitive approach has yielded significant advances in our understanding of prospective memory processes. However, in this chapter, we argue that further insight can be gained by integrating motivational constructs. Specifically, we outline a new, goal-based motivational-cognitive model of prospective memory in which goal-related prospective memories are viewed as benefiting from both effortful and automatic processing throughout all phases of the prospective memory task. Drawing on contemporary goal frameworks, the new model views goals as knowledge structures with associative links to prospective memories. As a result of these associative connections, goal-related prospective memories are predicted (a) to be perceived as more important, (b) to benefit from greater use of mnemonic strategies, (c) to show greater accessibility in memory, (d) to show preferential allocation of attention during retrieval and performance, and (e) to benefit from automatic retrieval processes. Consequently, these processes are predicted to contribute to superior performance for goal-related prospective memories. In this chapter, we also review evidence that supports our new model. By guiding research into the motivational processes contributing to prospective memory, we hope to contribute to a more complete and ecologically valid understanding of prospective memory performance.

INTRODUCTION

The second author has a reputation for forgetting to do things he is supposed to do. Just recently, for instance, he was supposed to remember to mail a package. Although he thought about performing this task on several occasions, when the fateful time arrived it did not occur to him, and he forgot the task. Cognitive psychologists refer to his problem as a failure of prospective memory, which is defined as memory for activities to be performed in the future. Naturally occurring prospective memory tasks are ubiquitous and range from relatively mundane tasks (e.g., a parent remembering to pack a lunch for his or her child or a colleague remembering to include an attachment for an email message) to potentially highly consequential tasks (e.g., an airline pilot remembering to set the wing flaps for takeoff or a diabetic remembering to check blood sugar levels).

The second author's generally poor prospective memory performance is not always apparent: He does remember to do certain things. For instance, as a season ticket holder for the local university's men's basketball team, he has to remember to turn in his season ticket request each year by a specific date in order to keep his seats, which are in a prime location (tenth row). For the past five years, he has unfailingly performed this task. His performance record is also very good for important prospective memory tasks related to his job as a professor. For example, he has forgotten to attend only 1 of his 100+ committee meetings for graduate student theses and dissertations in the past nine years. These personal examples illustrate the fundamental point of this chapter: Motivational factors need to be considered in understanding prospective memory performance.

CURRENT STATE OF RESEARCH ON PROSPECTIVE MEMORY

Almost all research on prospective memory has been conducted by cognitive psychologists. Research on this topic is newer and less plentiful than research on retrospective memory, which refers to memory for past events or for information acquired in the past. However, in the past two decades, the field of prospective memory research has expanded greatly. For instance, there have been two international conferences devoted to the topic, and the second edited book on prospective memory is currently in press (Kliegel, McDaniel, & Einstein, in press). Although there are some similarities between prospective memory and retrospective memory, there is sufficient evidence to support the idea that prospective memory is a distinct construct (e.g., Salthouse, Berish, & Siedlecki, 2004). In fact, recent evidence has shown differences in brain activity underlying prospective and retrospective memory tasks (West, Bowry, & Krompinger, 2006; West & Krompinger, 2005; West & Wymbs, 2004).

Research on prospective memory has yielded significant advances in our understanding of the cognitive processes involved. First, prospective memory appears best conceptualized as a multiphase process (e.g., Ellis, 1996; Kliegel, Martin, McDaniel, & Einstein, 2002). In a model proposed by Kliegel et al. (2002), a prospective memory task includes four phases: intention formation, intention retention, intention initiation, and intention execution. An everyday example of these phases might include deciding to fill up the gas tank when starting the car (intention formation), maintaining this intention during the drive (the retention interval), noticing a gas station and retrieving the intended action from memory (intention initiation), and finally, turning in to the gas station and filling the tank (intention execution). Kliegel et al. (2002) provided support for this multiphase model with evidence showing that different types of executive processes in working memory support different phases of the prospective memory task.

Second, multiple studies have provided information on the role of attention resources in prospective memory. There is evidence that prospective memory performance can suffer when resources for strategic (attention demanding) processing are more scarce (e.g., Penningroth, 2005a; Smith, 2003). However, according to the multi-process theory of prospective memory (McDaniel & Einstein, 2000), retrieval of intentions can be relatively automatic or strategic, depending on characteristics of the task, the cue, the ongoing task, and the individual. If retrieval of intentions occurs automatically, the impact of scarce attention resources should be less significant. In fact, prospective memory performance has been found to utilize both automatic and strategic processes. For example, using a computerized prospective memory task, Einstein et al. (2005) were able to demonstrate either controlled monitoring for the prospective memory cue (e.g., increased RT in the concurrent ongoing task) or spontaneous retrieval (e.g., no increase in RT in the ongoing task). Consistent with predictions of the multi-process model, the type of retrieval processing depended on manipulations of task features. For example, when the ongoing task required focal processing of potential prospective memory cues, prospective memory retrieval was more spontaneous.

The findings presented above illustrate just a few of the developments that have occurred in prospective memory research. Clearly, a cognitive approach to prospective memory research has led to significant advances in our understanding of this complex task. However, we argue that this research has been limited by its predominantly "cold" cognitive focus. More specifically, we argue for integrating "hot" motivational constructs into the study of prospective memory. As illustrated by the second author's personal anecdotes described in the beginning of this chapter, all prospective memories are not alike. Some are more important. Understanding the contribution of motivation to prospective memory performance may advance our current understanding.

RATIONALE FOR INVESTIGATING MOTIVATIONAL FACTORS IN PROSPECTIVE MEMORY

Our proposal for incorporating motivational variables into the study of prospective memory is based on three justifications. First, this approach will improve the ecological validity of prospective memory research. An examination of everyday prospective memory tasks for an individual reveals multiple tasks that must be coordinated with each other and with other activities of the day. Under what circumstances is a person more likely to forget to perform a prospective memory task? We argue that motivational variables may help to explain when an individual is likely to exhibit superior or inferior prospective memory performance. Second, researchers in the field of prospective memory have recognized the need to also study motivational variables in prospective memory (e.g., Ellis, 1996, Kliegel et al., 2002; McDaniel & Einstein, 2000).

Third, a motivational approach might also inform research on prospective memory and aging, which has produced paradoxical findings. On laboratory tasks, young adults usually outperform older adults (e.g., Cherry, et al., 2001; Dobbs & Rule, 1987; for exceptions, see Einstein & McDaniel, 1990; Einstein, McDaniel, Richardson, Guynn, & Cunfer, 1995). However, in naturalistic settings, older adults usually perform as well as, or even better than, young adults (e.g., Rendell & Thomson, 1999). For instance, older adults have been shown to outperform young adults on such naturalistic tasks as telephoning the experimenter over the course of two weeks (Moscovitch, 1982), mailing postcards to the experimenter (Patton & Meit, 1993), and performing assigned tasks during their real-life activities that approximated intentions like taking medications (Rendell & Craik, 2000). The reasons for this paradox are still unclear, and they will probably prove to be complex, but motivational factors seem to be likely contributors to an explanation for the paradoxical findings (e.g., Rendell & Craik, 2000).

A MOTIVATIONAL-COGNITIVE MODEL OF PROSPECTIVE MEMORY: THE INFLUENCE OF GOALS

The study of motivation within psychology has been marked in the past by a diversity of "classic" theories (Allport, 1950; Freud, 1923; Maslow, 1954; Rogers, 1961). Today, however, researchers interested in motivation are in agreement about its basic underlying cognitive and affective processes (Bandura, 1986, 1999; Carver & Scheier, 1998; Deci & Ryan, 1985; Gollwitzer & Bargh, 1996; Higgens & Sorrentino, 1990; Kruglanski, 1996; Mischel, Cantor, & Feldman, 1996). A construct that is fundamental in these contemporary conceptions of motivation is goals.

Contemporary Goal Models

A goal refers to a mental representation of the aim of a course of action (Kruglanski, 1996; Locke & Latham, 1990). Goals appear to be organized hierarchically. For instance, one may have the goals of reading Steinbeck's *Of Mice and Men*, joining a writing group, and completing a bachelor degree in English. Although these are separate goals, and each may require different skills, they cohere for the individual, who sees them all as contributing to the larger goal of becoming a writer. Also, goals can vary in terms of whether they are temporarily adopted or chronically accessible. For instance, a runner might have the current goal of getting knee surgery so that she can run again. This goal is likely to be temporary and will no longer exist after the surgery. However, that same individual might also have the goal of being a good parent to her son, which is a more permanent goal. Goals differ along a number of other qualitative and quantitative dimensions, as well, including content, specificity, level of challenge or difficulty, and proximity (Locke & Latham, 1990).

Goal representations have been shown to influence attention, thoughts, affect, and behavior (e.g., Bargh, Chen, & Burrows, 1996; Bargh & Gollwitzer, 1994; Roberson, 1989). In short, goals are motivating. For instance, goals direct people's attention to goal-related activities that are required for goal success (Rothkopf & Billington, 1975), influence thinking about activities related to the goal (Klinger, Barta, & Maxeiner, 1980), lead to feelings of satisfaction or dissatisfaction depending on how goal-related performances are subjectively evaluated (Carver & Scheier, 1990; Higgins, 1987), and enhance effort and persistence for behaviors that lead to goal success (Earley, Wojnaroski, & Prest, 1987; Huber & Neale, 1987).

Goals also have been found to be embedded in larger cognitive networks, networks that would appear to be involved in prospective memory performance. In the goal systems theory developed by Kruglanski, Shah, and colleagues, goal representations are linked to representations for the "means" for achieving the goals (e.g., Kruglanski et al., 2002; Shah & Kruglanski, 2003). For example, a person might have the goal of being intelligent, and this goal representation might be linked to the representation for the activity of studying. We suggest that prospective memories, as more specific intentions, are represented at a level subordinate to representations for activities. For example, a person might have the prospective memory "study tomorrow at 2pm in the library," which is linked to the activity of studying, which itself is linked to the goal of being intelligent. In this scenario, the prospective memory would be linked to the goal through associative links and would benefit from such associative connections.

There is evidence that entities in goal networks are associatively linked, including evidence that goals influence the accessibility and performance of subordinate constructs. For instance, there is evidence of top-down activation from goals to means (e.g., Fishbach, Shah, & Kruglanski, 2004). Further, Sheeran, Webb, and Gollwitzer (2005) tested whether superordinate goals influence the performance of related implementation intentions. Implementation intentions are formed by consciously rehearsing a detailed implementation plan (e.g., "If situation X occurs, then I will perform behavior Y;" Gollwitzer, 1993). Sheeran et al. (2005) found that implementation intentions worked better (e.g., participants solved more puzzles) if they were related to an active or strong superordinate goal (e.g., speed). Therefore, superordinate goals again showed "top-down" activation, but, in this case, for a specific type of intention learned in the lab (implementation intentions). These lines of evidence from goals research strengthen our central argument: Namely, top-down activation from goals will influence performance for naturally occurring intentions, or real-life prospective memories.

Overview of the Model

Our new motivational-cognitive model of prospective memory is summarized in Figure 1. This is a working model that represents possible relationships between some of the motivational and cognitive variables in prospective memory. That is, some of the proposed links in the model have been tested empirically, but some of the links have not yet been tested. Thus, we hope that this model serves as both an organizing aid for existing evidence and a guide for future research. Central to the model is the notion that prospective memory performance is influenced by goal representations. Specifically, we argue that prospective memories related to goals will be more "motivated," and as such will benefit from top-down "hot" motivational influences. As a result, we argue that goal-related prospective memories will be viewed as more important. The influence of these motivational processes will be such that goal-related (more important) prospective memories will benefit from both effortful and automatic processing throughout all phases of the prospective memory task.

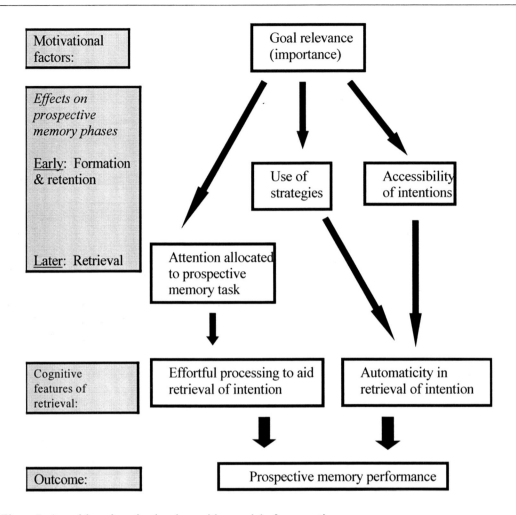

Figure 1. A goal-based motivational-cognitive model of prospective memory.

Evidence for the Goal-Based Motivational-Cognitive Model of Prospective Memory

In the remainder of this chapter, we review evidence supporting our goal-based motivational cognitive model of prospective memory. First, we will review evidence supporting our prediction that goal-related prospective memories will be viewed as subjectively more important. We then present evidence that prospective memories related to goals show benefits in processing (effortful or automatic processing) in various phases of the task. Specifically, we present new evidence showing that goal-related prospective memories show benefits in early phases of the task, from greater use of mnemonic strategies. We also present new findings that show that goal-related prospective memories are more accessible than other prospective memories during the intention retention phase. Finally, we review past research that shows that prospective memory tasks that are linked to an active goal are performed better, apparently because of increased attention allocated to monitoring for the prospective memory cue.

A Study to Test Whether Goal-Relevant Prospective Memory Tasks are Judged as More Important

In our model, we predicted a positive correlation between goal relatedness of prospective memories and perceived task importance. Specifically, individuals ought to rate tasks related to their personal goals as more important than tasks that are not related to their personal goals.

To test this prediction, we used a questionnaire method to assess real-life prospective memories and goals in a sample of 27 college students (age 18 – 30). In the questionnaire, participants were asked to list five prospective memories, or specific examples of things they wanted to remember to do (defined as appointments, tasks, and other things they wanted to remember to do). They then rated the importance of each of these prospective memory tasks. In a later section of the questionnaire, participants considered each prospective memory task they had listed and then indicated if the tasks were related to their goals in specific categories. The categories were adapted from Nurmi (1992). Fourteen goal categories were listed, including "profession/occupation," "property/possessions," "your education," and "your health." Thus, for each of their five prospective memory tasks, participants first indicated whether the task was related to a personal goal they had for profession/occupation, then for property/possessions, and so on. In the questionnaire section that preceded this goal-category task, participants had listed up to four of their own specific personal goals. Two independent raters later categorized these listed goals into the same 14 goal categories.

We then categorized participants' listed five prospective memory tasks into two categories, "goal-related" and "not goal-related." We used a fairly conservative method for defining prospective memory tasks as "goal-related," requiring such tasks to meet two criteria. First, the participant must have indicated that the prospective memory task was related to a specific goal category (from the 14 goal categories listed). Second, that goal category had to be highly accessible for the participant. Goal categories were defined as highly accessible if the participant had listed a personal goal in that category in the section of the questionnaire that asked respondents to list four current goals. For example, the prospective memory task *go to Biology study group* would be classified as "goal-relevant" if (a) the participant had specified that that particular task was related to his or her goals for education, and (b) the participant had listed at least one current goal that was categorized as an education goal by the independent raters. Therefore, goal-relatedness of prospective memory tasks was a within-groups variable. The dependent variable was rated importance of the prospective memory task.

In short, we found that prospective memory tasks that were related to personal goals were rated as more important (see Figure 2). These results support our claim that prospective memory task importance is really measuring goal relevance. In other words, we argue that another way to think about important tasks is as tasks that are related to one's current goals. Goals can be self-chosen or assigned (e.g., when an experimenter assigns participants the goal of prioritizing the prospective memory task over the ongoing task) and can be short-term or long-term. Therefore, in the studies described in the remainder of this chapter, we equate prospective memory task importance with goal-relatedness.

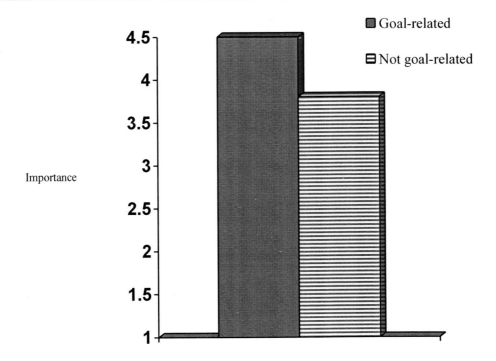

Figure 2. Mean importance ratings for real prospective memory tasks, by goal-relatedness. Note: Importance ratings: 1 = low, 2 = low-medium, 3 = medium, 4 =medium-high, and 5 = high.

Influences of Goals During Early and Middle Phases of the Prospective Memory Task

Two Studies to Test Whether People Use Strategies More Frequently for Goal-Relevant Prospective Memory Tasks

One way individuals try to increase remembering of prospective memories is to use external reminders or other strategies. Strategies can be used at the earliest phase of the prospective memory task, during intention formation. For example, an individual might form the intention to stop at an ATM after work and immediately create an external reminder by writing "cash" on his or her hand. Strategies can also be used at any time during the retention interval. For example, someone who is driving home might form the intention to get an oil change for the car on the next Saturday, but not record this intention as a written note on the calendar until after arriving home.

In a recent study (Penningroth, 2005b), we wanted to test whether people used strategies differently for two types of prospective memory tasks: prospective memory tasks related to their goals and prospective memory tasks not related to their goals. We operationally defined "goal-relatedness" for prospective memory tasks as perceived importance. That is, because we had found in a separate study that goal-relevant prospective memory tasks were perceived as more important, we used task importance as a measure of goal-relevance. We asked 197 college students about their use of strategies for real-life prospective memory tasks. Specifically, we assessed their use of 12 specific strategies, which fell into three categories: external strategies (e.g., placing something in a special place), internal strategies (e.g., using mental rehearsal), or conjunction strategies (e.g., tying the intention to another event). Participants reported on their strategy use separately for very important tasks and less important tasks. For instance, in the section on very important tasks, they were instructed to think about times when they have to remember to do things that are very important. Then, they rated the frequency of using each specific strategy (e.g., mental rehearsal) for important tasks using a 7-point Likert scale (*1* = *never, 2* = *up to two times in the last six months, 3* = *two or fewer times in the last four weeks, 4* = *two or fewer times in the last two weeks, 5* = *three to five times in the last two weeks, 6* = *six to ten times in the last two weeks, and 7* = *11 or more times in the last two weeks*). In the section on less important prospective memory tasks, participants received the same instructions, but with the words *less important* substituted for *very important.*

We predicted that overall strategy use would be more frequent for very important prospective memory tasks than less important prospective memory tasks. We also predicted that people would use better strategies more frequently for important (versus less important) prospective memory tasks. External strategies are more effective than internal strategies (Maylor, 1990; West, 1988), and conjunction strategies appear to be more effective than external strategies (Maylor, 1990). Therefore, we predicted an interaction between importance and strategy type. Specifically, we predicted bigger "importance effects" for better strategies, that is, for external strategies, and possibly for conjunction strategies. We found support for the first prediction, but not for the second prediction. For important intentions, participants reported using strategies more frequently. However the type of strategy used did not differ for very important and less important prospective memory tasks.

In a second study, we attempted to replicate the results with a new sample of 91 college students. A specific purpose in this replication was to rule out a possible alternative explanation for importance effects in the first study. In the first study, the preliminary instructions required participants to think about times when they have to do things that are very important (or less important*)*. It is possible that participants recalled more tasks in the *very important* condition than in the *less important* condition (Penningroth, 2006). Because the dependent measure of strategy frequency was assessed with an absolute scale (e.g., *11 or more times in the last two weeks*), participants may have reported higher frequencies of strategy use for important tasks simply because they had retrieved more instances of very important tasks than less important tasks. To rule out this possible alternative explanation, in the second study, we changed the frequency response options from an absolute scale to a relative scale (new response options included *never, 1/4 of the time, 1/3 of the time, etc.*). The pattern of results replicated those found in the first study.

In summary, across two studies, participants reported using strategies more frequently for very important than for less important prospective memory tasks, but participants did not use better strategies for important tasks. Therefore, these studies provide some support for our motivational-cognitive model of prospective memory. Goal-related prospective memory tasks (important tasks) appear to benefit from more frequent use of mnemonic strategies during early phases of the task.

Evidence for Goal-Related Influences in the Middle Phase of the Prospective Memory Task

We predicted that goal-related prospective memory tasks would be more accessible in memory during the intention retention phase. We have conducted two studies and a pilot study to test this prediction. In the first two studies, we measured the goal-relevance of prospective memory tasks as rated importance. We defined accessibility in terms of earlier retrieval in a brief recall session. Thus, our specific prediction was that prospective memory tasks an individual considered to be more important would be retrieved earlier than prospective memory tasks considered to be less important.

In the first study, 87 college students performed a recall task in which they listed their real-life prospective memory tasks for the next day, week, or year (depending on condition). For example, in the "week" condition, they were instructed to spend four minutes listing appointments, tasks, and other things they intended to do in the next week. They summarized each item with one or two words to control for individual differences in writing speed (Maylor, Chater, & Brown, 2001). After listing their prospective memory tasks, participants rated the importance of each task. Results showed that, as predicted, prospective memory tasks that were retrieved earlier (that were more accessible) were rated higher in importance (there were no differences between the different timeframe conditions—i.e., day, week, and year). These results support the conclusion that prospective memory task importance increases the accessibility of some prospective memory tasks during the retention interval.

In a second study, we wanted to replicate these results with a new sample ($N = 49$) and to control for a possible alternative explanation. We had found that intentions that were retrieved earlier were rated as more important. We interpreted this result as showing that prospective memory task importance caused heightened accessibility for select (i.e., important) prospective memory tasks. However, the design of the study was correlational, not experimental. Therefore, an alternative explanation is that the relationship was in the opposite direction with accessibility driving the importance ratings. That is, participants' importance ratings might have been biased by their knowledge of task retrieval order. In the second study, we controlled for this possible confound by having participants rate the importance of their prospective memory tasks after the tasks had been randomly ordered. With this procedural control, we replicated the results of the first study. Therefore, we are more confident in concluding that the importance (goal-relevance) of a prospective memory task increases accessibility, and not the other way around.

Finally, we have some preliminary data from a study in which we directly asked participants to identify which of their prospective memory tasks were related to their personal goals. Our prediction was that goal-related prospective memory tasks would be more accessible in memory than other prospective memory tasks. These data were collected with a mailed survey sent to a middle-aged sample. Respondents were instructed to list their personal strivings (e.g., Emmons, 1986, 1989), which are personal goals that represent what a person is typically trying to do every day (e.g., "be honest" or "look attractive"). They then listed their real-life intentions (prospective memory tasks) for the upcoming week. Finally, they indicated which intentions were related to specific goals. Each of a participant's prospective memory tasks was therefore categorized as goal-related or not goal-related, based on the participant's own categorization.

The outcome measure of interest was accessibility of the prospective memory, defined as order retrieved. Because we have only received data from five respondents so far, we pooled the intentions across participants, which resulted in 56 individual intentions. Results from this preliminary data set do support our predictions. That is, on average, prospective memory tasks that individuals perceived as related to their personal goals were retrieved earlier than other prospective memory tasks. These preliminary findings offer some support for the hypothesized link in our model between the goal-relatedness of a prospective memory task and greater accessibility in memory.

Effects of Goal-Relatedness in Later Phases of the Prospective Memory Task

One approach to examining the effects of motivational factors in later phases of the prospective memory performance has been to experimentally manipulate importance in a computerized task. For example, Kliegel, Martin, McDaniel, and Einstein (2004) used a computerized prospective memory task (i.e., remembering to spot target words or target letters in words that would be presented on a computer screen) with an ongoing task of simultaneously rating the words on four dimensions (e.g., pleasantness). One group of participants was told that the prospective memory task was more important and the other group was told that the ongoing task of rating the words on four dimensions was more important.

Results showed better prospective memory performance overall when the prospective memory task was perceived as more important than the ongoing task. In addition, other findings from the same study suggested one mechanism for importance effects on prospective memory performance. That is, task importance improved prospective memory performance more when cognitive resources were scarce (i.e., when participants were required to perform an auditory digit detection task while monitoring for prospective memory targets). Thus, one way that importance might benefit prospective memory performance is by causing a reallocation of limited attention resources to monitoring for the prospective memory target. In our motivational-cognitive model of prospective memory, we would interpret these task importance effects as effects of goal influence. That is, when participants were instructed to prioritize the prospective memory task over the ongoing task, they formed a goal to perform well on the prospective memory task.

CONCLUSION

In summary, we have presented a motivational-cognitive model of prospective memory. Specifically, this model characterizes motivation in terms of goals, which we argue influence multiple phases of the prospective memory task. We have presented new evidence from our lab that supports some of the hypothesized links in the model. We have drawn on other investigators' findings that support our model, as well. We hope that the model also serves as a guide for future research on links between goals and cognitive processes in prospective memory.

REFERENCES

Allport, G. W. (1950). *Becoming.* New Haven: Yale University Press.

Bandura, A. (1986). *Social foundations of thought and action.* Englewood Cliffs, NJ: Prentice-Hall, Inc.

Bandura, A. (1999). Social cognitive theory of personality. In D. Cervone & Y. Shoda (Eds.), The coherence of personality: Social cognitive bases of consistency, variability, and organization (pp. 185-241). New York: Guilford Press.

Bargh, J. , Chen, M. & Burrows, L. (1996). Automaticity of social behavior: Direct effects of trait construct and stereotype activation on action. *Journal of Personality and Social Psychology, 71(2),* 230 – 244.

Bargh, J., & Gollwitzer, P. M. (1994). Environmental control of goal-directed action: Automatic and strategic contingencies between situations and behavior. In W. D. Spaulding (Ed.), *The Nebraska symposium on motivation,* (Vol. 41, pp. 71 – 124). Lincoln, NE: University of Nebraska Press.

Carver, C. S., & Scheier, M. F. (1990). Origins and functions of positive and negative affect: A control process view. *Psychological Review, 97,* 19-35.

Carver, C. S. & Scheier, M. F. (1998). *On the self-regulation of behavior.* New York: Cambridge University Press.

Cherry, K. E., Martin, R. C., Simmons-D'Gerolamo, S. S., Pinkston, J. B., Griffing, A., & Gouvier, W. D. (2001). Prospective remembering in younger and older adults: Role of the prospective cue. *Memory, 9,* 177 – 193.

Deci, E. & Ryan, R. (1985*). Intrinsic motivation and self determination in human behavior.* New York: Plenum Press.

Dobbs, A. R., & Rule, B. G. (1987). Prospective memory and self-reports of memory abilities in older adults. *Canadian Journal of Psychology, 41,* 209 – 222.

Earley, P. C., Wojnaroski, P., & Prest, W. (1987). Task planning and energy expended: Exploration of how goals influence performance. *Journal of Applied Psychology, 72,* 107-114.

Einstein, G. O., & McDaniel, M. A. (1990). Normal aging and prospective memory. *Journal of Experimental Psychology: Learning, Memory, and Cognition, 16,* 717 – 726.

Einstein, G. O., McDaniel, M. A., Richardson, S. L., Guynn, M. J., & Cunfer, A. (1995). Aging and prospective memory: Examining the influences of self-initiated retrieval processes. *Journal of Experimental Psychology: Learning, Memory, and Cognition, 21,* 996 – 1007.

Einstein, G. O., McDaniel, M. A., Thomas, R., Mayfield, S., Shank, H., Morrisette, N., et al. (2005). Multiple processes in prospective memory retrieval: factors determining monitoring versus spontaneous retrieval. *Journal of Experimental Psychology: General, 134,* 327 – 342.

Ellis, J. (1996). Prospective memory or the realization of delayed intentions: A conceptual framework for research. In M. Brandimonte, G. O. Einstein, and M. A. McDaniel (Eds.), *Prospective memory: Theory and applications* (pp. 1 - 22). Mahwah, NJ: Lawrence Erlbaum Associates.

Emmons, R. A. (1986). Personal strivings: An approach to personality and subjective well-being. *Journal of Personality and Social Psychology, 51(5),* 1058 – 1068.

Emmons, R. A. (1989). The personal striving approach to personality. In L. A. Pervin (Ed.) *Goal Concepts in Personality and Social Psychology,* pp. 87 – 126, Hillsdale, NJ: Erlbaum.

Fishbach, A., Shah, J. Y., & Kruglanski, A. W. (2004) Emotional transfer in goal systems. *Journal of Experimental Social Psychology, 40,* 723 – 738.]

Freud, S. (1923). *The ego and the id.* Standard Edition (Vol. 18, pp. 12-66). London: Hogarth Press, 1961.

Gollwitzer, P. M. (1993). Goal achievement: The role of intentions. In W. Stroebe & M. Hewstone (Eds.), *European review of social psychology, Volume 4,* pp. 142 – 185. New York: J. Wiley and Sons.

Gollwitzer, P.M. & Bargh, J. A. (Eds.) (1996). *The psychology of action: Linking cognition and motivation to behavior.* New York: Guilford.

Higgins, E. T. (1987). Self-discrepancy: A theory relating self and affect. *Psychological Review, 94,* 319-340.

Higgins, E. T., & Sorrentino, R. M. (Eds.) (1990). *Handbook of motivation and cognition* (Vol. 2) New York: Guilford.

Huber, V. L., & Neale, M. A. (1987). Effects of self- and competitor goals in performance in an interdependent bargaining task. *Journal of Applied Psychology, 72,* 197-203.

Kliegel, M., Martin, M., McDaniel, M. A., & Einstein, G. O. (2002). Complex prospective memory and executive control of working memory: A process model. *Psychologische Beitrage, 44,* 303 – 318.

Kliegel, M., Martin, M., McDaniel, M. A., & Einstein, G. O. (2004). Importance effects on performance in event-based prospective memory tasks. *Memory, 12,* 553 – 561.

Kliegel, M., McDaniel, M. A., & Einstein, G. O. (Eds.). (in press). *Prospective memory: Cognitive, neuroscience, developmental, and applied perspectives.* Mahwah, NJ: Lawrence Erlbaum Associates.

Klinger, E., Barta, S. G., & Maxeiner, M. E. (1980). Motivational correlates of thought content frequency and commitment. *Journal of Personality and Social Psychology, 39,* 1222 – 1237.

Kruglanski, A. W. (1996). Goals as knowledge structures. In P. M. Gollwitzer & J. A. Bargh (Eds.), *The psychology of action: Linking cognition and motivation to behavior.* (pp.599 - 618). New York: Guilford Press.

Kruglanski, A. W., Shah, J. Y., Fishbach, A., Friedman, R., Chun, W. Y., & Sleeth-Keppler, D. (2002) A theory of goal systems. In M. P. Zanna (Ed.), *Advances in experimental social psychology* (Vol. 34, pp. 331 - 378). New York: Academic Press.

Locke, E. A., & Latham, G. P. (1990). *A theory of goal setting and task performance.* Englewood Cliffs, NJ: Prentice-Hall.

Maslow, A. H. (1954). *Motivation and personality.* New York: Harper.

Maylor, E. A. (1990). Age and prospective memory. *Quarterly Journal of Experimental Psychology, 42A,* 471 – 493.

Maylor, E. A., Chater, N., & Brown, G. D. A. (2001). Scale invariance in the retrieval of retrospective and prospective memories. *Psychonomic Bulletin & Review, 8,* 162 – 167.

McDaniel, M. A., & Einstein, G. O. (2000). Strategic and automatic processes in prospective memory retrieval: A multiprocess framework. *Applied Cognitive Psychology, 14,* S127-S144.

Mischel, W., Cantor, N., & Feldman, S. (1996). Principles of self-regulation: The nature of willpower and self-control. In E. T. Higgens & A. W. Kruglanski (Eds.), *Social psychology: Handbook of basic principles* (pp. 329-360). New York: Guilford.

Moscovitch, M. (1982). A neuropsychological approach to memory and perception in normal and pathological aging. In F. I. M. Craik and S. Trehub (Eds.), *Aging and cognitive processes* (pp. 55 – 78). New York: Plenum Press.

Nurmi, J. (1992). Age differences in adult life goals, concerns, and their temporal extension: A life course approach to future-oriented motivation. *International Journal of Behavioral Development, 15,* 487 – 508.

Patton, G. W., & Meit, M. (1993). Effect of aging on prospective and incidental memory. *Experimental Aging Research, 19,* 165 – 176.

Penningroth, S. L. (2005a). Effects of attentional demand, cue typicality, and priming on an event-based prospective memory task, *Applied Cognitive Psychology, 19,* 885 – 897.

Penningroth, S. L. (2005b, July). Strategy differences for remembering important and less important real-life intentions. Paper presented at the 2nd International Conference on Prospective Memory, Zurich, Switzerland.]

Penningroth, S. L. (2006). Accessibility of real-life prospective memory task varies with importance. Unpublished manuscript.

Rendell, P. G., & Craik, F. I. M. (2000). Virtual week and actual week: Age-related differences in prospective memory. *Applied Cognitive Psychology, 14,* S43 – S62.

Rendell, P. G., & Thomson, D. M. (1999). Aging and prospective memory: Differences between naturalistic and laboratory tasks. *Journal of Gerontology: Psychological sciences, 54B(4),* P256 – P269.

Roberson, L. (1989). Assessing personal work goals in the organizational setting: Development and evaluation of the work concerns inventory. *Organizational Behavior and Human Decision Processes, 44,* 345 – 367.

Rogers, C. (1961). *On becoming a person.* Boston: Houghton Mifflin.

Rothkopf, E. Z., & Billington, M. J. (1975). A two-factor model of the effect of goal descriptive directions on learning from text. *Journal of Educational Psychology, 67,* 692-704.

Salthouse, T. A., Berish, D. E., & Siedlecki, K. L. (2004). Construct validity and age sensitivity of prospective memory. *Memory & Cognition, 32,* 1133 – 1148.

Shah, J. Y., & Kruglanski, A. W. (2003). When opportunity knocks: Bottom-up priming of goals by means and its effects on self-regulation. *Journal of Personality and Social Psychology, 84,* 1109 – 1122.

Sheeran, P., Webb, T.L., & Gollwitzer, P. M. (2005). The interplay between goal intentions and implementation intentions. *Personality and Social Psychology Bulletin, 31,* 87 – 98.

Smith, R. E. (2003). The cost of remembering to remember in event-based prospective memory: Investigating the capacity demands of delayed intention performance. *Journal of Experimental Psychology: Learning, Memory, and Cognition, 29,* 347 – 361.

West, R. L. (1988). Prospective memory and aging. In M. M. Gruneberg, P. E. Morris & R. N. Sykes (Eds.), *Practical aspects of memory: Current research and issues,* (Vol. 2, pp. 119 – 125). Chichester: Wiley.

West, R., Bowry, R., & Krompinger, J. (2006). The effects of working memory demands on the neural correlates of prospective memory. *Neuropsychologia, 44,* 197 – 207.

West, R., & Krompinger, J. (2005). Neural correlates of prospective and retrospective memory. *Neuropsychologia, 43,* 418 - 433.

West, R., & Wymbs, N. (2004). Is detecting prospective cues the same as selecting targets? An ERP study. *Cognitive, Affective, & Behavioral Neuroscience, 4,* 354 – 363.

In: Psychology of Motivation
Editor: Lois V. Brown, pp. 129-140

ISBN: 978-1-60021-598-8
© 2007 Nova Science Publishers, Inc.

Chapter 8

THE ROLE OF GOAL FACILITATION AND GOAL CONFLICT IN MOTIVATION

Winifred A. Gebhardt[*]

Leiden University Institute for Psychological Research
Clinical, Health and Neuropsychology
Leiden University, The Netherlands

ABSTRACT

Psychological theories on motivation generally focus on one single attitude object, or goal, at a time. However, people always hold multiple goals simultaneously. Therefore, motivation with respect to one goal should be considered within the context of other goals that are part of the individual's personal goal system. Some goals coincide when the attainment of one goal leads to goal progress of another. Others goals may be in conflict with one another. A conflict in goals occurs when various equally desired end states are mutually exclusive, either because they draw from similar limited resources or because they are logically incompatible. Conflict in goals may lead to mixed emotions about a goal and to feelings of ambivalence. Empirical research within the field of health behavior strongly suggests that examining behavior within the context of the personal goal structure adds significantly to our understanding of behavioral change.

INTRODUCTION

People have an innate desire to feel competent, to determine their own lives (deCharms, 1968; Deci & Ryan, 1985; White, 1959) and to have significant relationships with others (Baumeister, 1995; Deci & Ryan, 1985). They want to express and develop unique

---

[*] Address: P.O. Box 9555, 2300 RB Leiden, The Netherlands; Gebhardt@fsw.leidenuniv.nl + 31-71 5274084 (phone); + 31-71 5274678 (fax)

characteristics of the self related to these needs. In the process of doing so, they seek positive feedback that is consistent with their own view of the self.

From a unique history of past learning experiences within one's own culture and social context, people define the content of their self-conceptions, i.e., how they view themselves and how they wish others to look upon them. Looking for opportunities to affirm positive views of the self, we are almost habitually occupied with the "I". For this, we rely on self-definitions that are more or less stable over time (e.g., "I am a good-natured soul") and search for ways to express what we consider central elements of the self. In addition, we attempt to develop our abilities to reach our perceived full potential (e.g., "I could really be good at writing"), serving a need for personal growth. Driven by the inkling that achieving certain desired possible future states (i.e., I become a writer), will lead to satisfaction and to feeling good about the self, we attempt to progress towards these states. As such, we act to bring out evaluations of the self that match our identity standards. In line with this perspective, personal goals have been defined as desired future states that people seek to obtain, maintain or avoid (e.g., Austin & Vancouver, 1996) through action (e.g., Kruglanski, 1996). The ultimate aim of goal-striving lies in affirming, sustaining or enhancing the self (e.g., Stets & Burke, 2000; Sedikides, Gaertner & Toguchi, 2003; Van Empelen, Gebhardt & Dijkstra, 2006). For instance, we do not primarily wish to lose weight in order to achieve a lesser body weight. Rather, we expect to gain positive emotional consequences in terms of enhanced self-conceptions when we actually attain this goal.

Summarizing, people have a basic need to feel competent, autonomous and connected to others. They select those goals that are believed to –once achieved- lead to fulfillment of these needs and to corresponding positive emotions. They wish to have a consistent and positive view of themselves now and in the future within all domains that relate to the basic needs. Therefore, they do not only wish to have fulfilling social relationships, they also yearn to be successful in work and in leisure pursuits, and they are keen on remaining or becoming "healthy, wealthy, and wise".

PERSONAL GOALS

Goal–setting is preceded by an awareness of a discrepancy between a desired state and the present state. For example, Carver and Scheier (1999) suggest that the input of the process of behavioral change is a person's perception of the present condition, that is evaluated against a measure (a comparator), which represents the desired state. In case of a discrepancy, a person will be motivated to reduce the difference between the two states. Similarly, Higgins' self-discrepancy theory (1987; 1996) is based on the assumption that people are motivated to reach certain states in which the self-concept matches personally relevant "self-guides". Self-guides are defined as representations of attributes that someone would hope to possess in the future. These representations have been frequently referred to as "possible" selves (see Màrkus & Nurius, 1986). Possible selves include both the "ideal selves" that refer to hopes, wishes and desires, and their opposites, the "feared selves", that refer to the self one does not want to be (Carver, Lawrence & Scheier, 1999). Possible selves also encompass the "ought selves", or who one is morally required to be, relating to perceived duties, obligations and responsibilities. Thus, someone may wish to be regarded as a very attractive person (ideal self), who is not lazy or passive (feared self), and as someone who should provide healthy meals for the family (ought self). Similarly a person may want to be regarded as a sociable and "cool" person (ideal self), but worries that one's drinking habits could eventually lead to becoming a drunk (feared self), and thinks that one is morally obliged to set strict drinking standards for oneself (ought self). Research indicates that possible selves may remain relatively stable and balanced over time (Frazier, Hooker, Johnson & Kaus, 2000) and may be the means through which behaviors become part of the enduring aspects of the self (Stein, Roeser & Markus, 1998).

Whether a discrepancy between the actual state and the desired state is actually experienced, is likely to depend on its availability and the accessibility (Higgins, 1987). The availability of a discrepancy is based on the number of matches and mismatches within a discrepancy and on the magnitude of the differences. Thus, a person may find oneself kind and caring during certain encounters (matches), but rather impatient during other interactions (mismatches). Similarly, a person may find oneself to have lean legs and to be slim around the waist (matches), but at the same time to have rather heavy hips (mismatch). Accessibility of a discrepancy is determined by the frequency of its activation, the recency of the activation and the applicability to the situation. When a person has recently been exposed to an ideal standard, e.g., a billboard of a slim photo-model, the likelihood of re-activation increases, which then may cause a self-perpetuating loop. That is, the more frequently the discrepancy is activated, the more likely it is to be activated in the situations that follow. Furthermore, if the situation is ambiguous and is possibly connected to the discrepancy, the discrepancy will be elicited during the primary evaluation of the situation. In short, availability and accessibility govern the likelihood of activation of the discrepancy, i.e., whether a difference between the current and wished-for states is experienced.

Generally spoken, people will commit themselves to the goal that has the highest priority at a specific moment in time (Heckhausen, 1991). However, all goals remain cognitively represented and may be activated fairly easily to the extent that they override previous action tendencies. Once a goal is prioritized, a behavioral strategy is required for the course of action that is in line with future situations and that is expected to lead to the desired outcome. The strategy encompasses, for example, plans regarding the timing of the behavior and the type of situations within which the behavior should occur (e.g., implementation intentions, see Gollwitzer, 1999).

Subsequently, initial action leads to outcomes, which may be or may not be in line with expectations. It has been argued that the evaluation of whether a discrepancy still exists is not the main determinant of the valence and intensity of the emotions that accompany the process of change. Instead, the relative progress toward the goal -as compared to the expected progress- determines these emotions and as such shapes the remainder of the behavioral process (Boldero & Francis, 2002). Correspondingly, Rothman (2000) suggested that satisfaction with the outcome of initial behavioral change predicts whether people will relapse to previous behavior or will continue to persist in goal pursuit. For example, he observed that women who had reported more benefits related to weight loss directly after a weight reduction program were far more likely to have maintained their weight loss at the one year follow-up, than those who had experienced fewer benefits. It is important to note that the two groups of women had not differed in their initial weight or in the amount of weight lost during the program.

In the process of evaluating the relative speed of progress towards the goal, a person will utilize attributions related to the cause of the outcomes (causal attributions, see Weiner 1986) and will compare own achievement with the successfulness of others at attaining comparable goals (social comparisons, see Festinger, 1954). The attributions and social comparisons are generated to "make sense" of expected or unexpected effects of the newly instigated behavior. For example, people will attempt to evaluate whether their (lack of) achieving positive results is attributable to themselves or not. In the process of doing so, they may select people who are clearly more successful (upward comparison) or who are less so (downward comparison). Not the outcomes by themselves, but rather how they are interpreted and emotionally experienced, serve as new sources of information. The more people are satisfied with their advancement towards the goal, the more they are inclined to continue their efforts. If, however, they are disappointed with the outcomes of their endeavors, they are likely to adopt other behavioral strategies (e.g., Cropanzano, Citera & Howes, 1995), to adjust their goal (e.g., Brandstädter & Renner, 1990) or to disengage from the goal all together (e.g., Wrosch, Scheier, Miller, Schulz & Carver, 2003)[1].

Behavior certainly has an impact on the environment. During the process of behavioral change, however, other factors than behavior may influence the environmental context. These factors may elicit different goals. The process is considered to be a continuous one with behavior and "disturbing" factors incessantly changing the environment, which, in turn, calls for the occurrence of new behavior. Thus, once the behavior is initiated, behavior and its outcome are part of a continuous process of behavioral change (e.g., Bandura, 1978).

MULTIPLE GOALS

As mentioned, people have basic needs to fulfill. Furthermore, based on their current and future self-conceptions they pursue multiple goals concurrently (Gebhardt, 2006). Some of the goals may be independent from each other. In such instances the pursuit of the one goal does not have a direct positive or negative influence on the pursuit of the other goal.

Some other goals may be aligned to the extent that the pursuit of one goal increases the chance of attaining another. This phenomenon has been labeled goal congruence (Brunstein, Schultheiss & Grassman, 1998), goal coherence (Sheldon & Kasser, 1995), goal integrity (McGregor & Little, 1998) or inter-goal facilitation (Riediger, 2001; Maes, ter Doest & Gebhardt, 2005; ter Doest, Maes, Gebhardt & Koelewijn, 2006). Sheldon and Kasser (1995) distinguish between a horizontal and a vertical degree of coherence (goal-facilitation). Horizontal coherence represents the degree to which a goal leads to the attainment of another

---

[1] Fishbach and Dhar (2005), however, find support for the opposite hypothesis, i.e. that progress towards one goal increases the chance of disengagement and the pursuit of other conflicting goals. For example, in one of their studies, female dieters who had been manipulated to believe that they had made substantial progress towards their goal of loosing weight were significantly more likely to choose a chocolate bar over an apple as a parting gift, than those who were led to believe that they had hardly progressed. They conclude that frequently expected or actual progress towards a goal leads to distancing oneself from it. This effect, however, seems to be fully mediated by the level of commitment to - and accessibility of the superordinate goal (Fishbach, Dhar & Zhang, 2006). For example, participants who had been manipulated to believe that they exercised more than others were less inclined to maintain a healthy diet and exercise than those who were led to believe that they exercised less than others. However, this pattern was reversed when the superordinate goal of keeping in shape was primed.

goal at the same level of abstraction, for example, when cycling to the store results in both having done the errands and having exercised or when participating in cooking classes because one would like to learn to cook tastier and healthier meals coincides with meeting new people in the area one has just moved to. A high level of horizontal coherence leads to relatively low demands on personal resources. Vertical coherence refers to the degree to which a proximal or subordinate goal serves one or more distal or superordinate goals. It occurs, for example, when exercising three times a week is expected to improve one's overall fitness level and health.

In many other instances, a conflict between goals may exist. Riediger's (2001) review of theoretical frameworks on the interrelationships between goals indicates that two main sources of goal conflict can be distinguished: (1) conflict based on resource limitations and (2) logical incompatibilities between goals. The first source of goal conflict includes time-based conflicts, when the time necessary for the fulfillment of one goal is at the expense of the time needed to accomplish another goal. It also encompasses strain-based conflicts when the energy required for the pursuit of one goal affects one's functioning when pursuing another goal. These types of conflicts are typical, for example, for those who struggle with both demanding work - and family responsibilities. Goal incompatibility refers to those instances when the attainment of one goal directly results in the non-fulfillment of another goal. For example, when one accepts and eats the home-made high-calorie cake baked by one's mother in order to be kind, this may immediately frustrate one's simultaneously held goal of losing weight. These types of conflicts involve, amongst others, the conflict between short- and long-term goals, which is typical for many health behaviors.

When goal conflict occurs, individuals are likely to regard each of the corresponding goals both positively and negatively at the same time. They are both wanting and at the same time not wanting the same goal object. In such instances of ambivalence, they may have strong mixed emotions, such as feeling torn (e.g., Newby-Clark, McGregor & Zanna, 2002). These emotions, in turn, are likely to influence whether or not a goal is prioritized. For example, if one is convinced that condoms are an effective means of reducing the risk of contracting sexually transmitted infections, but also associates the use of condoms with a lack of trust in one's partner, one will experience ambivalence towards the goal of "having protected sex".

EMPIRICAL EVIDENCE: EXAMPLES FROM HEALTH BEHAVIOR RESEARCH

The social-cognitive perspective on behavioral change, which includes theories such as the Theory of Planned Behavior (Ajzen, 1985), the Health Belief Model (Rosenstock, 1974), the Protection Motivation Theory (Rogers, 1983) and Bandura's social learning theory (Bandura, 1978), has predominated the field of health behavior research during the past few decades. This perspective focuses on the expected outcomes of a specific behavior as well as on the perceived ease with which one believes to be able to perform the behavior to the level that outcomes will be reached. Accordingly, if the person expects that the behavior will lead to many positive outcomes (high desirability) and that it is relatively easy to perform the behavior (high feasibility), it has a high likelihood of being adopted.

One of the main criticisms on this view is that it does not take into account the notion that individuals have multiple goals (e.g., Gebhardt & Maes, 2001; Abraham & Sheeran, 2003). It has been argued that for a more accurate prediction of behavioral change, there is a definite need to consider the behavior within the context of other goals a person is pursuing. Even adding merely one or two alternative behavior(s) next to the behavior under study has been found to substantially increase the predictive power (e.g., Sheppard, Hartwick & Warshaw, 1988). For example, Jaccard (1981) found that attitude towards the use of birth control pills was a stronger predictor of behavior when it was analyzed in juxtaposition to attitudes towards using condoms or using the diaphragm, then when it was studied in isolation. In the following, several examples of research within the field of health behavior will be presented to further illustrate the significance of investigating behavior within the context of the – multiple- goals people are pursuing.

For example, Simons and Carey (2003) conducted a study among 592 young adults on marijuana use in relation to their self-generated ten most important personal strivings. Each participant rated the influence they expected that six different levels of marijuana use, ranging from abstinence to using marijuana everyday, would have on their strivings. They found that the extent to which marijuana was expected to interfere with their strivings was associated with both marijuana initiation and frequency of use.

Similarly, McKeeman and Karoly (1991) examined the role of structural goal conflict in the process of smoking cessation among 114 undergraduate students. The sample consisted of 38 smokers, 40 smokers who had made a serious but unsuccessful attempt to quit in the previous 4 months, and 36 successful quitters, who had stopped smoking for one to four months. The participants stated eight of their most important life goals, of which the five most important were selected for further analysis. They subsequently indicated the degree to which each goal might have interfered with their attempts to stop smoking. It was observed that the measure of goal conflict successfully discriminated between the groups of (ex)smokers, i.e. quitters reported significantly lower levels of inter-goal conflict when compared to smokers and relapsers. The authors concluded that motivation to change is not sufficient for successful adoption of new behavior. It is of equal importance to resolve the potential conflict that behavioral change will elicit in other life domains.

In a series of studies based on the Health Behavior Goal Model (Gebhardt, 1997; Gebhardt & Maes, 2001; Maes & Gebhardt, 2000), goal conflict differentiated between 312 non-exercisers, 466 exercisers who trained once or twice a week, and 202 individuals who exercised at least three times a week. The sedentary participants had stronger beliefs that regular exercise would interfere with day-to-day activities, such as social activities, household chores, and watching TV than the other two groups. Furthermore, the impediment of these activities was expected to be aggravating, reflecting the relevance of the underlying goals (Gebhardt & Maes, 1998; Gebhardt, van der Doef & Maes, 1999). In a one-year follow-up study (Gebhardt, 1997) goal conflict was a significant predictor of the initiation of regular exercise as well as for falling back to a sedentary life-style. Participants who were sedentary but who became regular exercisers at the follow-up had perceived less goal conflict at baseline than those who remained sedentary. Additionally, those who exercised regularly three or more times a week, but who relapsed to being sedentary at the follow-up reported more conflict at baseline than those who remained to be regular exercisers. Gebhardt et al. (in prep) also investigated whether the extent that exercise was expected to facilitate important personal goals was related to exercise levels in a group of 1287 adolescents. Sedentary and active adolescents reported a similar order of ten specific goals with respect to the likelihood of being positively influenced by exercise. The frequency of the reported facilitation for each of the goals, however, was lower for the sedentary subgroup than for those who exercised once or twice a week, who in turn scored lower than those who exercised at least three times a week. It was concluded from the study that exercise is likely to support other valued personal goals, and that the level of goal facilitation is directly related to the activity level of the individual. Furthermore, when exercise is incorporated in the personal goal system, this may be an important motivator to start or remain exercising.

In a prospective diary study among 81 adults who had just started exercising conflict between exercise and three other self-generated personal goals led to higher levels of negative affect and inter-goal facilitation led to higher levels of positive affect (Riediger & Freund, 2004). The extent to which exercise facilitated the other three goals predicted the amount of effort and time spent on pursuing any of the four goals. Goal conflict, however, did not appear to predict goal involvement.

Karoly and co-workers (2005) asked 399 psychology students to generate their most important academic, social and work or family goals. They then indicated three of their non-exercise as being the goals which most interfered with their exercise goal. For irregular exercisers competing goals were of greater importance than the exercise goal, while for regular exercisers the exercise goal and alternative goals were equally significant. Irregular exercisers also showed other goal regulatory thoughts that favored their interfering goals above the exercise goals. For example, they reported significantly lower levels of self-monitoring, social comparison, planning and self-reward for their exercise goal than for their interfering goals. In contrast, the regular exercise group construed the exercise and interfering goals in a very similar manner.

Gebhardt, Kuyper and Greunsven (2003) observed in a sample of 470 Dutch adolescents that those who always used condoms and those who did not use them consistently, differed from each other with regard to the underlying motives for having sex. After controlling for variables incorporated in the Theory of Planned Behavior, lower scores on the motive to express love through having sex and a lower need for intimacy in relationships significantly added to the variance of whether or not they had protected sex with a steady partner. Conversely, consistent condom use with casual partners was related to a high need for intimacy in relationships. In another study with 133 young females, Gebhardt, Kuyper and Dusseldorp (2006) found that condom use with a new sexual partner was negatively related to the motive for having sex to cope with negative emotions, but unrelated to motives such as expressing love, experiencing pleasure, or pleasing others. Both studies indicate that the functionality of behavior, such as the reasons for having sex, determines at least partly the choices made, such as using a condom.

As a final example, among a sample of 453 university students who had intended to use condoms with a new partner, Abraham and colleagues (1999) observed that the importance attached to having sexual intercourse relative to the importance of having protected sex predicted condom use. Thus, not so much the relevance of using condoms itself, but rather how this importance relates to another significant goal, in this instance having sexual intercourse, was significant for whether or not those who had intended to use a condom actually did. The authors conclude that a multi-goal model of action control contributes substantially to the prediction of health behavior.

In summary, these findings indicate that the more a specific goal or behavior is congruent with other goals, the more likely it is to be adopted and sustained. Similarly, the more a behavior hinders prominent other goals, the less likely it is to be adopted and sustained. This implies that Austin and Vancouver (1996) are correct in stating that "single goals cannot be understood when isolated from other goals and from the cognitive, behavioral and affective responses organized in pursuing goals" (p.338).

BRINGING GOALS IN LINE

Having a great number of different goals to attend to necessitates control systems to continuously determine whichever goal is going to be prioritized above the other goals at any certain moment in time. It appears important that alternative goals are "forgotten" in the process of goal pursuit (e.g., Kuhl, 1985). In other words the goal needs to be "shielded" from other goals (Shah, Friedman & Kruglanski, 2002), and the intra-goal conflict needs to be efficiently managed (McKeeman & Karoly, 1991). Strategies related to how to cope with distractions in the form of alternative goals need to be part of the contingency plans.

One possibility of enabling this is to strengthen the salience by repeatedly linking the behavioral goal to the self-generated "possible selves" of the individual. Activation of goal salience in terms of how it facilitates certain desired states should increase the openness of the individual to recognize goal-related opportunities. High levels of goal salience should also increase the accessibility of the goal to counteract the potential threat of obstacles and temptations. Another possibility to reduce the negative impact of conflict is to anticipate and prepare for it by enhancing one's self-regulatory strategies. These preparations include self-regulatory skills to cope with the conflict, for example by trying to bring the conflicting goals in alignment, or to cope with the negative emotions that accompany the conflict. For example, Koestner, Lekes, Powers and Chicoine (2002) asked students to think of three possible distractions that might occur during the pursuit of their self-generated goal for the weekend, and of three strategies for the management of those distractions. This procedure had a positive effect on subsequent goal progress. Sheldon, Kasser, Smith and Share (2002) also successfully instructed participants to regard the distress and discomfort during the pursuit of their (mostly academic) semester goals as indicators of the necessity to apply coping strategies, rather than as feelings that should be avoided. This method, thus, could possibly counteract the incapacitating effect of ambivalent feelings (e.g., "I wish to attain the goal, but I do not like the process"). Further research should discern whether such techniques prove to be effective not only for the initiation of behavior but also for behavioral maintenance.

CONCLUSION

Both goal conflict and goal facilitation have a substantial influence on the adoption and maintenance of a variety of health behaviors. Thus, whether a behavior is adopted and given priority over and above other purposes depends on the strength of its connections to valued goals and the relative lack of goal conflict (see Health Behavior Goal Model; Gebhardt 1997; Maes & Gebhardt, 2000). This implies, for example that much of the behavior that seems irrational, e.g. because it is detrimental to one's health, is in fact embedded in a structure of other goals that are far more relevant to the person. It is likely that people have accepted the consequences of their behavior because they believe that it is consistent with their other self-conceptions at that moment in time (e.g., Buchanan, 2006).

In this contribution, I have argued that one should be aware that humans always pursue more than one goal at a time. It is therefore highly relevant to determine whether a specific goal is likely to interfere with other short- or long-term aims or whether it in fact assists their attainment. By expanding the knowledge on the role of inter-goal relationships, we will most certainly enhance our basic understanding of human behavior.

REFERENCES

Abraham, C., Sheeran, P., Norman, P., Conner, M, De Vries, N. & Otten, W. (1999). When good intentions are not enough: Modeling postdecisional cognitive correlates of condom use. *Journal of Applied Social Psychology*, 29, 2591-2612.

Abraham, C. & Sheeran, P. (2003). Implications of goal theories for the Theories of Reasoned Action and Planned Behavior. *Current Psychology*, 22, 264-280.

Ajzen, I. (1985). From intentions to actions: A theory of planned behavior. In J. Kuhl & J. Beckman (Eds.). *Action control: From cognition to behaviour* (p.11-39). Heidelberg: Springer Verlag.

Austin, J.T. & Vancouver, J.B. (1995). Goal constructs in psychology: Structure, process, and content. *Psychological Bulletin*, 120, 3338-375.

Bandura, A. (1978). The self-system in reciprocal determinism. *American Psychologist*, 33, 344-360.

Baumeister, R.F. & Leary, MR. (1995). The need to belong: Desire for interpersonal attachments as a fundamental human motivation. *Psychological Bulletin*, 117, 497-529.

Boldero, J. & Francis, J. (2002). Goals, standards, and the self: Reference values serving different functions. *Personality and Social Psychology Review*, 6, 232-241.

Brandstädter, J. & Renner, G. (1990). Tenacious goal pursuit and flexible goal adjustment: Explication and age-related analysis of assimilative and accommodative strategies of coping. *Psychology and Aging*, 5, 58-67.

Brunstein, J.C., Schultheiss, O.C. & Grässman, R. (1998). Personal goals and emotional well-being: The moderating role of motive dispositions. *Journal of Personality and Social Psychology*, 75, 494-508.

Buchanan, D. (2006). Moral reasoning as a model for health promotion. *Social Science and Medicine*, 63, 2715-2726.

Carver, C.S. , Lawrence, J.W. & Scheier, M.F. (1999). Self-discrepancies and affect: Incorporating the role of feared selves. *Personality and Social Psychology Bulletin*, 25(7), 783-792.

Carver, C.S. & Scheier, M.F. (1999). Stress, coping, and self-regulatory processes. In: L.A. Pervin & J.P. Oliver (Eds). *Handbook of personality theory and research* (pp.553-575). New York, NY: The Guilford Press.

Cropanzano, R., Citera, M & Howes, J. (1995). Goal hierarchies and plan revision. *Motivation and Emotion*, 19, 77-98.

DeCharms, R. (1968). *Personal causation: The internal affective determinants of behavior.* New York, NY: Academic Press.

Deci, E.L. & Ryan, R.M. (1985). *Intrinsic motivation and self-determination in human behavior.* New York, NY: Plenum.

Fishbach, A. & Dhar, R. (2005). Goals as excuses or guides: The liberating effect of perceived goal progress on choice. *Journal of Consumer Research, 32,* 370-377.

Fishbach, A., Dhar, R. & Zhang, Y. (2006). Subgoals as substitutes or complements: The role of goal accessibility. *Journal of Personality and Social Psychology, 91,* 232-242.

Frazier, L.D., Hooker, K., Johnson, P.M. & Kaus, C.R. (2002). Continuity and change in possible selves in later life: A 5-year longitudinal study. *Basic and Applied Social Psychology, 22,* 237-243.

Festinger, L. (1954). A theory of social comparison processes. *HumanRelations, 7,* 117-140.

Gebhardt, W.A. (1997). *Health behaviour goal model: Towards a theoretical framework for health behaviour change.* Leiden University Press: Health Psychology Series, No 2.

Gebhardt, W.A. (2006). Contextualizing health behaviors: The role of personal goals. In: D. de Ridder & J. de Wit (Eds.). *Self-regulation in health behavior.* Hoboken, NJ: Wiley.

Gebhardt, W.A., Kuyper, L. & Dusseldorp, E. (2006). Condom use at first intercourse with a new partner in female adolescents and young adults: The role of cognitive planning and motives for having sex. *Archives of Sexual Behavior, 35,* 217-223.

Gebhardt, W.A., Kuyper, L., & Greunsven, G. (2003). Need for intimacy in relationships and motives for sex as determinants of adolescent condom use. *Journal of Adolescent Health, 33,* 154-164.

Gebhardt, W.A., van der Doef, M.P. & Maes, S. (1999). Conflicting activities for exercise. *Perceptual and Motor Skills, 89,* 1159-1160.

Gebhardt, W.A. & Maes, S. (2001). Integrating social-psychological frameworks for health behavior research. *American Journal of Health Behavior, 25,* 528-536.

Gebhardt, W.A. & Maes, S. (1998). Competing personal goals and exercise behaviour. *Perceptual and Motor Skills, 86,* 755-759.

Gebhardt, W.A., Ter Doest, L., Dijkstra, A., Maes, S., Garnefski, N., Kraaij, V. & de Wilde, E.J. (in prep). The facilitation of important personal goals through exercise.

Gollwitzer, P.M. (1999). Implementation intentions: Strong effects of simple plans. *American Psychologist, 54,* 493-503.

Heckhausen, H. (1991). *Motivation and action.* New York, NY: Springer Verlag.

Higgins, E.T. (1996). Ideals, oughts, and regulatory focus: Affect and motivation from distinct pains and pleasures. In: P.M. Gollwitzer & J.A. Bargh (Eds.). *The psychology of action: Linking cognition and motivation to behavior* (p.91-114). New York, NY: The Guilford Press.

Higgins, E.T. (1987). Self-discrepancy: A theory relating self and affect. *Psychological Review, 94*(3), 319-340.

Jaccard, J. (1981). Attitudes and behavior: Implications of attitudes towards behavioral alternatives. *Journal of Experimental Social Psychology, 17,* 286-307.

Karoly, P., Ruehlman, R.S., Okun, M.A., Lutz, R.S., Newton, C. & Fairholme, C. (2005). Perceived self-regulation of exercise goals and interfering goals among regular and irregular exercisers: a life space analysis. *Psychology of Sport and Exercise, 6,* 427-442.

Koestner, R., Lekes, N., Powers, T.A. & Chicoine, E. (2002). Attaining personal goals: Self-concordance plus implementation intentions equals success. *Journal of Personality and Social Psychology*, 83, 231-244.

Kruglanski, A.W. (1996). Goals as knowledge structures. In: P.M. Gollwitzer & J.A. Bargh (Eds.). *The psychology of action: Linking cognition and motivation to behavior* (p.599-618). New York, NY: The Guilford Press.

Kuhl, J. (1985). From cognition to behavior: Perspectives for future research on action control. In J.Kuhl and J. Beckman (Eds.). *Action control: From cognition to behavior* (pp.267-276). New York, NY: Springer Verlag.

Maes, S. & Gebhardt, W.A. (2000). Self-regulation and health behaviour: The health behaviour goal model. In: M. Boekaerts, P.R. Pintrich & M. Zeidner (Eds.). *Handbook of self-regulation* (pp.343-368). San Diego, CA: Academic Press.

Maes, S., ter Doest, L. & Gebhardt, W.A. (2005). *The goal facilitation inventory-workplace version: Factor structure and psychometric properties*. Leiden, The Netherlands: Leiden University.

Markus, H. & Nurius, P. (1986). Possible selves. *American Psychologist*, 41, 954-969.

McGregor, I. & Little, B.R. (1998). Personal projects, happiness, and meaning: On doing well and being yourself. *Journal of Personality and Social Psychology*, 74, 494-512.

McKeeman, D. & Karoly, P. (1991). Interpersonal and intrapsychic goal-related conflict reported by cigarette smokers, unaided quitters and relapsers. *Addictive Behaviors*, 16, 543-548.

Newby-Clark, I.R., McGregor, I. & Zanna, M.P. (2002). Thinking and caring about cognitive inconsistncy: When and for whom does attitudinal ambivalence feel uncomfortable. *Journal of Personality and Social Psychology*, 82, 157-166.

Riediger, M. (2001). *On the dynamic relations among multiple goals: Intergoal conflict and intergoal facilitation in younger and older adulthood*. Berlin: Free University of Berlin (dissertation).

Riediger, M. & Freund, A.M. (2004). Interference and facilitation among personal goals: Differntial associations with subjective well-being and persistent goal pursuit. *Personality and Social Psychology Bulletin*, 12, 1511-1523.

Rogers, R.W. (1983). Cognitive and physiological processes in fear appeals and attitude change: A revised theory of protection motivation. In: J.T. Cacioppo & Petty, R.E. (Eds.). *Social psychophysiology: A sourcebook* (153-176). New York: Guilford Press.

Rosenstock, I.M. (1974). The health belief model and preventive health behaviour. *Health Education Monographs*, 2, 354-386.

Rothman, A.J. (2000). Toward a theory-based analysis of behavioral maintenance. *Health Psychology*, 19(S), 64-49.

Sedikides, C., Gaertner, L. & Toguchi, Y (2003). Pancultural self-enhancement. *Journal of Personality and Social Psychology*, 84, 60-79.

Shah, J.Y., Friedman, R. & Kruglanski, A.W. (2002). Forgetting all else: On the antecedents and consequences of goal shielding. *Journal of Personality and Social Psychology*, 83, 1261-1280.

Sheldon, K.N. & Kasser, T. (1995). Coherence and congruence: Two aspects of personality integration. *Journal of Personality and Social Psychology*, 68, 531-543.

Sheldon, K. M., Kasser, T., Smith, K., & Share, T. (2002). Personal goals and psychological growth: Testing an intervention to enhance goal attainment and personality integration. *Journal of Personality, 70, 5-31.*

Sheppard, B.H., Hartwich, J. & Warshaw, P.R. (1988). The Theory of Reasoned Action: A meta-analysis of past research with recommendations for modifications and future research. *Journal of Consumer Research,* 15, 325-343.

Simons, J.S. & Carey, K.B. (2003). Personal strivings and marijuana use initiation, frequency, and problems. *Addictive Behaviors,* 28, 1311-1322.

Stein, K.F., Roeser, R., & Markus, H.R. (1998). Self-schemas and possible selves as predictors and outcomes of risky behaviors in adolescents. *Nursing Research,* 47, 96-106.

Stets, J.E. & Burke, P.J. (2000). Identity theory and social identity theory. *Social Psychology Quarterly,* 63, 224-237.

Ter Doest, L, Maes, S., Gebhardt, W.A. & Koelewijn, H. (2006). Personal goal facilitaton through work: Implications for employee satisfaction and well-being. *Applied Psychology: An International Review,* 55, 192-219.

Van Empelen, P., Gebhardt, W.A. & Dijkstra, A. (2006). The silent need for a positive self: Why physical health is not the central human motive in unhealthy and healthy behaviours. *Netherlands Journal of Psychology,* 62, 42-50.

Weiner, B. (1986). *An attributional theory of motivation and emotion.* New York, NY: Springer Verlag.

White, R.W. (1959). Motivation reconsidered: The concept of competence. *Psychological Review,* 66, 297-333.

Wrosch, C., Scheier, M.F., Miller, G.E., Schulz, R. & Carver, C.S. (2003). Adaptive self-regulation of unattainable goals: Goal disengagement, goal reengagement, and subjective well-being. *Personality and Social Psychology Bulletin,* 29, 1494-1508.

In: Psychology of Motivation
Editor: Lois V. Brown, pp. 141-151

ISBN: 978-1-60021-598-8
© 2007 Nova Science Publishers, Inc.

Chapter 9

THE IMPLICIT NATURE OF GOAL-DIRECTED MOTIVATIONAL PURSUITS

Jay L. Wenger
HACC: Central Pennsylvania's Community College
Lancaster Campus, Pennsylvania, USA

ABSTRACT

During the past 20 years, there's been an abundance of research that has addressed the distinction between implicit and explicit cognitive processes. Implicit processes are those that can occur spontaneously and without conscious intent or awareness; explicit processes are those that occur with such intent and awareness. Recently, several of these studies have included addressing the effects of various motivational pursuits – in particular, goal-directed pursuits.

Researchers who investigate the implicit nature of goal-directed pursuits usually propose that such endeavors are represented as organized knowledge structures housed within a person's overall network of underlying associations. As a result, these structures can be activated in the same way that other concepts are activated. In other words, if appropriate cues are presented in the environment, these structures become activated; in turn, they operate toward completion, and both the activation and the operation can occur without the need for conscious awareness and/or maintenance.

As examples, consider two experiments. In one experiment, participants who were incidentally exposed to words related to the goal of achievement (e.g., succeed, attain, master), tended to perform better on a task, compared to participants who were not primed with the same words (Bargh, Gollwitzer, Lee-Chai, Barndollar, & Trotschel, 2001). In a second experiment, participants who were asked to concentrate on specific characteristics of a close friend, tended to express more willingness to help in a subsequent situation, compared to participants who were not asked to concentrate on characteristics of a friend (Fitzsimons & Bargh, 2003). In these experiments, the goals that were activated were achievement and helpfulness, respectively. In both cases, the goals apparently operated without the need for conscious awareness or maintenance.

INTRODUCTION

"Most of a person's everyday life is determined not by their conscious intentions and deliberate choices but by mental processes that are put into motion by features of the environment and that operate outside of conscious awareness and guidance" (Bargh & Chartrand, 1999, p. 462).

One of the most investigated topics during the past 20 years in psychology has been the study of cognitive processes that "operate outside of conscious awareness." Generally, they have been termed implicit processes, and they have been contrasted with explicit processes – those that occur with conscious intent and awareness (e.g., Banaji, 2001; Blair, 2001). The implicit and explicit distinction is similar to others in psychology, in that it incorporates aspects of automatic processes versus controlled processes, respectively, and nonconscious versus conscious levels of cognitive processing (Bargh & Chartrand, 1999).

Most of the research that has addressed the implicit/explicit distinction has investigated beliefs about topics that are considered fairly personal and sensitive in nature (Greenwald et al., 2002). For example, there's an abundance of experiments that have demonstrated that participants who report very little bias toward a specific racial or ethnic group at the explicit level of awareness, indeed manifest a detectable bias when evaluated at the implicit level of awareness (for reviews, see Blair, 2001; Brauer, Wasel, & Neidenthal, 2000). The reason the implicit/explicit distinction is important for topics that are personal and sensitive in nature, is that for these topics it is not always wise to trust what participants might report at the explicit level of awareness. Too often, participants are prone to present themselves in a more favorable manner than should be believed (e.g., Dovidio & Fazio, 1992). Furthermore, it's likely they cannot actually know, let alone understand, all the complex subtleties of their beliefs (Wenger, 2007).

The primary way in which investigators have studied implicit processes is by using various kinds of incidental activation strategies. Participants are exposed to certain stimuli in a way that they cannot be fully aware of how the stimuli, along with other influences, might affect subsequent responses. In other words, the associations between the incidental exposures and the subsequent responses occur without the need for conscious awareness. In many cases, these incidental exposures occur spontaneously and the responses need to be given very quickly. Thus, the speed of the exposure-to-response associations is part of what keeps participants from being fully aware of the implicit influences that are being investigated. As such, they will be less likely to respond in self-enhancing ways (Dovidio & Fazio, 1992).

Most researchers argue that implicit influences occur within a person's organized network of underlying associations (e.g., Anderson, 1992; Collins & Loftus, 1975). Within these networks, the activation of one concept readily spreads to other concepts that are closely related (Collins & Loftus, 1975). Thus, associated concepts tend to be activated together or in close succession. Recently, several investigators (e.g., Aarts, Gollwitzer, & Hassin, 2004; Bargh & Chartrand, 1999; Kruglanski, 1996) have proposed that goal-related information is also represented within these overall networks of associations. Thus, goal-related information can be activated and operate in the same way that other information is activated, and it can yield effects from that initial activation. In other words, goal-related information can be activated and operate implicitly.

IMPLICIT ASSOCIATION TEST

Probably, the most popular task that has been used to evaluate implicit processes has been the Implicit Association Test – IAT (Greenwald, McGhee, & Schwartz, 1998). The IAT is a computer-based task in which participants respond very quickly to variety of words that fit into four separate categories. When they need to respond in the same way (using the same response key) to words that fit into two closely-related categories, it is easier, than when they need to respond in the same way to words that fit into two less-related categories. The IAT has been very effective in evaluating the underlying aspects of beliefs that are considered personal and sensitive in nature. In particular, many studies have used the IAT to evaluate aspects of stereotypic beliefs.

However, only recently has the IAT been used to investigate constructs directly linked to the psychology of motivation (see Brunstein & Schmitt, 2004; Hausmann & Ryan, 2004). In one example, Wenger and Yarbrough (2005) used the IAT to investigate the implicit nature of two types of motivation – intrinsic motivation and extrinsic motivation. Intrinsic motivation refers to the reason why we perform certain activities for inherent satisfaction or pleasure; you might say performing one of these activities is reinforcing in-and-of itself. Extrinsic motivation refers to our tendency to perform activities for known external rewards, whether they be tangible (e.g., money) or psychological (e.g., praise) in nature (Deci & Ryan, 1985).

Using the IAT, Wenger and Yarbrough (2005) investigated the intrinsic and extrinsic motivations of individuals who pursued religion. In particular, they had religious participants respond to words that were associated to themselves (e.g., me, my, mine) and words that were associated to other people (e.g., they, them, their). Also, the participants needed to respond to phrases associated with intrinsic motivations for pursuing religion (e.g., learn about religious beliefs, seek God's presence) and phrases that were associated with extrinsic motivations for pursuing religion (e.g., receive comfort during trouble, meet friends at religious events).

Results indicated that participants who reported higher levels of intrinsic motivation at the explicit level of awareness (reported via anonymous surveys), then also manifested higher levels of intrinsic motivation at the implicit level of awareness (manifested via the IAT). In other words, intrinsically-motivated individuals were relatively fluent in using the same response key for combining words associated with self and phrases associated with intrinsic motivation, at the same time they needed to combine words associated with others and phrases associated with extrinsic motivation. They were not as fluent in using the same response key for combining words associated with self and phrases associated with extrinsic motivation, at the same time they needed to combine words associated with others and phrases associated with intrinsic motivation.

This research is compatible with several studies that have demonstrated a consistency between what participants report at the explicit level of awareness and what they manifest at the implicit level (e.g., Nosek, Banaji, Greenwald, 2002; Wittenbrink, Judd, & Park, 1997). But, the Wenger and Yarbrough (2005) research only required participants to respond quickly to various concepts during a single task. While such a task can indicate what concepts tend to be closely associated and activated together, the task does not indicate how the activation might affect subsequent behavior. Later in this chapter, I will present research that demonstrates such influence.

GOAL-DIRECTED MOTIVATIONAL PURSUITS

One of the most investigated topics in the psychology of motivation has been the study of goal-directed pursuits. However, most of these studies have emphasized the roles of both conscious choice and conscious maintenance in such pursuits (e.g., Deci & Ryan, 1985; Locke & Latham, 1990). Recently, there have been several studies that have used incidental priming strategies to demonstrate how human behavior often results from automatic processes that occur without conscious awareness – this includes the activation and operation of goal-directed motivational pursuits.

Several researchers propose that all learned motivational pursuits are represented as organized knowledge structures, and these structures are housed within a person's overall network of underlying associations (e.g., Bargh & Chartrand, 1999; Kruglanski, 1996). In particular, Aarts et al. (2004) define a goal as "a mental representation of a desired state that may pertain to a behavior (e.g., to engage in a puzzle task, to work hard) or an outcome (e.g., to own money, to be proud of oneself). Goals are thought to guide organisms to select and persist in activities that are instrumental in attaining these goals" (p. 24).

As knowledge structures, goals can then be activated in the same way that other concepts are activated. If appropriate cues are presented in the environment, goals become activated. In turn, they operate toward completion, and both the activation and the operation can occur without the need for conscious awareness and/or maintenance. It should be noted that while it's possible for a person to be consciously aware of their behaviors during these situations, they are not completely aware of the underlying processes that are affecting the behaviors. In short, the more we pursue anything, whether it's a goal or not, corresponding associations are strengthened, and the need for conscious awareness is reduced. This is compatible with several well-established theories of learning (e.g., Anderson, 1992; Newell & Rosenbloom, 1981).

Moskowitz, Li, and Kirk (2004) provide a great example of how we can relate to the implicit nature of everyday goal pursuit – both the automatic activation and operation of a pursuit. Imagine the situation in which you are trying to remember something – perhaps it's someone's name or perhaps it's something that needs to be done. Either way, you are motivated to retrieve this memory, and thus a goal has been activated and currently operating toward completion. But, you have difficulty retrieving the memory, even though it seems to be on the "tip of your tongue." So eventually you give-up, and you start to pursue another task in some other situation and/or context. Consciously, you have stopped pursuing the goal of retrieving the information; or so it seems.

Then after a period of time, the "name" or the "something to do" comes to mind; it's been retrieved after all. Moskowitz et al. (2004) propose that what occurred is that the goal to retrieve the memory was initially activated (consciously), and the operation of the goal was also in effect (consciously), albeit to no avail. But, the operation remained in effect (nonconsciously), and after a period of time, the retrieval was indeed successful.

DEMONSTRATIONS OF IMPLICIT GOAL INFLUENCE

Probably the classic set of experiments that has demonstrated the implicit nature of goal pursuits was conducted by Bargh, Gollwitzer, Lee-Chai, Barndollar, and Trotschel (2001). In their first experiment, participants were asked to perform word-search puzzles for about ten minutes. For some participants, many of the words in the puzzles were associated with high achievement – for example, succeed, attain, and master. For other participants, the words were neutral with respect to achievement – for example, carpet, river, and shampoo. The participants who were incidentally exposed to the achievement-related words showed superior performance in finding words, compared to the participants who were not exposed to the achievement-related words.

In a subsequent experiment, Bargh et al. (2001) interrupted participants two minutes into the word-search task. The participants were literally told to "stop" the task. Nonetheless, those who were incidentally primed with words associated with achievement were more likely to continue a bit longer with the task – despite the instructions to stop. In both of these experiments, Bargh et al. argue that the exposure to achievement-related words activated the goal structure for achievement. In turn, that structure activated appropriate behavioral tendencies, and those tendencies continued even when there were specific instructions to not continue.

Fitzsimons and Bargh (2003) conducted an interesting goal-pursuit experiment in an airport setting. They simply approached travelers and asked if they would be willing to complete a short questionnaire that would only last about one minute. During that minute, participants were asked to concentrate and think about either a close friend or an acquaintance from work who they know fairly well. In doing so, the participants needed to respond to several questions about the characteristics of the target person and some aspects of their relationship with the target person.

After participants completed the short questionnaire, the researchers asked if they would be willing to participate in a subsequent study that would take about 10-15 minutes longer. The participants who had just focused on a close friend, compared to those who focused on a well-known acquaintance, expressed more willingness to "help" in the subsequent study. Fitzsimons and Bargh (2003) argue that activating the cognitive representation of a friend spread to activate the corresponding goal structure for helping. In turn, behavioral tendencies were activated to achieve the goal, and thus participants expressed more willingness to help. Apparently, this sequence of underlying activations occurred "entirely outside conscious awareness" (p. 149).

Recently, Aarts et al. (2004) conducted a series of experiments to show that certain goal-directed motivations can be activated by implicitly inferring motivations from other people. In one of their experiments, participants initially read a story about a hypothetical person who was engaged in some work-related activity before taking a vacation with friends. In one condition, the hypothetical person was working on a farm; the implication in this condition was that the person was working to earn money. In the second condition, the hypothetical person was simply volunteering time to work within the community; this condition does not suggest the goal of earning money.

Then, all participants were led to believe that they would have an opportunity to earn some money for themselves, if enough time remained at the end of the experimental session.

But, to get to that opportunity a short intermediate task needed to be completed. Interestingly, participants who read about the hypothetical person who was working at a farm (to earn money), were more likely to complete that task faster, than the participants who read about the person who worked as a volunteer within the community. In other words, they completed the intermediate task faster so they would have an opportunity to earn money for themselves. Aarts et al. (2004) argue that these participants implicitly inferred the goal of earning money from the fictitious person, and that inference activated their own goal representation for earning money.

CHARACTERISTICS OF IMPLICIT GOAL PURSUIT

Bargh and Chartrand (1999, p. 472) have identified two "hallmark" characteristics involved in the operation of goal-directed motivations; they are "evaluation" and "persistence." Like the activation and operation of goals, both of these characteristics can occur without conscious awareness or maintenance (see also Moskowitz et al., 2004).

First, as participants pursue a goal, they will tend to "evaluate" the effectiveness of their pursuit. In particular, implicit processes will be engaged to monitor the difference between the current state of goal incompleteness and the desired state of goal achievement. If this evaluation indicates a discrepancy of some sort, then "compensatory" processes will be put into effect to try reduce the discrepancy (Moskowitz et al., 2004, p. 323). Second, as participants pursue a goal, they will tend to "persist" toward the completion of the goal, even if an obstacle occurs (Bargh & Chartrand, 1999). As described earlier, an interruption to stop a task constitutes one type of obstacle (Bargh et al., 2001).

In a creative experiment, Moskowitz (2002) used an incidental priming paradigm with college athletes to demonstrate the implicit "evaluation" of a goal pursuit. Athletes are participants who presumably have well-established goals to achieve, especially in sports. In his research, athletes were led to believe that they were participating in two unrelated tasks. In the first task, they were asked to concentrate and reflect on a time when they were either successful or unsuccessful in a sport competition (i.e., success or failure). As part of this reflection, they needed to describe (a) what actions they performed in the competition, (b) how their actions affected the outcome, (c) emotions they felt at the time, and (d) how their actions affected others.

In the second task, ostensibly unrelated, participants performed a Stroop (1935) task; they simply needed to identify the font color of words as fast as possible. Some of the words were related to athletic success (e.g., agile, strong), while other words were related to academic success (e.g., smart, studious). Interestingly, college-athlete participants who focused on a personal failure in sports/athletics were slower in responding to the words that were related to athletic success, than college-athlete participants who focused on a personal success in sports/athletics.

Moskowitz (2002) explains these results in terms of "compensatory processes." When participants concentrate on a failure, it not only activates the goal structure related to athletic achievement, but it also primes a sense of incompleteness – goal incompleteness. In turn, this sense of incompleteness activates attentional processes to seek-out information that might be relevant in rectifying the sense of incompleteness. You might say the athlete's cognitive system is looking for a chance to redeem itself. Thus, even when the athlete does not need to pay attention to the content of upcoming information (the task only required that they identify the font color of words), they nonetheless notice information related to athletic success more than other information, including information related to other kinds of success (e.g., academic success). Moskowitz argues that this extra processing of particularly relevant information is what led to the slower response times.

While Moskowitz (2002) demonstrated the attentional processes that can accompany a sense of goal incompleteness, Wenger (2007) demonstrated how such a sense can actually affect the "persistence" of subsequent behavior. Instead of using college athletes as participants, Wenger used college students who were serious in pursuing religion – participants who were intrinsically motivated in pursuing religion. The construct of intrinsic religious motivation is one of the most investigated topics in the psychology of religion (see Kirkpatrick & Hood, 1990). In short, it is considered to be an approach to religion in which a person genuinely tries to "live" their religious faith. In contrast, extrinsic religious motivation is considered to be an approach to religion in which a person "uses" religion for external benefits such as personal comfort and/or social status (Allport & Ross, 1967).

The construct of intrinsic motivation has also been one of the most popular topics in the psychology of motivation (see Deci & Ryan, 1984), and it seems there should be an important link between such motivation and implicit goal-directed motivational pursuits. Both imply an internalization for some kind of prioritized activity. As Lepper, Corpus, & Iyenger (2005) state, intrinsic motivation is "the desire to engage in behaviors for no reason other than sheer enjoyment, challenge, pleasure, or interest" (p. 184). One possibility for this internalization is that the construct of intrinsicness is subsumed as a type of implicit goal pursuit, and Wenger's (2007) research provides support.

Wenger (2007) used an experimental methodology similar to that of Moskowitz (2002). There were two phases. In the first phase, religious participants responded to a survey. Part of the survey evaluated their levels of motivation for intrinsic religious pursuit, while another part required that they concentrate and reflect on either a success or a shortcoming in their pursuit of religion. During the reflection, they needed to describe (a) what actions they performed in the situation (e.g., success or shortcoming), (b) how their actions violated their religious standards, (c) emotions they felt at the time, and (d) how their actions affected others. As in Moskowitz's research, these questions tended to force participants to genuinely focus on their successes or shortcomings.

In the second phase, each participant had the opportunity to spend time reading a short story that included information about pursuing religion, along with a bit of a challenge to live life consistently based on one's chosen religious pursuit. Results indicated that religious individuals who initially focused on a religious shortcoming tended to spend more time reading that story than religious individuals who focused on a religious success. Furthermore, this effect was most pronounced for participants who reported higher levels of intrinsic motivation for their religious pursuit.

Again, these results can be couched in terms of Moskowitz's (2002) "compensatory processes." Focusing on a goal-related shortcoming, in this case a religious shortcoming, activates a sense of goal incompleteness. In turn, this sense activates cognitive processes to reduce the discrepancy between the current state and the desired state – in other words, compensatory processes. Thus, the participants were motivated to seek-out information toward goal completeness. In this case, they spent more time reading a story that was relevant to their religious pursuit. But, Wenger's (2007) study extends Moskowitz's research, because it suggests a link between the motivational construct of intrinsic motivation and the cognitive construct of implicit processing. While the nature of that link is still unclear, one hypothesis is that it involves the degree to which a person's underlying sense of self is associated with the cognitive representation of the particular goal (see Gollwitzer & Wicklund, 1985).

CONCLUSION

During our everyday lives, there are probably times when several different goals will be activated during one situation. For example, on a relaxing Sunday afternoon, I might experience goals of (a) reading something academic, (b) visiting relatives, and (c) watching a sporting event on TV. Presumably, these goals would be involved in a competition of sorts for my time, and one of them will probably have a stronger influence. But, which one, and why? Several researchers provide possible answers – answers based on theories about how implicit goals might achieve a kind of priority status. Here are four possibilities.

First, Bargh (1990) suggests that underlying goals will achieve a kind of priority status via frequency of use and activations – in other words, a practice effect. In his view, cognitive representations of goals become associated with various cues in the environment. Thus, when certain cues present themselves, a goal structure is activated, and in turn, behavioral tendencies are set in place to achieve the desired state. As a goal becomes associated with more and more situational cues, then the pursuit of that goal will occur more often. As such, the goal will be activated in more instances, which suggests it has achieved a higher status.

Second, Custers and Aarts (2005) posit that goal representations can include information about "affect" – including positive affect. This is an intriguing possibility. It seems very likely that we are naturally motivated to pursue anything that would be considered positive in value; after all, this is the "hallmark of incentive theory" (Custers & Aarts, 2005, p. 130). Thus, any goal structure that includes particularly positive affective information will then maintain a higher priority status, and it will be more likely to be chosen in situations in which all other information is equal.

Third, Moskowitz et al. (2004) present a view that is similar to both Bargh's (1990) emphasis on frequency and Custers and Aarts' (2005) emphasis on affective information. Moskowitz et al. argue that goals can achieve a priority status like a habit. They state that the "habitual pursuit of some goals over other goals can lead to those goals acquiring a chronic state of heightened accessibility" (p. 320). Thus, frequency plays a role. However, unlike Bargh's emphasis, these goals do not necessarily require specific cues to be presented in the environment before they are activated. Instead, the representation of the goal itself apparently includes the "chronic" or priority status. This is similar to, but not exactly the same as, incorporating positive affective information within the goal's representation, ala Custers and Aarts.

Fourth, Gollwitzer and Wicklund (1985) propose that goals can achieve a priority status based on their closeness to a person's underlying sense of self. This view assumes that a person's own sense of self is somehow central within the person's organization of underlying associations. As such, any structures, including goal structures, that are closely-linked to the representation of self, will be considered important. In other words, these closely-associated goal structures should be readily activated in any situation that involves a heightened sense of self.

So reconsider: on a relaxing Sunday afternoon, which activity will I be likely to pursue – reading something academic, visiting relatives, or watching sports on TV? I have enjoyed sports throughout my life. I have a variety of memorabilia in my office at home, and my conversations with neighbors often involve something about sports. So I live with a variety of cues to presumably activate the goal of watching sports (Bargh, 1990). But, perhaps I've also fostered a more general desire to keep in touch with sports and subsequently watch sports on TV (when I can). As a result, this desire might be incorporated within an underlying representation of wanting-to-pursue-sports. While this representation might include positive affect (Custers & Aarts, 2005), it might simply be a representation with an overall heightened (chronic) readiness to be activated (Moskowitz et al., 2004). Finally, it might be that over time, my own involvement in sports has led to a close association between the pursuit of sports and my underlying sense of self (Gollwitzer & Wicklund, 1985). Either way, let's watch a game!

REFERENCES

Aarts, H., Gollwitzer, P.M., Hassin, R.R. (2004). Goal contagion: Perceiving is for pursuing. *Journal of Personality and Social Psychology, 87,* 23-37.

Allport, G.W., & Ross, J.M. (1967). Personal religious orientation and prejudice. *Journal of Personality and Social Psychology, 5,* 432-443.

Anderson, J.R. (1992). Automaticity and the ACT-Super(*) theory. *American Journal of Psychology, 105,* 165-180.

Banaji, M.R. (2001). Implicit attitudes can be measured. In H.L. Roediger III, J.S. Nairne, I. Neath, & A.M. Surprenant (Eds.), *The nature of remembering: Essays in honor of Robert G. Crowder* (pp. 117-150). Washington, DC: American Psychological Association.

Bargh, J.A. (1990). Auto-motives: Preconscious determinants of social interaction. In E.T. Higgins & R.M. Sorrentino (Eds.), *Handbook of motivation and cognition* (Vol. 2, pp. 93-130). New York: Guilford Press.

Bargh, J.A., & Chartrand, T.L. (1999). The unbearable automaticity of being. *American Psychologist, 54,* 462-479.

Bargh, J.A., Gollwitzer, P.M., Lee-Chai, A., Barndollar, K., & Trotschel, R. (2001). The automated will: Nonconscious activation and pursuit of behavioral goals. *Journal of Personality and Social Psychology, 81,* 1014-1027.

Blair, I.V. (2001). Implicit stereotypes and prejudice. In G.B. Moskowitz (Ed.), *Cognitive social psychology: Princeton symposium on the legacy and future of social cognition* (pp. 359-374). Mahwah, NJ: Lawrence Erlbaum Associates.

Brauer, M., Wasel, W., & Niedenthal, P. (2000). Implicit and explicit components of prejudice. *Review of General Psychology, 4,* 79-101.

Brunstein, J.C., & Schmitt, C.H. (2004). Assessing individual differences in achievement motivation with the Implicit Association Test. *Journal of Research in Personality, 38,* 536-555.

Collins, A.M., & Loftus, E.F. (1975). A spreading activation theory of semantic processing. *Psychological Review, 82,* 407-428.

Custers, R., & Aarts, H. (2005). Positive affect as implicit motivator: On the nonconscious operation of behavioral goals. *Journal of Personality and Social Psychology, 89,* 129-142.

Deci, E.L., & Ryan, R.M. (1985*). Intrinsic motivation and self-determination in human behavior.* New York: Plenum Press.

Dovidio, J.F., & Fazio, R.H. (1992). New technologies for the direct and indirect assessment of attitudes. In J.M. Tanur (Ed.), *Questions about questions: Inquiries into the cognitive bases of surveys* (pp. 204-237). New York: Russel Sage Foundation.

Fitzsimons, G.M., & Bargh, J.A. (2003). Thinking of you: Nonconscious pursuit of interpersonal goals associated with relationship partners. *Journal of Personality and Social Psychology, 84,* 148-164.

Greenwald, A.G., Banaji, M.R., Rudman, L.A., Farnham, S.D., Nosek, B.A., & Mellott, D.S. (2002). A unified theory of implicit attitudes, stereotypes, self-esteem, and self-concept. *Psychological Review, 109,* 3-25.

Greenwald, A.G., McGhee, D.E., & Schwartz, J.L.K. (1998). Measuring individual differences in implicit cognition: The Implicit Association Test. *Journal of Personality and Social Psychology, 74,* 1464-1480.

Gollwitzer, P.M., & Wicklund, R.A. (1985). The pursuit of self-defining goals. In J. Kuhl & J. Beckmann (Eds.). *Action control: From cognition to behavior* (pp. 61-85). Heidelberg, Germany: Springer-Verlag Publishers.

Hausmann, L.R.M., & Ryan, C.S. (2004). Effects of external and internal motivation to control prejudice on implicit prejudice: The mediating role of effects to control prejudiced responses. *Basic and Applied Social Psychology, 26,* 215-225.

Kirkpatick, L.A., & Hood, R.W. (1990). Intrinsic-extrinsic religious orientation: The boon or bane of contemporary psychology of religion? *Journal for the Scientific Study of Religion, 29,* 442-462.

Kruglanski, A.W. (1996). Goals as knowledge structures. In P.M. Gollwitzer & J.A. Bargh (Eds.), *The psychology of action: Linking cognition and motivation to behavior* (pp. 599-618). New York: Guilford Press.

Lepper, M.R., Corpus, J.H., & Iyengar, S.S, (2005). Intrinsic and extrinsic motivational orientations in the classroom: Age differences and academic correlates. *Journal of Educational Psychology, 97,* 184-196.

Locke, E.A., & Latham, G.P. (1990). *A theory of goal setting and task performance.* Englewood Cliffs, NJ: Prentice Hall.

Moskowitz, G.B. (2002). Preconscious effects of temporary goals on attention. *Journal of Experimental Social Psychology, 38,* 397-404.

Moskowitz, G.B., Li, P., & Kirk, E.R. (2004). The Implicit Volition Model: On the preconscious regulation of temporarily adopted goals. In M.P. Zanna (Ed.), *Advances in experimental social psychology,* (Vol. 36, pp. 317-413). San Diego, CA: Elsevier Academic Press.

Newell, A., & Rosenbloom, P. (1981). Mechanisms of skill acquisition and the law of practice. In J.R. Anderson (Ed.), Cognitive skills and their acquisition (pp. 1-55). Hillsdale, NJ: Lawrence Erlbaum Associates.

Nosek, B.A., Banaji, M.R., & Greenwald, A.G. (2002). Harvesting implicit group attitudes and beliefs from a demonstration web site. *Group Dynamics, 6,* 101-115.

Stroop, J.R. (1935). Studies of interference in serial verbal reactions. *Journal of Experimental Psychology, 18,* 643-662.

Wenger, J.L. (2007). The implicit nature of intrinsic religious pursuit. *The International Journal for the Psychology of Religion, 17,* 47-60.

Wenger, J.L., & Yarbrough, T.D. (2005). Religious individuals: Evaluating their intrinsic and extrinsic motivations at the implicit level of awareness. *The Journal of Social Psychology, 145,* 5-16.

Wittenbrink, B., Judd, C.M., & Park, B. (1997). Evidence for racial prejudice at the implicit level and its relationship with questionnaire measures. *Journal of Personality and Social Psychology, 72,* 262-274.

In: Psychology of Motivation
Editor: Lois V. Brown, pp. 153-165

ISBN: 978-1-60021-598-8
© 2007 Nova Science Publishers, Inc.

Chapter 10

PROCRASTINATION AND MOTIVATIONS FOR HOUSEHOLD SAFETY BEHAVIORS: AN EXPECTANCY-VALUE THEORY PERSPECTIVE

Fuschia M. Sirois[*]

Department of Psychology, University of Windsor, Windsor, Canada

ABSTRACT

Research into why individuals do or do not engage in important health behaviors is often approached from the perspective of expectancy-value theories of motivation. Such theories suggest that the motivation to engage in a behavior is regulated by the outcome expectancies for the behavior and the value of the outcome. However, the relationship of expectancies and values to stable individual differences known to affect motivation are often overlooked. In this chapter the links between procrastination, a behavioral style known to be linked to poor health behaviors, and household safety behaviors were examined using an expectancy-value theory (EVT) framework. Adults (N = 254) recruited from the community and the Internet completed self-report measures of procrastination, health self-efficacy, household safety behaviors, previous experiences with household accidents, and questions about the importance of keeping their homes free from potential accidents. Despite the fact that chronic procrastinators were more likely to have experienced a household accident that could have been prevented, procrastination was negatively related to the performance of household safety behaviors. Procrastination was also negatively related to health-self-efficacy and household safety value. Hierarchical regression testing the EVT variables found support for the predictive value of both outcome expectancies (self-efficacy) and value, but not their product, in explaining household safety behaviors after controlling for procrastination. Separate path analyses tested whether self-efficacy and valuing household safety mediated the

---

[*] Correspondence concerning this article should be addressed to Fuschia M. Sirois, Ph.D. (Psychology), B.Sc. (Biochemistry/Nutrition), Department of Psychology, University of Windsor, 401 Sunset Ave., Windsor, Ontario, Canada   N9B 3P4. Tel: 1 519 253-3000, ext. 2224; Fax: 1 519 973-7021; E-mail: fsirois@uwindsor.ca

relationship between procrastination and household safety behaviors. Safety value and self-efficacy each partially mediated the procrastination-household safety behaviour relationship after controlling for procrastination. These findings suggest that EVT may be useful for explaining motivations for household safety behaviors in general, and may also provide insight into the lack of motivation for these behaviors demonstrated by procrastinators.

INTRODUCTION

The reasons why people do or do not engage in important health-related behaviors has become an increasingly important topic in health psychology and related disciplines in recent years. Understanding the motivational factors involved in the performance of health-promoting and health-protective behaviors is key for developing interventions at both the individual and societal level that may increase the performance of these behaviors. Expectancy-value theories of motivation are often used as conceptual frameworks for examining "why" people practice health-protective behaviors. Expectancy-value theory (EVT) suggests that people will choose to engage in those behaviors that they expect to succeed in and that have outcomes that are valued (Feather, 1982b). However, a growing body of research on the role of individual differences in predicting health behaviors suggests that investigating "who" practices health-protective behaviors is an equally important line of inquiry (Booth-Kewley & Vickers, 1994; Friedman, 2000). When these individual differences involve motivational difficulties, this question may be even more important to ask. Yet, the relationship of expectancies and values to stable individual differences known to affect motivation are often overlooked. In this chapter, the links between procrastination, a behavioral style associated with motivational problems, and household safety behaviors were examined using an EVT framework.

EXPECTANCY-VALUE THEORIES AND HEALTH BEHAVIOUR

From the perspective of expectancy value theory, people are viewed as goal-directed beings who will choose a behavior to achieve a specific end (Feather, 1982a; Fishbein, 1967). The strength of a person's motivation to engage and persistent in a particular activity depends upon the value or importance of the expected outcome of the behaviour, the expectations about how successful one will be in undertaking the activity, and the product of these values and expectancies (Feather, 1992). The expectations within EVT as described by Feather (1992) are conceived as being comprised of two specific types of expectancies which can fuel motivation for a behaviour. Consistent with Bandura's Social Cognitive theory (1977), efficacy-expectancies involve the confidence that one can successfully engage in a behaviour to produce desired outcomes, and outcome-expectations refer to the belief that a given behaviour will result in a particular outcome. Within Social Cognitive theory (Bandura, 1977) efficacy-expectancies in particular are viewed as powerful determinants of behaviour by promoting persistence in the face of difficulties and a strong conviction to follow through with behaviour. Similarly, Feather (1992) suggests that values themselves may function as motives to influence the effort and commitment that is put into an activity.

A number of widely used models and theories for predicting health behaviour are based on the core assumptions of EVT. For example, the initial formulation of the Theory of Reasoned Action (TRA) by Ajzen and Fishbein (1969) evolved out of an EVT framework. Along with its successor the Theory of Planned Behaviour (TPB; Ajzen, 1985), the TRA focuses on the role of attitudes, values and expectancies in the formation of intentions to perform a behaviour. The Health Belief Model (HBM; Rosenstock, 1974) is another EVT based model often used to explain people's motivations for health protective behaviors. These models have been applied to predict a variety of health-related behaviors with varying results depending upon the type of health behaviour (Abraham & Sheeran, 2000; Conner & Sparks, 1996). However, very few studies have employed a basic EVT model for understanding health behaviour (Pligt & Vries, 1998; Rogers, Deckner, & Mewborn, 1978), with researchers favoring more elaborate models such as the TPB and HBM.

Evidence from studies of health behaviors suggest that expectancy-value theories such as the TRA, TPB, and HBM may be useful tools for explaining safety behaviors (Conner & Norman, 1996; Norman, Abraham, & Conner, 2000). However, safety behaviors related to bicycle use and the use of seatbelts have tended to be the focus of these investigations (Gielen, Joffe, Dannenberg, Wilson, & Beilenson, 1994; Quine, Rutter, & Arnold, 2000). A recent review of the use of social science theories for explaining safety behaviour found that there was very little research that applied EVT theories such as the TRA, TPB, or the HBM for understanding the practice of safety-related behaviors (Trifiletti, Gielen, Sleet, & Hopkins, 2005). Moreover, the few studies which did were more likely to examine road-related safety behaviors rather than household safety behaviors. Nonetheless, household safety behaviors, such as maintaining electrical appliances, and eliminating trip and fall hazards in the home, are key for minimizing the risk of unintentional injuries and deaths from accidents in the home. Recent estimates suggest that in the United States there are nearly 20,000 deaths due to unintentional home injuries per year, and an average of 21 million medical visits resulting from injuries in the home (Home Safety Council, 2004). In addition, 13.3% of Canadians age 12 and over sustain personal injuries in the home each year (Statistics Canada, 2002). Applying EVT to understanding the factors that motivate household safety behaviors may provide some much needed insight into understanding the factors associated with this neglected area of health-protective behaviors.

PROCRASTINATION AND HEALTH BEHAVIORS

Procrastination is a common and pervasive problem characterized by self-regulation difficulties which take the form of delaying the start and/or completion of necessary and important tasks (Ferrari & Tice, 2000). Chronic procrastination can be viewed as a trait like construct that affects behaviour across a variety of life domains, including health-related behaviour. Recent studies have found that procrastination is associated with less frequent practice of a variety of health protective behaviors including wellness behaviors (e.g., proper diet and exercise), and medical visits (Sirois, 2004; Sirois, Melia-Gordon, & Pychyl, 2003).

The motivational factors that may explain why procrastinators engage in fewer health-related behaviors have not been fully explored. Using the TPB as a conceptual framework, one study examined the role of health-related efficacy beliefs in the strength of procrastinators' intentions to engage in health-protective behaviors (Sirois, 2004). Although the health behaviors identified were those which participants believed would have protected them from a retrospectively recalled illness experience, procrastinators reported weaker intentions to perform these important behaviors in the future. Consistent with the TPB, these weaker intentions were explained by the procrastinators' lower health-related self-efficacy beliefs, but not their ability to consider the future consequences of their current actions. To date this is the only investigation that has explored the reasons why chronic procrastination is associated with fewer health behaviors. However, this study examined intentions to engage in, but not the performance of, health behaviors. Further research is therefore needed to assess the role of efficacy beliefs and other factors for understanding the poor motivation of procrastinators with respect to health protective behaviors.

THE PRESENT STUDY

Although expectancy value theory (EVT) has been somewhat supplanted by more elaborate EVT based models for understanding the motivations for health-related behaviors, the studies that have investigated health behaviors using a basic EVT framework have found support for the utility of both efficacy beliefs and values (Pligt & Vries, 1998; Rogers et al., 1978). Moreover, preliminary research on the links between procrastination and the intentions to engage in important health behaviors suggests that health efficacy beliefs may play a role in procrastinators' lack of motivation for health behaviors (Sirois, 2004). An EVT approach may therefore be beneficial for understanding why some individuals put off important health behaviors such as keeping the home safe and free from potential accidents. The purpose of this study was to examine household safety behaviors in a community-dwelling population and their association with chronic procrastination, using an expectancy-value theory (EVT) framework. According to EVT, efficacy beliefs, values, and their product should each explain unique variance in safety behaviors. In addition, it was expected that procrastination would be negatively associated with household safety behaviors, and that the importance of these behaviors and health-related efficacy would mediate this relationship.

METHODS

Participants and Procedure

A sample of 254 people recruited online and from the community completed the survey package[1]. The majority of the sample was female (70.0%), and from Canada (59.3%) and the

---

[1] The results reported in the current chapter are based on a secondary analysis of data from a research study on procrastination and health. The results from the original study are reported in: Sirois, F. M. (2007). "I'll look after my health, later": A replication and extension of the procrastination-health model with community-dwelling adults. *Personality and Individual Differences, 43 (1),* 15-26.

United States (36.8%), with the remaining participants from Europe (1.6%) and Australia (1.6%). The mean age of the participants was 33.8 years (SD = 12.4), and ranged from 16 to 74 years. The majority of the participants self-identified as Caucasian (73.7%), and the remainder were Asian (17.5%), African American (2.8%), Hispanic (2.8%), Aboriginal (1.6%), and other (1.6%).

Online recruitment notices were placed on sites advertising psychological studies, and on various message boards. Notices and questionnaire displays advertised the study in several community centers in Windsor, Canada. Participants were given the choice of completing the survey online or having the survey sent by mail. The majority of participants (217) completed the survey online.

Materials

The mail-in and online surveys contained the same sets of questions and measures, including a set of demographic questions and measures of dispositional procrastination, health self-efficacy, household safety behaviors, previous experiences with household accidents, and questions about the importance of keeping the home free from potential accidents.

Procrastination

The revised Adult Inventory of Procrastination (AIP-R; McCown & Johnson, 2001) is a recently revised 15-item measure of chronic procrastination motivated by avoiding task unpleasantness. Except for the addition and removal of one item, it is identical to the original AIP measure. Due to the pejorative nature of procrastination, the scale creators recommend using distracter items in between the scale items. The current study included 5 distracter items in addition to the 15 regular items. The AIP-R includes 7 positively and 8 negatively keyed items scored on a 7-point Likert-type scale ranging from 1 (*Strongly Disagree*) to 7 (*Strongly Agree*). High scores indicate a greater tendency towards task avoidant procrastination. Previous studies have demonstrated that the AIP-R has good internal consistency (alpha = .84, N = 984; McCown & Johnson, 2001). The Cronbach's alpha for the current study was .88.

Health Self-Efficacy

Health-specific self-efficacy was assessed with the Health Efficacy subscale of the Control Beliefs Inventory (Sirois, 2003). This subscale contains 8 items that assess feelings of competence and confidence in one's ability to carry out actions important for the maintenance of health. The scale includes 5 items such as "I am confident that I can successfully look after my health" that are scored in the positive direction as well as 3 reverse scored items. Response options are rated on 6-point Likert-type scale ranging from 1 for *strongly disagree* to 6 for *strongly agree*. The Health Efficacy subscale has demonstrated good psychometric properties with good convergent validity (r = .45; Sirois, 2003) with the Generalized Self-Efficacy scale (Schwarzer & Jerusalem, 1995), and has shown good internal consistency in previous studies (e.g., Cronbach's alpha = .84; Sirois, 2004). The internal consistency for the current sample was very good (Cronbach's alpha = .81).

Household Safety Behaviors

The performance of behaviors necessary for maintaining safety at home was assessed with the 8-item Household Safety Behaviors Questionnaire (HSBQ) created for this study. Items such as "I make sure that the smoke alarm is tested regularly to ensure that it is functioning properly (e.g., has fresh batteries)" and "I make sure that stairs and walkways at home are free of clutter and other tripping hazards" were scored on a 5-point scale with response options ranging from 1 (*false*) to 5 (*true of me*). In the case that participants may not have been responsible or capable of attending to these tasks they were instructed to answer according to any actions that were taken to ensure that the person who was responsible was made aware of what needed to be done. Reliability analysis of the HSBQ revealed good internal consistency (alpha = .84).

Household Emergency Preparation and Experience

Four additional questions assessed whether participants had taken the necessary steps to prepare their household for dealing with potential emergencies. Respondents indicated "yes" or "no" to whether they had a working fire extinguisher in the kitchen, a carbon-monoxide detector installed, a first aid kit in the home, and a working flashlight and/or candles easily accessible in case of a power blackout. One final question asked participants about their previous experience with household accidents: "Has there ever been an accident in your household that could have been prevented had you or someone else taken the necessary precautions?" Participants responded "yes" or "no" to this question.

Household Safety Value

Two questions were used to measure the value of performing household-safety related behaviors. Participants answered "How important to you is keeping your household prepared for dealing with potential accidents?" and "How important to you is keeping your household safe and free from potential accidents?" on a 10-point rating scale with response options from 1 (*not important at all*) to 10 (*extremely important*). The mean of the two items served as an index of household safety value.

RESULTS

Data Screening

Electronically received surveys were screened to ensure that each was a unique response. Duplicates and surveys that were missing 20 percent or more of the required responses were not included in the analyses of the final sample of 254.

Descriptive Statistics

The proportion of people who had prepared for household emergencies varied depending upon the specific task. The majority of the sample had a first aid kit in their home (67.3%), and reported having a working flashlight or candles in case of a blackout (93.7%). However, less than half of the sample had a working fire extinguisher (47.2%) or a carbon monoxide detector (46.9%). There were no differences in the procrastination scores of those who were and were not prepared for emergencies by having a first aid kit, fire extinguisher, or carbon monoxide detector. However, the few people who were not prepared for a blackout had significantly higher procrastination scores (No, $M = 54.29$, $SD = 9.46$; Yes, $M = 46.01$, $SD = 14.8$, $t (252) = 3.24$, $p < .01$).

Although the majority of the sample indicated that they had not previously experienced a household accident that could have been prevented had preventive actions been taken, 28% reported that they had such an experience. Interestingly, those who had experienced a previous household accident also had higher procrastination scores (No, $M = 45.45$, $SD = 14.7$; Yes, $M = 49.34$, $SD = 14.1$, $t (252) = -1.95$, $p = .05$).

Table 1 presents the bivariate relations among procrastination, health self-efficacy, and the household safety variables. Procrastination was negatively related to health-self-efficacy, household safety value, and to the performance of household safety behaviors.

Table 1. Bivariate correlations, means and standard deviations for the procrastination, health self-efficacy, and household safety variables

Variable	1	2	3	4
1. Procrastination	---			
2. Health Self-efficacy	.79**	---		
3. Household safety behaviors	.17**	.15*	---	
4. Household safety value	.13*	.18**	.20**	---
Mean	46.53	4.27	3.84	8.15
Standard deviation	14.6	0.76	0.72	1.58

Note: $*p < .05$, $**p < .01$.

Test of the Expectancy-Value Theory

To test the predictive power of the expectancy value theory variables for explaining household safety behaviour, a hierarchical multiple regression was conducted with procrastination entered in the first step, household safety value and health self-efficacy entered in the second step, and their interaction term entered in the final step. Following the recommendations of West, Aiken, and Krull (1996), the interaction term was calculated as the mean-deviated product of health self-efficacy and household safety value. Moderation is supported if the hierarchical regression analysis indicates that the interaction term is significantly related to the outcome variable. The results of this analysis are presented in Table 2. Although procrastination, health self-efficacy, and household safety value were each uniquely related to the general household safety behaviors questionnaire (GHSB), the interaction term was not. Together these variables accounted of 48% of the variance in the GHSB, with the majority of this variance explained by household safety value.

Table 2. Hierarchical regression analyses testing the expectancy-value theory model variables for explaining household safety behavior.

Step	Variable(s) Entered	Step 1			Step 2			Step 3		
		Beta	t	ΔR^2	Beta	t	ΔR^2	Beta	t	ΔR^2
1.	Procrastination	-.41**	-7.15	.17**	-.22**	-4.44	.32**	-.22**	-4.45	.00
2.	Health self-efficacy	---	---		.13**	2.72		.13**	2.64	
	Household safety value	---	---		.55**	11.56		.55**	11.52	
3.	Health self-efficacy X Household safety value	---	---		---	---		-.03	-.67	
	Total equation	$R^2 = .17**$			$R^2 = .48**$			$R^2 = .48**$		

$*p < .05, ** p < .01$

Testing Mediation of Procrastination and Household Safety Behaviors

To examine whether health self-efficacy and household safety value individually mediated the link between procrastination and household safety behaviors, separate multiple regression analyses were conducted using the general procedures of Baron and Kenny (1986) to assess mediation. According to these guidelines mediation is implied when it is demonstrated that the predictor variable is related to the outcome variable and the proposed mediator variable, and the mediator variable is also related to the outcome variable after controlling for the predictor variable. Finally, full mediation is established when, after controlling for the mediating variable, the predictor variable exerts no effect upon the outcome variable. Partial mediation is also possible when the addition of the mediator produces a significant drop in the effect of the predictor variable on the outcome variable. Because the Baron and Kenny procedure may not be very sensitive to detecting partial or full mediation in larger samples it has been suggested that a Sobel test be used to assess the significance of the indirect effect of the predictor on the outcome variable (Preacher & Hayes, 2004).

The results of the regression analyses are presented in Table 3. Overall, both health self-efficacy and household safety value met the first three criteria of Baron and Kenny (1986). Although the effect of procrastination on household safety behaviors was reduced after the addition of the mediator in both analyses, this effect was still significant. The significance of the indirect effects of each mediator were therefore tested using the procedure outlined by Preacher and Hayes (2004), with 3,000 bootstrapped resamples to estimate the size and significance of each effect. The indirect effect is said to be significant if the 95% confidence interval (CI) does not include zero. According to the bootstrapping analyses the mean mediation effects from procrastination through household safety value (95% CI: -0.011, -0.004) and through health self-efficacy (95% CI: -0.007, -0.002) to household safety behaviors were each significant, indicating that household safety value and health self-efficacy each partially mediated the relationship between procrastination and household safety behaviors. The magnitude of the household safety value effect was $\beta = .25$ X $.63 = .158$, indicating that 15.8% of the variance in self-reported household safety behaviors was explained by the household safety value effect in the procrastination- safety behaviors model.

Similarly, 12.9% of the variance in self-reported household safety behaviors through procrastination was explained by the partial mediation of health self-efficacy.

Table 3. Regression analyses of the mediational roles of safety value and health self-efficacy in the link between procrastination and household safety behaviors

Outcome variable	Predictor variable	β	t	R^2 change
Household safety value				
Household safety behaviors	Procrastination	-.41**	-7.21**	.17**
Household safety value	Procrastination	-.25**	-4.16**	.07**
Household safety behaviors	Household safety value	.63**	13.00**	.40**
Household safety behaviors	1. Household safety value	.57**	11.89**	.30**
	2. Procrastination	-.27**	5.61**	.07**
Health self-efficacy				
Household safety behaviors	Procrastination	-.41**	-7.21**	.17**
Health self-efficacy	Procrastination	-.38**	-6.43**	.14**
Household safety behaviors	Health self-efficacy	.34**	5.78**	.12**
Household safety behaviors	1. Health self-efficacy	.22**	3.60**	.04**
	2. Procrastination	-.33**	-5.49**	.10**

Note: When two predictor variables are included in the same analyses, the regression statistics reflect the effect of each variable when entered into the regression equation last.

When 1 predictor is entered, F value is for (1, 251) degrees of freedom; when two predictors are entered, F value is for (1, 252) degrees of freedom.

$N = 254$, * $p < .05$, ** $p < .01$, *** $p < .001$.

CONCLUSION

The purpose of the current study was to examine the links between procrastination and household safety behaviors, and to test the possible motivational factors involved using a basic EVT framework. As expected, the measure of general household safety behaviors was negatively related to trait procrastination, and individuals who were not prepared for a blackout also had higher procrastination scores. The test of health self-efficacy and household safety value for predicting safety behaviors partially supported the utility of the EVT framework. After controlling for procrastination, both health self-efficacy and a belief that keeping the home safe from potential accidents was important were each uniquely related to household safety behaviors, but the interaction term was not. Nonetheless, these variables combined explained 48% of the variance in household safety behaviors. The mediation analyses with the EVT variables provided further insight into the motivational factors involved in the poor safety behaviors reported by procrastinators in the current study. Both health self-efficacy and household safety value each partially mediated the relationship between procrastination and safety behaviors.

The links among procrastination, safety behaviors, and health self-efficacy is consistent with the tenets of EVT (Feather, 1992) and Bandura's Social Cognitive theory (1977; 1986), which suggest that strong efficacy beliefs promote behavior initiation and persistence whereas weak efficacy beliefs can contribute to behavior avoidance. Thus, procrastinators are less motivated to engage in behaviors to keep the household safe partially because they believe that they are not capable of performing these behaviors. Considering that these behaviors involve such things as putting away hazardous tools right after they are used, checking the fire alarm batteries, and fixing broken things around the house in a timely manner, it is not surprising that individuals who chronically procrastinate do not feel confident in their ability to keep the household safe.

In the current study household safety value was the more potent predictor of safety behaviors, both in general and for procrastinators. A belief that keeping the home safe and free from potential accidents accounted for the majority of variance in household safety behaviors. This finding is line with other studies that found that values were an important predictor of health behaviour (Pligt & Vries, 1998). According to Feather (1982a), when an individual believes the outcome associated with a behaviour is important they will be more motivated to engage in the behaviour. The results from the current study indicate that household safety is not very important to individuals who chronically procrastinate and therefore they are less likely to follow through with the necessary tasks to keep their household safe. The importance of safety behaviors does not appear to be amendable by previous experiences with household accidents either. Individuals who had experienced a previous household accident also had higher procrastination scores. This finding also suggests a possible causal chain between procrastination, the practice of household safety behaviors and the occurrence of household accidents that future research should examine more closely. Given this possibility and the current findings, interventions that target increasing the value of practicing household safety behaviors may be necessary to improve motivation and subsequent safety behaviors in chronic procrastinators.

Despite the promising findings in the current study with respect to EVT, there are several limitations that should be addressed. The measures of health self-efficacy used in the current study assessed a more general efficacy belief regarding one's health rather than efficacy beliefs about performing safety behaviors. According to Bandura (1977) self-efficacy should be assessed with domain specific scales that address the confidence for performing specific tasks. The relationship of safety behaviors to health-efficacy beliefs in the current study may therefore have been underestimated. Future studies using an EVT framework should strive to include more specific efficacy expectancy measures. Safety behaviors were assessed by a self-report scale as opposed to the actual performance of these behaviors and this may also have influenced the results.

The unique Internet sampling method employed in the present study may have introduced limitations with respect to the sample characteristics. Although Internet users may be expected to have higher socio-economic status than non-users, obtaining a sample by this means may also be a potential strength of the study. An internet-based survey may be an ideal methodology for obtaining a representative sample of procrastinators especially given that researchers have described the Internet as "a virtual procrastination field" (Lavoie & Pychyl, 2001). In addition, it has been demonstrated that samples obtained from Internet recruiting are larger and more heterogeneous than those obtained from the community, and accordingly may be more representative than their community-based counterparts (Krantz & Dalal, 2000).

Overall, the results from the present study highlight the importance of values for predicting household safety behaviors and suggest that EVT may provide a useful and parsimonious framework for explaining motivations for household safety behaviors. Given the human and medical costs of unintentional injuries in the home, and that safety issues within the home can affect all household members, the links between procrastination and household safety behaviors indicated in the current study warrants further investigation. Together, these findings indicate that EVT may provide additional insight into the lack of motivation for safety behaviors demonstrated by procrastinators, and suggest that interventions that target the perceived importance of keeping the home safe and the confidence to carry out safety behaviors are key to improving household safety.

ACKNOWLEDGEMENTS

This research was supported by a research grant (# 410-2005-0094) from the Social Sciences and Humanities Research Council (Canada). Gratitude is expressed to Shanesya Kean and Sabrina Voci for their assistance with data collection.

REFERENCES

Abraham, C., & Sheeran, P. (2000). Understanding and changing health behavior: From health beliefs to self-regulation. In P. Norman & C. Abraham & M. Conner (Eds.), *Understanding and changing health behavior: From health beliefs to self-regulation* (pp. 3-24). Amsterdam: Harwood.

Ajzen, I. (1985). From intentions to actions: A theory of planned behavior. In J. Kuhl & J. Beckman (Eds.), *Action control: From cognition to behavior*. Heidelberg: Springer.

Ajzen, I., & Fishbein, M. (1969). The prediction of behavioral intentions in a choice situation. *Journal of Experimental Social Psychology, 5*, 400-416.

Bandura, A. (1977). Self-efficacy: Toward a unifying theory of behavioral change. *Psychological Review, 84*(2), 191-215.

Baron, R. M., & Kenny, D. A. (1986). The moderator-mediator variable distinction in social psychological research: Conceptual, strategic and statistical considerations. *Journal of Personality and Social Psychology, 51*, 1173-1182.

Booth-Kewley, S., & Vickers, R. R. (1994). Associations between major domains of personality and health behavior. *Journal of Personality, 62*(3), 281-298.

Conner, M., & Norman, P. (1996). *Predicting health behavior*. Buckingham: Open University Press.

Conner, M., & Sparks, P. (1996). The theory of planned behavior and health behaviors. In M. Conner & P. Norman (Eds.), *Predicting health behavior* (pp. 121-162). Buckingham: Open University Press.

Feather, N. T. (1982a). Human values and the prediction of action: An expectancy-valence analysis. In N. T. Feather (Ed.), *Expectations and actions: Expectancy-value models in psychology.* (pp. 263-289). Hillsdale, NJ: Erlbaum.

Feather, N. T. (1992). Values, valences, expectations, and actions. *Journal of Social Issues, 48*, 109-124.

Feather, N. T. (Ed.). (1982b). *Expectations and actions: Expectancy-value models in psychology.* Hillsdale, NJ: Erlbaum.

Ferrari, J. R., & Tice, D. M. (2000). Procrastination as a self-handicap for men and women: A task-avoidance strategy in a laboratory setting. *Journal of Research in Personality, 34*, 73-83.

Fishbein, M. (1967). Attitude and the prediction of behavior. In M. Fishbein (Ed.), *Readings in attitude theory and measurement*. New York: Wiley.

Friedman, H. S. (2000). Long-term relations of personality and health: Dynamisms, mechanisms, tropisms. *Journal of Personality, 68*(6), 1089-1107.

Gielen, A. C., Joffe, A., Dannenberg, A. L., Wilson, M. E. H., & Beilenson, P. L. (1994). Psychosocial factors associated with the use of bicycle helmets among children in counties with and without helmet use laws. *Journal of Pediatrics, 124*, 204–210.

Home Safety Council (2004). The State of Home Safety in America: The Facts About Unintentional Injuries in the Home, Second edition. Wilkesboro: Home Safety Council.

Krantz, J. H., & Dalal, R. (2000). Validity of web-based psychological research. In M. H. Birnbaum (Ed.), *Psychological experiments on the Internet*. San Diego: Academic Press.

Lavoie, J. A. A., & Pychyl, T. A. (2001). Cyberslacking and the procrastination superhighway: A web-based survey of online procrastination, attitudes, and emotion. *Social Science Computer Review, 19*(4), 431-444.

McCown, W. G., & Johnson, J. L. (2001). *The Adult Inventory of Procrastination revised.* Unpublished manuscript.

Norman, P., Abraham, C., & Conner, M. (2000). *Understanding and changing health behavior: From health beliefs to self-regulation*. Amsterdam: Harwood.

Pligt, J., & Vries, N. K. (1998). Belief importance in expectancy-value models of attitudes. *Journal of Applied Social Psychology, 28*(15), 1339-1354.

Preacher, K. J., & Hayes, A. F. (2004). SPSS and SAS procedures for estimating indirect effects in simple mediation models. *Behavior Research Methods, Instruments, and Computers, 36*, 717-731.

Quine, L., Rutter, D. R., & Arnold, L. (2000). Comparing the Theory of Planned Behaviour and the Health Belief Model: the example of safety helmet use among schoolboy cyclists. In P. Norman & C. Abraham & M. Conner (Eds.), *Understanding and Changing Health Behaviour: From Health Beliefs to Self-Regulation* (pp. 73-98). Amsterdam: Harwood.

Rogers, R. W., Deckner, C. W., & Mewborn, C. R. (1978). An expectancy-value theory approach to the long-term modification of smoking behavior. *Journal of Clinical Psychology, 34*(2), 562-566.

Rosenstock, I. (1974). Historical origins of the health belief model. *Health Education Monographs, 2*(4).

Schwarzer, R., & Jerusalem, M. (1995). Generalized self-efficacy scale. In J. Weinman & S. Wright & M. Johnston (Eds.), *Measures in health psychology: A user's portfolio. Causal and control beliefs* (pp. 35-37). Windsor, UK: Nfer-Nelson.

Sirois, F. M. (2003). *Beyond health locus of control: A multidimensional measure of health-related control beliefs and motivations.* Unpublished doctoral dissertation, Carleton University, Ottawa.

Sirois, F. M. (2004). Procrastination and intentions to perform health behaviors: The role of self-efficacy and the consideration of future consequences. *Personality and Individual Differences, 37*, 115-128.

Sirois, F. M., Melia-Gordon, M. L., & Pychyl, T. A. (2003). "I'll look after my health, later": An investigation of procrastination and health. *Personality and Individual Differences, 35*(5), 1167-1184.

Statistics Canada (2002). *Health Indicators, May 2002.*

Trifiletti, L. B., Gielen, A. C., Sleet, D. A., & Hopkins, K. (2005). Behavioral and social sciences theories and models: are they used in unintentional injury prevention research? *Health Education Research 20*(3), 298-307.

West, S. G., Aiken, L. S., & Krull, J. L. (1996). Experimental personality designs: Analyzing categorical by continuous variable interactions. *Journal of Personality, 64,* 1-48.

In: Psychology of Motivation
Editor: Lois V. Brown, pp. 167-179

ISBN: 978-1-60021-598-8
© 2007 Nova Science Publishers, Inc.

Chapter 11

STIMULUS AND INFORMATION SEEKING BEHAVIOR – A COMPARATIVE AND EVOLUTIONARY PERSPECTIVE

Wojciech Pisula[*]

Warsaw School of Social Psychology and Institute of Psychology,
Polish Academy of Sciences, Warsaw, Poland

ABSTRACT

Organisms need information about their own organism's state, and about the surrounding in order to survive and reproduce. Even the simple organisms, such as protozoans utilize instantly available information that is provided by oncoming stimulation. The very first form of stimulus seeking – testing movements - develops in Platyhelminthes. The further evolution of stimulus seeking behavior is discussed in terms of the theory of integrative levels. The new qualities emerging at the developing levels of integration change both mechanisms of behavior, and it's form. The major steps of information seeking behavior evolution are: orienting reflex, locomotor exploration, investigatory responses, perceptual exploration, manipulatory responses, play, and cognitive curiosity. The analysis of each behavioral activity is conducted on the basis of comparative method. The cognitive activity is presented as an product of exploratory activity and play evolution. Therefore, the multi factorial nature of motivation of information seeking is finally discussed.

1. INFORMATION AND STIMULATION

There are many definitions of the term "information", when applied to the behavior of animals and humans. Which one is adopted usually depends on the subject of a particular discussion or analysis. Hence, information can mean one pixel lighting up on the computer screen or the appearance of a new animal in a social group.

[*] Chodakowska 19/31; 03-815 Warsaw, Poland; wojciech.pisula@wp.pl

Organisms on different levels of biological organization are capable of processing and seeking information with various levels of sensory, formal (logical), and material complexity. Therefore, a definition of information that would allow us to compare the behavior of organisms on different steps of the evolutionary ladder must be both broad and detached from a narrow understanding of the specifics of one biological structure. Such definition should account for the functional aspect of information, i.e. its role in behavior regulation. For the purposes of the present analysis, information is defined as an event, accessible to the animal's receptory/perceptual apparatus, which plays a part in regulating behavior through the meaning given to the stimulus by the recipient. It should be noted that both conditions described above must co-occur for the event to be classified as information. A number of events in the environment or within the organism itself may be accessible to the animal's perceptual apparatus, but if the animal is incapable of using that stimulation as behavioral regulator, then it does not translate into information. A stimulus becomes a piece of information only if the recipient is capable of endowing it with that feature. The same sensory stimulus, e.g. a scent left by an animal, may carry social information for other representatives of the same species, and food-related message for a predator hunting for the animal that produced the stimulus. Thus, the concept of information, which is useful in the analysis of animal and human behavior, must be placed within the context of the entire biological and ecological system in which a given organism exists. Those events that may have informative properties constitute a subset of sensory stimulation accessible to the animal's sensory or perceptual apparatus. This general rule is demonstrated in Figure 1.

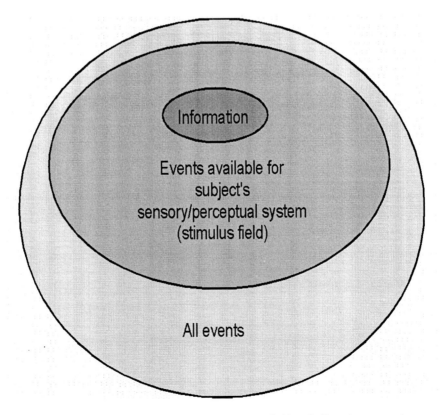

Figure 1. The position of the information within the stimulus field and all environmental events.

2. MAKING USE OF CONSTANTLY AVAILABLE INFORMATION

In some situations information is constantly available. Lower organisms often regulate their behavior based on information that is constantly available to their senses. This phenomenon was first described by H.S. Jennings (1906). In a plethora of experiments, Jennings documented the capability of simple organisms to use complex behavioral regulation based on external input. In his studies, the carriers of information were chemical, thermal, electric, and light stimuli. He came to fascinating conclusions. In the closing chapters of his monograph, Jennings described the ability of simple organisms to differentiate stimuli. This differentiation involves a negative (withdrawal) or positive (approach) [1] response to stimulus, a change of direction or the animal resuming or stopping its locomotion.

Behaviors regulated by information continuously available to the organism are classified as basic forms of behavior. And so, paramecium reacts to a light or thermal stimulus by performing a number of locomotor movements. Locomotion stops when the intensity of the stimulus becomes optimal for paramecium (Jennings, 1906). The example of *paramecium* is an excellent illustration of the principle described in item 1. Objectively speaking, stimulation has a certain intensity and direction. paramecium, however, is unable to use that second bit of information. The movements it performs are not oriented relative to the direction of the stimulus; they are classified as kineses. Similar behavior is found in woodlice, which initiate locomotion whenever the environment becomes too dry, and stop as soon as they reach damper ground (Gould, 1982). A higher form of behavior using continuously available information is taxis. Taxis involves the adoption of a specific body orientation relative to the direction of the stimulus, i.e. it is stimulus-oriented (Gould, 1982)

As it was rightly noted by K. Lorenz (1982), mechanisms of response to information continuously available to the organism are very common and can be found in all organisms. Behaviors such as tropism, kinesis, and taxis are indeed found in all animals. An important feature of all those forms of behavior is their response-based nature. The animal does not seek out information, but receives it from the environment and reacts to it depending on the capabilities of its sensory and executive apparatus.

3. TWO MILESTONES IN THE DEVELOPMENT OF INFORMATION SEEKING BEHAVIOR: TESTING MOVEMENTS AND LEARNING

When studying the behavior of flatworms, Jennings (1906) discovered a phenomenon, which he called *testing movements*. This is how he described it: "If the glinding Planaria comes to a region of considerably higher or lower temperature, it waves its head back and forth several times, apparently till it has determined the direction which leads back to the usual temperature, then turns and moves in that direction." (Jennings, 1906, p. 244). There is no doubt that what we have here is a description of the most basic form of information seeking. The animal receives information about the intensity of stimulation, and seeks information about the gradient of that intensity. Behavior of an organism taking the form of

---

[1]Positive vs. negative responses are elements of a broader theory of behavior regulation known as the Approach/Withdrawal theory (Maier, & Schneirla, 1935).

initiating testing movements in response to external information is found in all *Metazoa*, beginning with *Platyhelminthes*. Qualitatively new from the evolutionary perspective, this phenomenon may be related to the emergence of a new level of behavior control: a primitive brain in the form of *cephalic ganglia*.

In *Platyhelminthes*, there is also an advanced form of behavior modification, namely learning. For the purposes of the present paper, I adopted a broad definition offered by S.J. Shettleworth (1998, p. 100), which reads: "Learning or equivalent memory, is a change resulting from experience." Studies (Thompson and McConnell, 1955; Jacobson, Horowitz, and Fried, 1967) demonstrated that flatworms have the ability to make associations between pairs of events, in a Pavlovian pattern. The importance of that associative ability is often underrated. A couple of elements of that emergent quality in the regulation of behavior are important for the present analysis. Animals must be equipped with the ability to store information. This in turn opens new possibilities and creates new requirements. The emergence of memory enables the animal to compare a previously memorized stimulus with the one it is currently experiencing. At the same time, it forces the animal to make that comparison. If it was optional, it would cause incorrect responses and result in costs that would not have to be borne by individuals making such comparisons. At the basic level, the result of a comparison leads to simple conclusions about the stimulus, e.g. known (associated), unknown (no associations). Thus, even at the most basic level of integration, learning introduces a new element into behavioral regulation: the ability to differentiate between already familiarized and NOVEL stimuli. From that stage onwards, novel stimuli are a key element regulating information-seeking type behaviors. The two emergent qualities in the behavior of animals described above combine to create a new, far more advanced level of information-seeking integration.

4. THEORY OF INTEGRATING LEVELS AS THE TOOL FOR UNDERSTANDING BEHAVIOR DEVELOPMENT

The phrases "emergent quality" and "level of integration" used in the preceding paragraph refer to the approach called the "Integrative Levels" theory. The advanced version of that theory was put forward by J. Feibleman (1954).

Feibleman (1954) published a useful summary of this important concept.

- "Each level organizes the level or levels below it plus one emergent quality." (p. 59). Each behavioral act may be described in terms of muscle reflexes, but for some behaviors these will be not enough.
- "In any organization the higher level depends upon the lower." (p.60). Destruction of the sensory-motor system disturbs behavior, but the reverse is not the case.
- "For an organization at any given level, its mechanism lies at the level below and its purpose at the level above." (p.61). This is obvious when we consider that an analysis moves from the whole to its parts. Nerve cells can tell us about mechanisms of brain functioning, but not about the purpose or function of the brain processes.
- "It is impossible to reduce a higher level to the lower." (p.62). To reduce a higher to a lower level means to lose the quality which emerged at this level.

These descriptive points are supplemented by others which relate to explanation, especially of behavioral phenomena. Two of these are:

- "The analysis of the phenomenon must be at the lowest level which will provide sufficient explanation." (p.63). In fact, this rule has been widely accepted by comparative psychologists in another formulation known as "Morgan's cannon". I believe that it is worth quoting again: "In no case may we interpret an action as the outcome of the exercise of a higher psychical faculty, if it can be interpreted as the outcome of the exercise of one which stands lower in psychological scale." (Morgan, 1894, p. 53).
- "The reference of any organization must be to the highest level which its explanation requires." (p.64). That is to say: one cannot explain the phenomenon without bringing to the explanation elements belonging to the highest level of the phenomenon.

This approach was found to be useful for the purpose of behavior analysis (Pisula, 1998; Greenberg, Partrige, Weiss, & Pisula, 2004). In the next paragraphs, I am going to propose an application of the integrative levels theory to the analysis of the information seeking behavior.

5. TAXES AND ORIENTING REFLEX

Any analysis of behavior within the framework of the integrative levels theory must include three levels: descriptive, functional and that of mechanisms (Pisula, 1998). When analyzing the development of a given behavior, however, we must also take into account others, such as the level of phylogenetic and ontogenetic advancement. To a large extent, information-seeking behavior is represented by the animals' exploratory behaviors. Nevertheless, exploratory acts do not account for the entire range of information seeking behavior, e.g. for play.

One approach to the analysis of exploratory behavior from the point of view of the integrative levels theory was proposed by Pisula (1998). If we refer to the systematization presented in that paper, we can attempt to associate forms of exploration with the development of information seeking, from the simplest forms (orienting response), to more sophisticated ones (cognitive activity). It must be emphasized that any reference to information seeking stresses the animal's own activity, while the fundamental reaction of an organism to external information is by nature responsive, as it involves a reaction to stimuli received from the environment. This is characteristic of the aforementioned taxis, and the orienting reflex found in vertebrates. Without getting into details of the orienting reflex in vertebrates, we can conclude that it is released by a sudden, unexpected (for the organism) stimulus. Information seeking in response to a stimulus is mostly oriented towards finding its source. It is a strictly short-term response of an organism to a clear, unexpected sensory stimulus. The orienting reflex is typical for the behavior observed in vertebrates.

6. Further Advancement in the Development of Information Seeking Behavior – Locomotor Exploration

The basic form of information seeking is the behavior commonly referred to as locomotor exploration (Pisula, 1998). It involves covering the area available to the animal. Its main purpose is to learn topographical information about the surroundings. This form of gathering information develops in animals equipped with the ability to form representations of the space in which they exist. It is also the most basic form of information seeking, which can be described as controlled behavior (Pisula, 2001).

D. Berlyne (1963) classified locomotor exploration as one of three main forms of exploratory behaviors, along with orienting and investigatory reflexes. It is inevitable that such a general categorization places many different forms of behavior into one category. One of the forms of locomotor exploration is patrolling behavior. Birke and Archer (1983) used that term to describe behavior involving systematic traversing of familiar space, usually the animal's own territory. Obviously, "familiar space" is not a particularly precise term, as it begs the question *how familiar*? An animal functioning in its environment forms a representation of its surroundings. Such representation may be more or less complex. It can include objects with well-recognized features, represented in the form of the animal's mental representation or poorly defined objects, with a simple structure of representation. E.C. Tolman (1948) proposed a hypothesis, according to which the function of exploratory behavior is to construct a cognitive map. This was probably the first scientific attempt at analyzing animal behavior in the context of gathering information at the cognitive level.

Later studies by N. Tinbergen (1951) shed more light on the issue of cognitive maps. In his seminal research on the behavior of digger wasp, Tinbergen demonstrated that animals seek specific information. In terms of spatial orientation, they look for the so-called landmark, and subsequently direct their behavior relative to that spatial cue. This mechanism is a very common strategy of spatial orientation. Locomotor play is sometimes associated with exploration. It must be emphasized, however, that it provides a different kind of information, and is a form of behavior found in fewer animals compared with the very common locomotor exploration.

7. Information Seeking at the Lower Cognitive Level – Perceptual Exploration and Investigatory Responses

Locomotor exploration provides information about the location of important objects in space through mental representations the animal creates of this objects. However, learning the properties of these objects and their relationship to other elements in the environment occurs through perceptual exploration and investigatory responses (Pisula, 1998, 2004). The two forms of activity allow the animal to enrich existing representations of objects with their properties and attributes. Perceptual exploration makes it possible to replenish the existing representation of an object or area with information about its stimulatory properties. Manipulatory responses allow the animal to add information about the weight and structure of the object under exploration. They also enable it to form contingencies between a given behavior and the environment. Both forms of information gathering depend on the ability to construct complex cognitive representations of objects. It is therefore the prerequisite of higher forms of information seeking – knowledge seeking at the cognitive level.

An important new element appearing at this level of integration of information seeking is that the properties of an object become of key importance for the regulation of that behavior. Complex, novel stimuli (objects) become a powerful incentive to initiate exploratory and manipulative activities. There is also a new dimension to novelty. It involves not only a relocation of a familiar object in space or an appearance (or removal) of a new object. All that is required to set off exploration is a change in the object's properties.

8. COGNITIVE ACTIVITY AS INFORMATION SEEKING BEHAVIOR

Daniel Berlyne was probably the first researcher to notice the close relationship between exploratory behaviors and cognitive activity (Berylne, 1963). Berlyne used the term knowledge-seeking behavior. He emphasized the symbolic character of knowledge acquired in this manner. For the perspective adopted in this paper, it is worthwhile to evoke again the idea put forward in the introduction: the informative value of a stimulus depends on the recipient's ability to endow that stimulus with meaning. Thus it is obvious that if the subject is capable of symbolic operations, stimulation may be processed in this way. Consequently, the informative value of this stimulation for that recipient will be higher than for a recipient not equipped with symbolic processing abilities.

We should mention here once more the tenets of the integrative levels theory. It is obvious that symbolic behavior (knowledge-seeking) is dependent on the lower levels of behavior integration (e.g. exploration), and contains these lower-level components. However, this level of behavior cannot be reduced to lower levels (Pisula, 1998). Berlyne classified the following basic types of activity as the highest level of integration: epistemic observation, consultation and directed thinking. Within the integrative levels framework, epistemic observation must be categorized as a sophisticated form of perceptual exploration, while consultation rather belongs to information seeking, together with directed thinking. This modification does not seem to run counter to Berlyne's intentions, as hi placed directed thinking at a privileged position in terms of behavior regulation. What it does, on the other hand, is to take into account the integrative levels and ecological approach (Gibson, 1979) that emphasizes the dependence of the stimulus' meaning on the individual's perceptual abilities.

9. PLAY AS INFORMATION SEEKING BEHAVIOR

The adaptive function of play is typically defined in terms of gathering information by the playing animal. The information may be related to the animals own body movements (play with one's body, e.g. jumping, falling, sudden spurts, etc.) (Fagen, 1981). Gathering information through play may also be related to the properties of inanimate objects (toys). Researchers studying play behaviors were also interested in the social aspects of play, such as the social skills training. R. Fagen (1981), one of the most experienced researchers in the field, noted how closely it is connected with "underdefined" environment and equally underspecified behavior. This hypothesis was recently developed into a definition of play as training for the unexpected social or physical event (Spinka, Newberry, i Bekoff, 2001). This interpretation of play closely corresponds with the mechanism of behavior regulation proposed by Inglis (2000), namely uncertainty reduction.

Notably, individual forms of play, ordered from the simplest (solitary play) to the most complex (social play), reduce different types of uncertainty. We can conclude that they correspond to different, ever higher levels of integration of that form of information seeking. What clearly distinguishes play from other forms of information seeking is the motivational mechanism. It seems, however, that there is a certain overlap between various theoretical concepts. While we cannot rule out the possibility that receiving stimulation and information produces a certain type of pleasure (for higher organisms), we must note that the dominant role is played by uncertainty reduction. This uncertainty, regardless of the adopted theoretical approach, is invariably related to the aversive motivational state. However, play is dominated by hedonistic mechanisms (Bekoff, 2004), which are philogenetically more recent and which regulate the behavior of a smaller number of species.

10. THE PROBLEM OF NEOPHOBIA AND NEOPHILIA WITH RESPECT TO NOVELTY AND INFORMATION

In 1906, H. Jennings noted that there are two basic forms of responding to external stimuli: positive, involving approach, and negative (withdrawal), demonstrated by moving away from the source of the stimulus. This is a universal phenomenon, i.e. it is found in the simplest of organisms (e.g. amoeba) and complex eumetazoans. Building on Jennings' idea, T.C. Schneirla (Maier and Schneirla, 1935; Schneirla, 1959)put forward a dual process theory of behavior regulation, according to which weak stimulation triggers processes causing the organism to approach the source of the stimulus, while weak stimulation results in withdrawal. While in the case o simple organisms the terms approach and withdrawal emphasized the behavioral nature of the phenomenon, when talking about higher organisms, researchers prefer to use the terms seeking/approaching and avoidance. This way of thinking was present both in theoretical ideas on processing stimulation, and in papers devoted to the behavior of organisms towards novel stimuli. S.A. Barnett (1963) stressed the threatening aspect of novelty (neophobia), while D. Berlyne (1960) and M. Zuckerman (2003) put emphasis on novelty seeking. This traditional approach has its proponents today. J. Hogan (2005) expressed it very clearly "... I consider fear and exploration to be unitary system that is expressed as approach at low levels, withdrawal at moderate levels and immobility at high levels." p. 61. I will challenge this comprehensive approach, which treats neophobia and neophilia as two extremes of one dimension/process further on.

The key issue for the analysis of the rewarding aspects of novelty is the definition of novelty. Novelty is often defined as "change in stimulus conditions from previous experience" (Bevins, Klebaur, & Bardo, 1997, p. 114). It is therefore clear that the novelty effect only occurs when the organism is capable of learning. The rewarding properties of novelty have two components. The first one is related to the fundamental mechanism of sensory reinforcement, revealed in 1950s and incorporated into a theoretical system by D.O.

Hebb (1955)and Kish (1966). Sensory reinformcement is a primitive mechanism present in animal behavior, which is largely independent of novelty. Rats learn to push a lever in Skinner boxes by being rewarded with a weak light stimulus, and that effect does not disappear with progress in learning. Once a complete contingency between the behavior and stimulus exposition is established, the reinforcement mechanism does not fade. Animals still display instrumental reactions, despite the lack of novelty and the message that there is no element of uncertainty in a given situation. This phase of behavior can be described as stimulus-seeking behavior (Pisula & Matysiak, 1998). The heart of the controversy surrounding the rewarding properties of novelty is the concept of novelty itself. There is a general consensus that novelty should be viewed as a continuum stretching between complete familiarity and complete novelty (Bevins, 2001). Furthermore, it is well documented that with low stimulus intensity animals prefer novel stimuli (Berlyne, 1963; Bevins, 2001; Pisula, 2003; Pisula & Siegel, 2005). Interpretative problems emerge in the analysis of animals' behavior towards complete novelty. What needs to be determined here is whether complete novelty is merely a complete change in the configuration of the elements of the environment, or whether it should also include a change in the intensity of stimulation.

Rats are especially useful in detailed analysis of the relationship between neophobia and neophilia, because their behavior is characterized by two apparently contradictory trends: strong neophilia (novelty seeking) and strong neophobia (fear of novelty). Those properties of rats' behavior attracted the attention of the researchers who laid the foundations for the study of animal behavior (Barnett, 1963; Calhoun, 1963; Cowan, 1977). In the theoretical approach based on the unitary drives tradition (Jennigs, 1096; Mair & Schneirla, 1935; Hebb, 1955; Hogan 2004) it is a question of novelty intensity. Low or medium intensity produces approach, while high intensity results in withdrawal or immobility (Hogan, 2004). More recent data put a question mark over this concept. R.A. Rosellini & D. R. Widman (1989) demonstrated, that experiencing emotional pressure reduces the intensity and variety of the exploratory behaviors in rats. They interpreted this effect in terms of the rats' sensitization to predation resulting from the stress. Thus, they emphasized the ecological context of exploration measurements. Interestingly, in the rats subjected to stress in this study, the intensity of exploration of a new object increased with each session. In terms of the description based on the unitary drives theory, rats subjected to a stressor initially demonstrated withdrawal (Schneirla, 1959, 1965; Hogan 2004), while controls demonstrated approach. Results consistent with the above data were obtained by W. Pisula & J. Osinski (2000). Two psychogenetically selected sublines of Roman High-Avoidance (RHA) and Roman Low-Avoidance (RHA) rats were tested. There are reasons to interpret differences between those two sublines in terms of emotional reactivity, i.e. high reactivity of the RLA subline and low reactivity of the RHA subline (Gentsch, Lichsteiner, Driscoll and Feer, 1982; Pisula & Osinski 2000). Rats with high emotional reactivity demonstrated fewer and less varied exploratory behaviors than the low reactivity subline.

Thus it is established that the experience of emotional stress, whether caused by experimental manipulation (Rosellini & Widman ,1989) or individual traits (Pisula & Osinski, 2000), inhibits novelty seeking. Not every event in the environment, however, causes emotional anxiety. It seems that there are objective, novelty-independent parameters of stimulation that trigger an emotional response. Those are: intensity of stimulation and the pace at which that intensity is increasing (Osinski, 2003). The fact that exploration is inhibited by emotional stress is not in itself a proof o the integral relationship between those two mechanisms. K. Lorenz noted as early as 1982 that exploration occurs in a field devoid of tension. P.E. Cowan (1977) pointed out that neophobia is the animal's specific adaptation to environmental conditions in which it exists. This opinion is supported by current research. Following their detailed studies on exploration in parrots, C. Mettke-Hoffman, H. Winkler and B. Leisler (2002) concluded that neophobia and exploration evolved independently, and that "[they] are also functionally independent." (p. 269).

11. REWARDING VALUE OF NOVELTY AND INFORMATION

There is a lot of data in support of the claim that novelty has its own rewarding value, independent of other properties of a stimulus. W.H. Nissen (1930) demonstrated that rats are willing to endure electric shock if rewarded by being able to enter a maze. M.T. Bardo and R. A. Bevins (2000) showed that rats spent more time in the experimental cage zone previously associated with novelty. Nevertheless, it is difficult to decide whether the fact that the animal focuses on a stimulus is a result of its novelty, or its informational significance.

In a study on response to novelty in low-stress conditions (Pisula, 2003) responses to two types of change in a familiar setting were analyzed: spatial rearrangement and visual change of the pattern displayed on the computer screen. It was found that whereas rats can discriminate complex visual stimuli (Gaffan and Woolmore, 1996) and detect the changes in light brightness (Hughes, 1999), these findings show that when they are attracted by two distinct sorts of novelty (visual versus space rearrangement), they ignore the visual change and rather engage in investigation of the spatial properties of their surroundings. One may easily imagine that the potentially adaptive significance of spatial change is much greater than the change of location of a picture on the wall. Another study (Pisula & Siegel,2005) demonstrated that novelty and stimulus complexity have different impact on various forms of exploration. At the lower, locomotor level (see Pisula, 1998 for classification), it is the change itself that is significant. Both increasing and decreasing complexity of the setting resulted in increased intensity of exploration. By contrast, the analysis of rats' interactions with objects showed that their responses differed depending on sex and type of change. Males demonstrated markedly stronger responses to the introduction of a new object to the experimental cage and to removal of an object from the cage when compared to females. Both these studies (Pisula, 2003; Pisula & Siegel, 2005) revealed the difference in the effect of novelty itself and the significance of perceived change. Rats focused their attention on environmentally significant changes, such as a relocation of important objects in space (Pisula, 2003). In a study on complexity (Pisula & Siegel, 2005), male rats spent more time examining a new object than females. We can suspect that the stronger territoriality of male rats caused them to interpret the appearance of a new object differently than females. In all probability, the appearance of an unknown in a familiarized space was an important information for male rats, more so than for females.

The distinct role of novelty and informative value of a stimulus in behavior regulation was also demonstrated in another study (Pisula, Stryjek and Nałęcz-Tolak, 2006). Experiment II of the study involved a comparison of responses to novelty of rats habituated to stable vs. constantly changing environment. As was the case in previously cited studies, rats preferred changeable environment to static one (i.e. they spent more time in the former). Direct response to test event (introduction of a new object) resulted in a similar reaction in both groups of rats. However, rats used to a very changeable setting habituated quickly, while those that had not previously experienced changeability examined the new object much longer. We can suspect that they were not attracted by novelty, but by the informative value. Rats accustomed to changeability "knew" that a change in a section of the experimental cage did not imply the occurrence biologically important events. Rats used to a static environment ascribed a potentially greater environmental significance to an unfamiliar event. The study revealed the distinctiveness of a rewarding value of the novelty effect and a rewarding informative significance of an event, which is separate from novelty.

An interesting hypothesis about the reward mechanisms at the core of information seeking was recently published by I. Biederman and E. A. Vessel (2006). These researchers associate the phenomenon of perceptual pleasure with the opioid system and treat it as the key element of the motivational basis for information seeking.

12. CONCLUSIONS

Arguments and research results quoted above enable us to propose a number of statements describing the main functions of information seeking behavior and its status among other forms of behavior.

A. Animals make active use of environmental information. The informative value of a signal received is determined by its relationship to other biologically significant events in the animal's environment, as well as the animal's perceptual abilities and information processing skills.

B. The emergence of the ability to store information provided the basis for the development of novelty detection and active information seeking. This was a very early development, as it occurred concurrently with the appearance of ganglia in Platyhelminthes, if not earlier. From that developmental stage onwards, information seeking became the fundamental component of behavioral repertoire.

C. The development of information seeking behavior was possible due to the expanding capabilities of the perceptual apparatus and growing resources of the nervous system. The right tool for the analysis of this phenomenon is the integrative levels theory, as it is capable of accounting for newly emerging qualities in this category of behavior.

D. Due to its adaptive role, information seeking behavior has a very high/dominant position in the hierarchy of needs.

E. The mechanism driving behavior directed towards gathering new information is the reinforcing property of stimulation, information and novelty. In humans, perceptual pleasure and cognitive curiosity are the central elements of information seeking behavior.

REFERENCES

Bardo M.T. & Bevins R.A. (2000). Conditioned place preference: what does it add to our pre-clinical understanding of drug reward? *Psychopharmacology, 153,* 31-43.

Barnett, S.A. (1963). *The rat: a study of behaviour.* Chicago: Aldine.

Berlyne, D.E. (1963). Motivation problems raised by exploratory and epistemic behavior. W: S.Koch (Ed.) *Psychology: a study of science,* vol. 5, p 285-364. New York-Toronto-London: McGraw-Hill.

Bevins R.A. (2001). Novelty seeking and reward: implications for the study of high-risk behaviors. *Current Directions in Psychological Science, 10,* 189-193.

Bevins R.A., Klebaur J.E., & Bardo M.T. (1997). Individual differences in response to novelty, amphetamine-induced activity and drug discrimination in rats. *Behavioural Pharmacology, 8,* 113-123.

Biederman I., and Vessel E. A. (2006). Perceptual pleasure and the brain. *American Scientist, 94,* 247-253.

Calhoun, J.B. (1963). *The ecology and sociology of the norway rat.* Bethesda, Maryland: U.S. Department of health, education, and welfare.

Cowan P.E. (1977). Neophobia and neophilia: new-object and new-place reactions of three *Rattus* species. *Journal of Comparative and Physiological Psychology, 91,* 63-71.

Fagen, R. (1981). *Animal play behavior.* New York: Oxford University.

Feibleman, J.K. (1954). Theory of integrative levels. *The Brittish Journal for the Philosophy of Science, 5,* 59-66.

Gallistel, C.R. (1990). Representations in animal cognition: An introduction. *Cognition, 37,* 1-22.

Gentsch, C., Lichsteiner, M., Driscoll, P. and Feer, H. (1982). Differential hormonal and physiological responses to stress in Roman High and Low avoidance rats. *Physiology and Behavior, 28,* 259-263.

Gibson, J. J. (1979). *The ecological approach to visual perception.* Boston: Houghton Mifflin.

Gould, J. L. (1982). *Ethology. Mechanisms and Evolution of Behavior.* New York: W.W. Norton and Company.

Greenberg, G., Partrige, T., Weiss, E. & Pisula, W. (2004). Comparative psychology – A new perspective for the 21st century: Up the spiral staircase. *Developmental Psychobiology, 44,* 1-15.

Hebb, D.O. (1955). Drives and the C.N.S. (Conceptual nervous system). *Psychological Review, 62,* 243-254.

Hogan, J. A. (2005). Motivation. In: J.J. Bolhuis, and L. Giraldeau (Eds). *The behavior of animals: mechanisms, function, and evolution,* (pp 41-71). Oxford: Blackwell.

Hughes, R.N. (1999). Sex differences in novelty-related location preferences of hooded rats. *The Quarterly Journal of experimental Psychology, 52B,* 235-252.

Jacobson A.L., Horowitz S.D., and Fried C. (1967). Classical conditioning, pseudoconditioning, or sensitization in the planarian. *Journal of Comparative and Physiological Psychology, 64,* 73-79.

Jennings, H.S. (1906). *The behavior of lower organisms.* New York: Columbia University Press.

Kish, G.B. (1966). Studies of sensory reinforcement. In: W.K. Honig (Ed.) *Operant behavior*, (pp. 57-83). New-York: Appleton-Century-Crofts.

Lorenz, K.Z. (1982). *The foundations of ethology*. New York: Simon & Schuster.

Maier, N.R.F. & Schneirla, T.C. (1935). *Priciples of Animal Psychology*. New York: McGraw-Hill.

Mettke-Hoffman C., Winkler H. and Leisler B. (2002). The significance of ecological factors for exploration and neophobia in Parrots. *Ethology, 108*, 249-272.

Morgan C.L. (1894). *An introduction to comparative psychology*. London: Scott.

Nissen, H.W. (1930). A study of exploratory behavior in the white rat by means of the obstruction method. *Journal of Genetic Psychology, 37*, 361-367.

Osinski, J.T. (2003). The effect of gradual and sudden exposure to stressor on stimulus seeking behavior and emotional reaktivity in rats. *Polish Psychological Bulletin, 34*, 197-201.

Pisula W., Stryjek R. And Nałęcz-Tolak A. (2006). Response to novelty of various types in laboratory rats. *Acta Neurobiologiae Experimentalis, 66*, 235-243.

Pisula, W. (2003). The Roman high- and low-avoidance rats respond differently to novelty in a familiarized environment. *Behavioural Processes, 43*, 63-72.

Pisula, W. & Matysiak, J. (1998). Stimulus-seeking behavior. In: G. Greenberg & M.M. Haraway (Eds). *Comparative Psychology: A Handbook* (pp. 198-202). New York: Garland.

Pisula, W. & Siegel, J. (2005). Exploratory behavior as a function of environmental novelty and complexity in male and female rats. *Psychological Reports, 97*, 631-638.

Pisula, W. (1998). Integrative levels in comparative psychology - the example of exploratory behavior. *European Psychologist, 3*, 62-69.

Pisula, W. (2004). Exploratory behavior – inquisitiveness in animals. In: M. Bekoff (Ed.) *Encyclopedia of Animal Behavior* (pp. 574-581). Westport, Connecticut; London: Greenwood Press.

Rosellini R.A. & Widman D.R. (1989). Prior exposure to stress reduces the diversity of exploratory behavior of novel objects in the rat (Rattus norvegicus). *Journal of Comparative Psychology, 103*, 339-346.

Schneirla, T.C. (1959). An evolutionary and developmental theory of biphasic process underlying approach and withdrawal. In: M.J. Jones (Ed.), *Nebraska Symposium on Motivation* (vol. 7, pp. 1-42). Lincoln: University of Nebraska Press.

Schneirla, T.C. (1965). Aspects of stimulation and organization in approach/withdrawal processes underlying vertebrate behavioral development. In: D.S. Lehrman, R.A. Hinde, and E. Shaw (Eds). *Advances in the study of behavior* (pp. 1-71). New York: Academic Press.

Shettleworth, S.J. (1998). *Cognition, evolution, and behavior*. New York: Oxford University Press.

Spinka, M., Newberry, R.C., and Bekoff, M. (2001). Mammalian play: training or the unexpected. *The Quarterly Review of Biology, 76*, 141-168.

Thompson R., and McConnell J. (1955). Classical conditioning in the planarian, *Dugesia dorotocephala*. *Journal of Comparative and Physiological Psychology, 48*, 65-68.

Tinbergen, N. (1951). *The study of instinct*. London: Oxford University Press.

Tolman, E.C. (1948). Cognitive maps in rats and men. *Psychological Review, 55*, 189-208.

In: Psychology of Motivation
Editor: Lois V. Brown, pp. 181-190

ISBN: 978-1-60021-598-8
© 2007 Nova Science Publishers, Inc.

Chapter 12

PSYCHOSOCIAL CORRELATES OF PERSONAL NORMS

K. P. H. Lemmens, R. A. C. Ruiter,
I. J. T. Veldhuizen and H. P. Schaalma

Maastricht University; Sanquin Blood Bank, Southeast Region, The Netherlands

ABSTRACT

Personal norms are the main motivator of intention to perform pro-social behaviour. They reflect the beliefs people have about what is right and what is wrong. Schwartz's norm activation model states that awareness of consequences and ascription of responsibility are related to personal norms, but it is not clear how, as the norm activation model can be interpreted as a moderator and a mediator model. In this chapter we compared both interpretations of the norm activation model and found that our data support a mediator model. This means that personal norms are influenced by awareness of consequences and ascription of responsibility. Targeting awareness of consequences and ascription of responsibility would activate personal norms which increases the behavioural intention.

INTRODUCTION

We often do something just because we feel like we have to do it, and not because we like doing it or will benefit from the behaviour. This accounts for a great variety of behaviours in our daily life. Indeed, often we feel a moral obligation to do something. This moral obligation is reflected in the *personal norm* we have regarding that behaviour, and reflects our beliefs about what is right and wrong to do.

Personal norms have been found to be of importance in a wide variety of pro-social and pro-environmental behaviours, like helping in an emergency (Schwartz & Clausen, 1970; Schwartz & David, 1976), donating bone marrow (Schwartz, 1970, 1973), donating blood (Armitage & Conner, 2001; Lemmens et al., 2005; Lemmens et al., submitted), volunteering (Schwartz & Fleishman, 1978; Schwartz & Howard, 1980), eating organic foods (Sparks &

Shepherd, 2002; Sparks, Shepherd, & Frewer, 1995; Thøgersen, 2002), buying environmentally friendly products (Harland, 2001; Minton & Rose, 1997; Nordlund & Garvill, 2002), recycling behaviour (Bratt, 1999; Hopper & Nielsen, 1991; Nordlund & Garvill, 2002), reducing car use (Bamberg & Schmidt, 2003; Harland, 2001; Matthies, Klöckner, & Preißner, 2006; Nordlund & Garvill, 2002), energy conservation (Harland, 2001), and support environmental protection organizations (Gärling, Fujii, Gärling, & Jakobsson, 2003; Harland, 2001; Stern, Dietz, & Black, 1986).

As personal norm is an important motivator of behaviour, it is important to gain more insight in its determinants and how these are related to each other. Therefore, we will use Schwartz's norm activation model. This model has often been used to study personal norms in pro-social and pro-environmental behaviour. It suggests that personal norms only influence behaviour when two preconditions are met. First, individuals must be aware that their potential actions have consequences for the welfare of others (awareness of consequences). Second, they must feel a degree of personal responsibility for these actions and potential consequences (Schwartz, 1970).

It is not clear how awareness of consequences, ascription of responsibility, and personal norms are related to each other. The model can be interpreted in two ways. In the first interpretation, personal norms only influence intention when the individual is both aware of the consequences of not taking action (*awareness of consequences*) and when he feels some kind of responsibility to do something (*ascription of responsibility*).

According to this interpretation –the norm activation model as a moderator model– personal norms, awareness of consequences, as well as ascription of responsibility need to be targeted in order to make sure that personal norms increase behavioural intention. The second interpretation says that awareness of consequences and ascriptions of responsibility are the antecedents of personal norms and that personal norms, in turn, influence intention. This means that personal norms can be activated by targeting awareness of consequences and ascription of responsibility. This reflects a mediator model in which the effects of awareness of consequences and ascription of responsibility on behavioural intention are mediated through personal norms.

It is important to distinguish between a moderator and a mediator model. When the relationship between personal norms and intention is moderated by awareness of consequences or ascription of responsibility, these norms lead to a positive intention when awareness of consequences and ascription of responsibility are high, but it leads to a neutral or negative intention when both are low. Ignoring these moderators can lead to the erroneous conclusions that personal norms do not affect intentions. When personal norms mediate the relation between awareness of consequences and intention or ascription of responsibility and intention, this means that personal norms can be influenced by inducing awareness of consequences and ascription of responsibility and thus strengthen the effect of personal norm on behavioural intention.

Some studies have found evidence for the norm activation model as a moderator model. Schwartz (1968) asked students to decide what the main character of a story would do in various interpersonal moral situations (for example, getting up early and be ready when your friends arrive or stay in bed until the last moment and have your friends wait for you). They also completed a questionnaire measuring their scores on general awareness of consequences and ascription of responsibility. It appeared that personal norms had a stronger effect on behaviour scores when students were high in awareness of consequences, compared to those scoring low. For the students with high awareness of consequences, personal norms had a stronger impact on behaviour scores for students high in ascription of responsibility. In another study Schwartz (1973) showed that personal norms had only an effect on donating bone marrow intention for females high in ascription of responsibility, but not for those with low scores. Hopper and Nielsen (1991) showed that personal norms only influence recycling behaviour for people high in awareness of consequences.

Other studies have found evidence for the mediator interpretation of the norm activation model. Gärling et al. (2003) studied the role of personal norms in reducing car use. They found that intention to reduce car use was causally related to personal norm, which, in turn, was causally related to awareness of consequences and ascription of responsibility. Stern, Dietz, Abel, Guagnano, and Kalof (1999) showed that personal norms mediate the relationship between awareness of consequences, ascription of responsibility and intentions to support environmentalism (e.g. buy environmentally friendly household products, support environmental group, and pay higher taxes to protect the environment). Stern et al. (1986) showed that personal norms for industry action (e.g. attend public meetings about chemical waste, write letters to newspaper or legislators, and participating is boycotts and demonstrations against chemical waste) are predicted by ascription of responsibility and awareness of harmful consequences of hazardous chemicals. Bamberg and Schmidt (2003) found that car use for university routes among students was predicted by personal norm, which in turn, was predicted by awareness of consequences.

PERSONAL NORM AND BLOOD DONATION

Worldwide many lives depend on the availability of a safe blood supply. The Netherlands, just like many other countries, depend on voluntary and non-remunerated donation. Personal norm is an important determinant of the intention to donate blood (Armitage & Conner, 2001; Lemmens et al., 2005; Lemmens et al., submitted), but the role of awareness of consequences and ascription of responsibility have not yet been studied. Whether awareness of consequences and ascription of responsibility are related to personal norms in a moderator or mediator model has implications for health education.

PRESENT STUDY

In this chapter we compared both the moderator and the mediator interpretation of the norm activation model in the context of blood donation. Awareness of consequences, ascription of responsibility, personal norm, and intention to donate blood were measured and used to compare both the moderator and mediator model.

PARTICIPANTS AND PROCEDURE

A survey was conducted among Dutch adults to measure blood donation cognitions. Participants were recruited from psychology courses at the Open University in the

Netherlands or through an internet research agency. They received an email invitation to participate in an on-line survey, explaining that we were interested in the views of both donors and non-donors, assuring anonymity, providing the researcher's contact details and informing that questionnaire completion would take no more than 20 minutes

In total 2.875 invitations were sent out and 1278 participants completed and returned the questionnaire (response 44%). The sample included 1013 non-donors, 155 donors, and 109 ex-donors. Most were female (N = 920, 72%) and employed (N = 933, 73%). Ages ranged from 18 to 71 years (M = 28.0).

MEASURES

Apart from demographic measures, we measured awareness of consequences, ascription of responsibility, personal norm, and blood donation intentions for this study. All measures were based on 7-point Likert scales, ranging form totally agree to totally disagree. Scores were recoded such that higher scores represent stronger pro-donation views.

Awareness of Consequences

Five items measured awareness of consequences (α = .57; e.g. 'Without a safe blood supply, medical care is almost impossible' and 'having a safe blood supply saves many lives annually').

Ascription of Responsibility

Five items measured ascription of responsibility (α = 83; e.g. 'I would donate blood because of my personal values and beliefs' and 'I would donate blood because it is my responsibility to help others').

Personal Norm

Four items measured personal norms to donate blood (α = 87; e.g. 'I feel a personal responsibility to donate blood' and 'I feel a moral obligation to give blood').

Intention

Three items measured intention to become a blood donor (α = .94; e.g. 'Do you intend to register as a blood donor in the next months' and 'Do you intend to give blood in the next months?').

STATISTICAL METHOD

We applied Baron and Kenny's (1986) methods for testing moderation and mediation and further employed structural equation modelling (SEM) to test the relationship structure between four variables.

- To test whether the relationship between personal norms and intention is moderated by awareness of consequences and ascription of responsibility we followed Baron and Kenny's (Baron & Kenny, 1986) method with standardized, mean-centred variables. Moderation is said to occur when a model includes (a) the impact of personal norm as a predictor, (b) the impact of awareness of consequences as moderator, and (c) the interaction between these two, see Figure 1. The moderator hypothesis is supported if this interaction (c) is significant. Significant main effects of either the predictor or moderator are not directly relevant to testing the moderator hypothesis.
- To test for mediation we followed Baron and Kenny's (Baron & Kenny, 1986) steps for mediation analysis. Mediation is said to occur when three conditions are met, (a) the independent variable (e.g. ascription of responsibility) should be associated with the mediating variable (e.g. personal norm), (b) the independent variable should be associated with the dependent variable (e.g. intention), and (c) in a regression of the dependent variable on both the independent variable and the mediator, the independent variable (path b) should reduce to non-significance whereas the mediator (path c) should remain significant, see Figure 2. We tested the norm activation model as a mediator model in two steps: first, testing whether the relation between awareness of consequences and intention was mediated was mediated by personal norms, and second, testing whether the relation between ascription of responsibility and intention was mediated by personal norm.

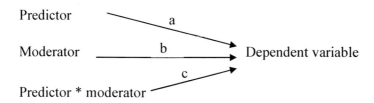

Figure 1. Moderator model (Baron & Kenny, 1986).

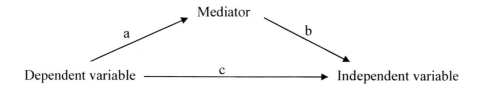

Figure 2. Mediator model (Baron & Kenny, 1986).

Structural equation modelling (SEM) was employed to test model fit for both the moderator and mediator model. We assessed the chi-square comparative fit index (CFI), the adjusted goodness of fit index (AGFI), and the root mean square error of approximation (RMSEA). These are less sensitive for sample size than χ^2. CFI > 0.90, AGFI > 0.99 and RMSEA < 0.50 indicate acceptable fit. Maximum likelihood solutions were used to test the models.

RESULTS

SPSS 12.0.1 was used for testing both models according to Baron and Kenny's (1986) methods for testing moderation and mediation. AMOS 5 was used to test both models according to structural equation modelling (SEM). Table 1 shows means, standard deviations and correlations between study measures.

Table 1. Means, standard deviations, and correlation

	1	2	3	4
Awareness of consequences	-			
Ascription of responsibility	.21***	-		
Personal norm	.29***	.31***	-	
Intention	.15***	.17***	.40***	-
Mean	5.32	4.69	3.75	3.00
Standard deviation	.79	1.14	1.50	1.83

ASSESSING MODERATION VS. MEDIATION

The results for moderation by awareness of consequences showed that the interaction between personal norm and awareness of consequences had no significant impact on intention as well ($B = .01$, $p = .84$). For moderation by ascription of responsibility we found again no significant interaction between personal norm and ascription of responsibility on intention ($B = .02$, $p = .44$). No support for the moderation model was thus found.

Mediation was tested in two steps. In step 1, the regression analyses showed (a) an effect of awareness of consequences on personal norm ($B = .29$, $p < .001$); (b) an effect of personal norm on intention ($B = .39$, $p < .001$); and (c) an effect of awareness of consequences on intention ($B = .15$, $p < .001$), that was no longer significant after including personal norm as a predictor ($B = .03$, $p = .25$). This mediation effect was statistically significant, $z = 5.16$, $p < .001$ (Kenny, Kashy, & Bolger, 1998), thus indicating that the effect of awareness of consequences on intention was mediated by personal norm.

In step 2, regression analyses showed (a) an effect of ascription of responsibility on personal norms ($B = .31$, $p < .001$); (b) an effect of personal norms on intention ($B = .38$, $p < .001$); and (c) an effect of ascription of responsibility on intention ($B = .17$, $p < .001$), that reduced in significance after including personal norm as a predictor ($B = .05$, $p = .051$). This mediation effect was statistically significant, $z = 7.00$, $p < .001$ (Kenny et al., 1998), thus indicating that also the effect of ascription of responsibility on intention was partly mediated by personal norm.

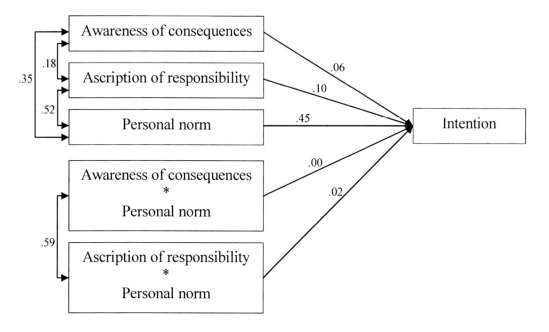

Figure 3. Moderator model with mean-centered variables.

STRUCTURAL EQUATION MODELLING

A SEM model for moderation using mean-centred variables fitted the data reasonably well, χ^2 = 27.7, p < .001; CFI = 0.96; AGFI = 0.98; RMSEA = 0.05. This model showed that both the interaction between awareness of consequences and personal norm and between ascription of responsibility and personal norm were not predictive for intention. Moreover, these interactions were highly correlated (r = 0.59), see Figure 3.

Next the model for mediation was tested, this model fitted the data well, χ^2 = 4.6, p = ns; CFI = 1.00; AGFI = 0.98; RMSEA = 0.03. This model showed that personal norms are predicted by awareness of consequences and ascription of responsibility. Intention is only predicted by personal norms. When adding a direct path from awareness of consequences to intention, this path was not significant (Beta = 0.07, p = ns). A direct path from ascription of responsibility to intention was not significant as well (Beta = 0.08, p = ns), see Figure 4.

CONCLUSION

Schwartz's Norm Activation Model has been used to study personal norms in pro-social and pro-environmental behaviour. This model has been interpreted both as a moderator and a mediator model; in this chapter we compared both interpretations. The results of the moderation/mediation analyses indicate that the mediator model better fits the data. This was confirmed by the structural equation modelling which showed that the mediator model better fitted the data.

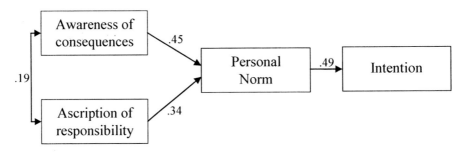

Figure 4. Mediator model.

In sum, personal norm to donate blood seems to be activated by the awareness of the consequences of not donating blood and ascription of responsibility to contribute to the blood supply. Subsequently, personal norm influences the intention to donate blood.

Only few other studies have compared both model interpretations. Osterhus (1997) applied the Norm Activation Model to energy conservation and found that support for both interpretations. The relation between awareness of consequences and intention to participate in the program was mediated by personal norm. The relation between personal norm and intention was moderated by ascription of responsibility. Thus, people who were aware of the consequences of high energy use and energy conservation had higher personal norms to participate in the program/conserve energy. But only people with high ascription of responsibility translated these norms into behaviour.

De Ruyter and Wetzels (2000) applied the Norm Activation Model to buying soccer club shares. They found support for the mediator interpretation of the model, ascription of responsibility activates personal norms which increase the intentions to buy shares. De Groot and Steg (submitted) compared both interpretations for several pro-environmental behaviours. They also found support for the mediator interpretation.

These studies all targeted pro-environmental behaviours to test the model. In this chapter, we compared both interpretations of the model for blood donation, a pro-social behaviour. The results suggest that in this context the model should be applied as a mediator model. This means that personal norms are positive when awareness of consequences and ascription of responsibility are positive. A positive personal norm, in turn, leads to a positive intention to donate blood. Personal norms to give blood can be activated by raising the awareness of the consequences of a shortage in safe blood and by increasing feelings or personal responsibility to contribute to the blood supply.

More research into awareness of consequences and ascription of responsibility is needed to be able to raise these and to increase personal norms accordingly.

REFERENCES

Armitage, C. J., & Conner, M. (2001). Social cognitive determinants of blood donation. *Journal of Applied Social Psychology, 31*, 1431-1457.

Bamberg, S., & Schmidt, P. (2003). Incentives, morality, or habit? Predicting students' car use for university routes with the models of Ajzen, Schwartz, and Triandis. *Environment and Behavior, 35*, 364-285.

Baron, R. M., & Kenny, D. A. (1986). The moderator-mediator variable distinction in social psychological research: Conceptual, strategic and statistical considerations. *Journal of Personality and Social Psychology, 51*, 1173-1182.

Bratt, C. (1999). The impact of norms and assumed consequences on recycling behavior. *Environment and Behavior, 31*, 630-656.

De Groot, J. I. M., & Steg, L. (Submitted for publication). Morality and prosocial behavior: The role of awareness, responsibility and norms in the norm activation model.

De Ruyter, K., & Wetzels, M. (2000). With a little help from my fans - Extending models of pro-social behaviour to explain supporters' intentions to buy soccer club shares. *Journal of Economic Psychology, 21*, 387-409.

Gärling, T., Fujii, S., Gärling, A., & Jakobsson, C. (2003). Moderating effects of social value orientation on determinants of proenvironmental behavior intention. *Journal of Environmental Psychology, 23*, 1-9.

Harland, P. (2001). *Pro-environmental behavior.* Universiteit Leiden, Leiden.

Hopper, J. R., & Nielsen, J. M. (1991). Recycling as altruistic behavior. Normative and behavioral strategies to expand participation in a community recycling program. *Environment and Behavior, 23*, 195-220.

Kenny, D. A., Kashy, D. A., & Bolger, N. (1998). Data analysis in social psychology. In Gilbert, D. T., Fiske, S. T. & Lindzey, G. (Eds.), *The Handbook of Social Psychology* (Vol. 1, pp. 233-265). New York: McGraw-Hill Companies.

Lemmens, K. P. H., Abraham, C., Hoekstra, T., Ruiter, R. A. C., De Kort, W. L. A. M., Brug, J., & Schaalma, H. P. (2005). Why don't young people volunteer to give blood? An investigation of the correlates of donation intentions among young adults. *Transfusion, 45*, 945-955.

Lemmens, K. P. H., Abraham, C., Ruiter, R. A. C., Veldhuizen, I. J. T., Dehing-Oberije, C. J. G., Bos, A. E. R., & Schaalma, H. (manuscript in preparation). Modeling antecedents of blood donation motivation among non-donors of varying age and education.

Matthies, E., Klöckner, C. A., & Preißner, C. L. (2006). Applying a modified moral decision making model to change habitual car use: How can commitment be effective? *Applied Psychology: An International Review, 55*, 91-106.

Minton, A. P., & Rose, R. L. (1997). The effects of environmental concern on environmentally friendly consumer behavior: An exploratory study. *Journal of Business Research, 40*, 37-48.

Nordlund, A. M., & Garvill, J. (2002). Value structures behind proenvironmental behavior. *Environment and Behavior, 34*, 740-756.

Osterhus, T. L. (1997). Pro-social consumer influence strategies: When and how do they work? *Journal of Marketing, 61*, 16-29.

Schwartz, S. H. (1968). Awareness of consequences and the influence of moral norms on interpersonal behavior. *Sociometry, 31*, 355-369.

Schwartz, S. H. (1970). Elicitation of moral obligation and self-sacrificing behavior: An experimental study of volunteering to be a bone marrow donor. *Journal of Personality and Social Psychology, 15*, 283-293.

Schwartz, S. H. (1973). Normative explanations of helping behavior: A critique, proposal, and empirical test. *Journal of Experimental Social Psychology, 9*, 349-364.

Schwartz, S. H., & Clausen, G. T. (1970). Responsibility, norms, and helping in an emergency. *Journal of Personality and Social Psychology, 16*, 299-310.

Schwartz, S. H., & David, A. B. (1976). Responsibility and helping in an emergency: Effects of blame, ability and denial of responsibility. *Sociometry, 39*, 406-415.

Schwartz, S. H., & Fleishman, J. A. (1978). Personal norms and the mediation of legitimacy effects on helping. *Social Psychology, 41*, 306-315.

Schwartz, S. H., & Howard, J. A. (1980). Explanations of the moderating effect of responsibility denial on the personal norm-behavior relationship. *Social Psychology Quarterly, 43*, 441-446.

Sparks, P., & Shepherd, R. (2002). The role of moral judgements within expectancy-value-based attitude-behaviour models. *Ethics & Behavior, 12*, 299-321.

Sparks, P., Shepherd, R., & Frewer, L. J. (1995). Assessing and structuring attitudes toward the use of gene technology in food production: The role of perceived ethical obligation. *Basic and Applied Social Psychology, 16*, 267-285.

Stern, P. C., Dietz, T., Abel, T., Guagnano, G. A., & Kalof, L. (1999). A value-belief-norm theory of support for social movements: The case of environmentalism. *Human Ecology Review, 6*, 81-97.

Stern, P. C., Dietz, T., & Black, J. S. (1986). Support for environmental protection: The role of moral norms. *Population and Environment, 8*, 204-222.

Thøgersen, J. (2002). Direct experience and the strength of the personal norm-behavior relationship. *Psychology & Marketing, 19*, 881-893.

In: Psychology of Motivation
Editor: Lois V. Brown, pp. 191-196
ISBN: 978-1-60021-598-8
© 2007 Nova Science Publishers, Inc.

Chapter 13

STRATEGIES INVOLVED IN THE MOTIVATION OF INDIVIDUALS TO PURSUE TESTING TO DETERMINE THE PRESENCE OF HIV

Brad Donohue[*], Courtney Irwin,
John Fordham and Daniel N. Allen
Department of Psychology, University of Nevada, Las Vegas, USA

ABSTRACT

HIV has become a worldwide pandemic. Indeed, there are a number of factors that are involved in the transmission and progression of HIV to AIDS. Therefore, this chapter first identifies the various behaviors that have contributed to the risk of contracting HIV. Although HIV testing is an essential component in the detection and transmission of HIV, individuals who are most at-risk of contracting HIV often fail to pursue such testing. This is unfortunate because knowledge of one's seropositivity can assist in the management of this disease, and reduce transmission of HIV to others. This chapter will highlight scientific advances in the detection of HIV, as well as methods of motivating individuals to effectively manage this potentially fatal condition.

Keywords: HIV, Testing, Motivation

Acquired Immunodeficiency Syndrome (AIDS) and its precursor human immunodeficiency virus (HIV), has become a worldwide pandemic, and is increasingly becoming a concern in the United States. Indeed, in 2002, at least 500,000 persons in the United States were estimated to be living with HIV or AIDS (Center for Disease Control, 2004), which probably significantly underestimates the magnitude of the problem given the

[*] Corresponding author. Bradley C. Donohue, Ph.D., Department of Psychology, University of Nevada Las Vegas, Box 455030, 4505 Maryland Parkway, Las Vegas, NV 89154-5030, USA. Tel.: +1.702.895.0181. FAX: +1.702.895.0195. E-mail: bradley.donohue@unlv.edu

absence of integrated surveillance of these conditions and the failure of individuals who are seropositive to undergo testing. For some time now it has been well-documented that teaching individuals to avoid behaviors that increase risk of HIV infection, and strict adherence to antiretroviral medication therapies post-infection, are effective in the prevention, spread and progression of HIV and AIDS. However, another relatively less studied prevention strategy would target increasing testing to detect the presence of the virus. While some early studies cast doubt on the usefulness of HIV testing and counseling as an effective means of primary prevention (Ickovics, Morrill, & Beren, 1994), more sophisticated applications that consider other important mediating factors such as motivation remain largely absent from the literature. Nevertheless, some recent progress along these lines is being made (Apanovitch, McCarthy, & Salovey, 2003). Potential benefits of increasing testing for HIV include enhanced awareness of the seriousness of the disease, and earlier detection when HIV is present so intervention strategies (e.g., medication management, engaging in behaviors that decrease the risk of spreading the virus to others) can be initiated. This later consideration is particularly important since the development of a number of antiretroviral therapies over the past 10 years that have substantially decreased AIDS associated mortality rates. Similarly, knowledge of a negative test result may motivate individuals to maintain their HIV negative status by decreasing high-risk behaviors. Unfortunately, groups who are most at-risk to contract HIV (e.g., low income ethnic minorities, poorly educated, intravenous drug users) are often particularly *unmotivated* to pursue testing. Therefore, this chapter will underscore issues relevant to HIV testing to assist mental health professionals in determining when HIV testing is indicated. Methods of enhancing motivation of individuals to engage in HIV testing, including obstacles that sometimes occur in the process, will also be emphasized.

Because HIV resides in bodily fluids such as blood, semen, and vaginal secretions it can be transmitted when these fluids are exchanged. Sexual activity involving broken or dysfunctional condoms (or sex without condom use), anal intercourse, and sharing of syringes or drug paraphernalia are the most common methods of transmissions (Coates & Schechter, 1988). In some countries transfusions of blood or blood clotting factor continue to remain a significant risk factor, although in the United States the risk for this type of transmission was greatest between 1978 and 1985, and since then has been almost entirely eliminated by screening and testing procedures. Other less common methods of transmission include tattooing or body piercing machines that are improperly cleaned, sharing of razors or toothbrushes when sores or cuts are present, or physical fights involving open cuts. Pregnant woman can pass HIV to their child during pregnancy, delivery, or during breast-feeding. However preventative anti-retroviral treatment initiated during pregnancy and prior to delivery can significantly decrease the likelihood of HIV transmission from the mother to infant before, during, and after birth. It may help to enhance motivation for women to be tested for HIV by informing them that with preventive anti-retroviral treatment, they have a 1 to 2 percent chance of transmitting HIV to their newborn, but 25 percent chance of doing so with no intervention. This is particularly important as women have traditionally been less motivated than men to be tested for HIV, although this is changing due to external pressures to be tested among other factors (Bond, Lauby, & Batson, 2005).

Those infected with HIV are often unaware of their contraction of this progressively debilitating virus because there are no initial physical manifestations, which may decrease motivation to pursue testing. Informing these individuals of the progression of HIV symptoms may assist in building motivation to pursue HIV testing so intervention strategies can be implemented shortly after infection, when HIV becomes present in the bloodstream. The virus is usually detected from the presence of antibodies that are produced by the body to protect T4 lymphocyte cells from being attacked by the virus. The period of detection from first infection varies, but is usually about 20 days, ranging up to one year unless very expensive and labor intensive testing procedures are utilized (i.e., polymerase chain reaction). The testing process usually consists of an initial screen (i.e., usually repeated reactive results from an enzyme-linked immunosorbant assay) followed by the more sensitive and costly Western blot test for those who are positive on screening. Although testing of blood is most commonly employed, urine and oral fluid tests are also available. The latter testing options are especially important when individuals lack motivation to be tested due to phobias that are relevant to blood withdraws (Lauby, Bond, Eroglu, & Batson, 2006). Testing results are usually available within 2 weeks. However, some individuals report they are reluctant to perform testing because they are concerned that the 2 week wait will cause them undue anxiety. To avoid this unnecessary concern, and potentially enhance motivation to be tested for the virus, rapid HIV screening tests are available that yield results in less than a half hour. However, these tests musts must be confirmed with the Western blot or equivalent method if a positive result is found. The Home Access test, approved by the Food and Drug Administration, is an excellent HIV testing methodology to employ when individuals lack motivation and/or transportation to visit HIV testing sites. This testing procedure also assists individuals who have fears related to visiting unfamiliar HIV testing sites or have concerns relevant to violations of confidentiality (e.g., fears of familiar persons seeing them enter an HIV testing site). Motivation for testing may also be enhanced by assisting in the scheduling of testing in familiar sites, such as their own private physician's office when testing is available (Bond et al., 2005). However, it is important to realize that if HIV/AIDS counseling is unavailable at these sites, or if rapport is not gained with medical staff, individuals who test positive for HIV may evidence poor adjustment necessitating ancillary services (Roberts, 2002; Mayer, 2004). When clients are concerned about HIV testing expenses, they should be informed of cost-free clinics, such as those indicated at the National HIV Testing Resources Center at the Center for Disease Control, which may be contacted 24 hours a day to assist in this process (i.e., 1-800-CDC-INFO).

As emphasized by Downing et al. (2001), populations that regularly engage in behaviors that significantly increase risk of contracting HIV (e.g., intravenous drug users, prostitutes) experience priorities (e.g., eviction, spouse abuse) that compete with HIV testing and decrease their perceptions of risk. Complicating this general lack of concern for or aversion to testing, individuals in these groups may be unaware they are engaging in HIV risk behaviors (Takahashi, Johnson, & Bradley, 2005). These considerations highlight the importance of devising prevention strategies that are tailored to address the aforementioned difficulties (e.g., see Fisher & Fisher, 1992). To illustrate this point, the following section underscores issues relevant to motivating individuals with substance use disorders to undergo testing for HIV. Indeed, it is essential to integrate HIV prevention strategies into the treatment plans of individuals who evidence substance use disorders. Along these lines, motivation to be tested for HIV is often enhanced when the client is uncertain about their exposure to HIV (Battle, Cummings, Yamada, & Krasnovsky, 1996). Many clients lack motivation to pursue testing due to fears that they will be unable to cope with positive HIV test results (Lauby et al., 2006; Ransom, Siler, Peters, & Maurer, 2005; Sonnex, Petherick, Hart & Adler, 1989). Therefore, it may be effective to suggest evidence-based methods of coping with HIV, such as available antiretroviral medication treatments(ARTs), to instill hope and desensitize potential test-related fears. When motivation to be tested for HIV is wanting, it is advisable to wait until client motivation improves, and then attempt to facilitate testing with a supportive and empathic attitude that emphasizes specific data purporting the benefits of testing (see Downing et al., 2001). Motivation to be tested for HIV can also be enhanced by pointing out recent sexual partners who are known to be HIV positive (at least with males) and soliciting significant others to encourage the client to be tested, when appropriate and within the limits of confidentiality (Bond et al., 2005). Other factors that appear to enhance motivation for testing include monetary token incentives, and making access to HIV testing convenient (e.g., Home Access Test, facilitating referral with client, driving client to testing facility). Innovative motivational procedures designed to increase testing include provision of psycho-educational information about AIDS in treatment programs that target individuals who are particularly at-risk to engage in HIV at-risk behaviors (Downing et al., 2001). It is also important to note that other factors in addition to level of motivation are important in influencing individuals to undergo testing for HIV and decreasing high-risk behaviors. For instance, Fisher and Fisher (1992) proposed a model for decreasing high-risk HIV behaviors that was composed of three determinants, including 1) information, 2) motivation, and 3) behavioral skills. Testing of this model indicated that motivation and information were independent predictors of risk reduction behavioral skills which in turn predicted AIDS preventative behaviors. Their model may also have direct applicability for increasing HIV testing, and highlights the importance of motivation as a necessary but not sufficient determinant of behavioral change. Of all therapeutic methodologies developed to enhance interest in being tested for HIV, motivational interviewing, first developed by William Miller (Miller & Rollnick, 1991), appears particularly promising. Indeed, this motivational approach has demonstrated efficacy in motivating individuals to seek out HIV testing and come back to learn about the test results, and to adhere to their antiretroviral medication regimes (see Foley et al., 2005). In motivational interviewing, information is presented in a non-confrontational manner that emphasizes empathy through reflective listening and non-judgmental responses. Motivation for change is brought about by objectively presenting the discrepancy between the participant's HIV/AIDS risk behaviors and goals of maintaining good health. Clients are gently encouraged to review their own personal benefits of disengaging from behaviors that compromise their health, rather than being told about potential generic benefits that might be expected to occur. The therapist attempts to intensify ambivalence about seropositive status, while supporting client-initiated goals that are incompatible with high-risk behaviors.

ACKNOWLEDGEMENT

This work was supported by funding from the National Institute on Drug Abuse (NIDA DA020548-01A1)

REFERENCES

Apanovitch, A. M., McCarthy, D., & Salovey, P. (2003). Using message framing to motivate HIV testing among low-income, ethnic minority women. *Health Psychology, 22*, 60-67.

Battle, R. S., Cummings, G. L., Yamada, K. A., & Krasnovsky, F. M. (1996). HIV testing among low-income african-american mothers. *AIDS Education and Prevention, 8*, 165-175.

Bond, L., Lauby, J., & Batson, H. (2005). HIV testing and the role of individual- and structural-level barriers and facilitators. *AIDS Care, 17*, 125-140.

Center for Disease Control and Prevention (1993). *HIV prevention counseling: A training program.* U S Department of Health and Human Services. Atlanta, GA: CDC

Center for Disease Control. *HIV/AIDS Surveillance Report, 2004, Vol.16*, Atlanta: US Department of Health and Human Services, Center for Disease Control, 2005, 1-46.

Coates, R. A., & Schechter, M. T. (1988). Sexual modes of transmission of the human immunodeficiency virus (HIV). *Annals of Sex Research, 1*, 115-137.

Downing, M., Knight, K., Reiss, T. H., Vernon, K., Mulia, N., Ferreboeuf, M., Carroll, A., & Vu, C. (2001) Drug users talk about HIV testing: Motivating and deterring factors. *AIDS Care, 13*, 561-577.

Fisher, J. D., & Fisher, W. D. (1992). Changing AIDS-risk behavior. *Psychological Bulletin, 111*, 455-474.

Foley, K., Duran, B., Morris, P., Lucero, J., Yizhou, J., Baxter, B., Harrison, M., Shurley, M., Shorty, E., Joe, D., Iralu, J., Davidson-Stroh, L., Foster, L., Begay, M., Sonleiter, N. (2005). Using motivational interviewing to promote HIV testing at an American Indian substance abuse treatment facility. *Journal of Psychoactive Drugs, 37*, 321- 329.

Ickovics, J. R., Morrill, A. C., & Beren, S. E. (1994). Limited effects of HIV counseling and testing for women: A prospective study of behavioral and psychological consequences. *Journal of the American Medical Association, 272*, 443-448.

Lauby, J. L., Bond, L. Eroglu, D., & Batson, H. (2006). Decisional balance, perceived risk and HIV testing practices. *AIDS and Behavior, 10*, 83-92.

Mayer, K. H. (2004). Recommendations for incorporating human immunodeficiency virus (HIV) prevention into the medical are of persons living with HIV. *Clinical Infectious Diseases, 38*, 104-121.

Miller, W.R., & Rollnick, S. (1991). *Preparing People to Change Addictive Behavior.* New York: Guilford Press.

Ransom, J. E., Siler, B., Peters, R. M., Maurer, M. J. (2005). Worry: Women's experience of HIV testing. *Qualitative Health Research, 15*, 382-393.

Roberts, K. J. (2002). Physician-patient relationships, patient satisfaction, and antiretroviral medication adherence among HIV-infected adults attending a public health clinic. *AIDS Patient Care and STDs, 16*, 43-50.

Sonnex, C., Petherick, A. Hart, G. J., & Adler, M. W. (1989). An appraisal of HIV antibody test counseling of injection drug users. *AIDS Care, 1*, 307-311.

Takahashi, T. A., Johnson, K. M. & Bradley, K. A. (2005). A population based study of HIV testing practices and perceptions in 4 U.S. states. *Journal of General Internal Medicine, 20*, 618-622.

Wortley, P. M., Chu, S. Y., Diaz, T., Ward, J. W., Doyle, B., & Davidson, A. J. (1995). HIV
    testing patters: Where, why and when were persons with AIDS tested for HIV? *AIDS, 9*,
    487-492.

In: Psychology of Motivation
Editor: Lois V. Brown, pp. 197-201

ISBN: 978-1-60021-598-8
© 2007 Nova Science Publishers, Inc.

Chapter 14

MOTIVATIONAL INCONTINENCE: PHILOSOPHICAL VIEWS ACROSS THE GAP BETWEEN NORMATIVE BELIEFS AND ACTIONS

Suzie Ferrie

School of Biosciences, University of Sydney, Australia

ABSTRACT

The familiar experience of a conflict between our actions and our normative beliefs was termed *akrasia* by the ancient Greeks. Philosophical theories of akrasia are helpful in illuminating situations of unwilling addiction as well as other disorders of motivation. The phenomenon of akrasia creates problems for theories of rational action, and this difficulty has meant that some philosophical approaches to akrasia have been forced to deny that akrasia really exists at all. If genuine akrasia is to be adequately characterised, it may be helpful to examine these attempts and their outcomes.

INTRODUCTION

The ancient Greeks are the first to have written about, and analysed, the phenomenon which they termed *akrasia*. This word, meaning 'lack of mastery', is also sometimes translated as 'weakness of the will' or 'incontinence'. Akrasia is said to occur when we intentionally act in a way that conflicts with our own better judgement. This seems to be a common, everyday experience for most of us: for example, we might find ourselves eating the whole family-sized block of chocolate, knowing that it would be better to stop after just one or two squares. For this to be considered genuine akrasia, we would have to be fully aware that we should stop eating the chocolate, and have the impression that we could stop at any time, and yet not stop. Unusually, the cognitive dissonance created by this conflict does not give rise to a reorganisation of beliefs to reduce the dissonance. Instead, it continues to cause discomfort due to the gap between the action and the belief or evaluation. Although this sort of situation is all too familiar, it creates problems for theories of rational action.

The 'folk' or naïve view of akrasia is that our knowledge of the best course of action is simply overwhelmed by our desire for some alternative, which is not as good for us overall but which is more pleasurable in the short term. As adults we learn to inhibit appetitive behaviours when needed, in order to achieve goals that are congruent with our normative beliefs, but occasionally our appetites and passions cause us to 'give in to temptation' despite knowing that we ought to do otherwise. Early thinkers such as Plato illustrated this idea by the use of images such as a charioteer (our rational mind) trying to control the direction of two horses (our appetites and our spirit or motivation). [1] Thus our passions drive us, but need to be kept under control by reason. [2] When our passions and appetites get out of hand, we do the wrong thing despite ourselves. In Plato's *Protagoras*, Socrates describes this naïve view of akrasia: '...a man often does evil knowingly, when he might abstain, because he is seduced and overpowered by pleasure...' [3] The essential elements of akrasia, as described here, are that we know what is best, we have the power to do what is best, and yet we intentionally do not do what is best because our knowledge is 'overmastered by anger, or pleasure, or pain, or love, or perhaps by fear, - just as if knowledge were a slave, and might be dragged about anyhow.'

At this point the first problem arises: if we are *truly* overwhelmed by our feelings, then it might not be true to say that we really feel we have the power to do what we ought to do. This would then not count as genuine akrasia, as others have pointed out. [4], [5] Socrates takes a different approach to the problem of akrasia, attacking the very idea that we can be 'overcome by pleasure' by rendering this explanation absurd. Suggesting that we judge actions to be good or evil on the basis of the pleasure or pain that they produce, Socrates then replaces the words "pleasure" and "pain" with "good" and "evil" in the original proposition, resulting in the ridiculous-sounding statement: 'I did evil, knowing it was evil, because I was overcome by good.' Similarly, 'I chose to do the more pleasurable action instead of the better action' becomes: 'I chose the better (more pleasurable) action instead of the better action'. On first glance this does seem absurd, but it is questionable whether pleasure and pain can be so simply equated with good and evil. Certainly, as Gerosimos Santas points out, it is not possible to do the same simple substitution with the other emotions that Socrates had said can "overmaster" us, such as anger, love and fear, [4] so it is unclear how effective this is as an attack on the overall explanation. Secondly, it is possible to interpret the 'absurd' statement in a way that still stands as a reasonable explanation: I did evil (to my future self, in the long term), knowing it was evil, because I was overcome by the desire for good (for my present self). It is this version of akrasia that is the next target of Socrates's attack.

Doing the wrong thing gives pleasure, or avoids pain, in the short term but causes pain in the future or robs us of other future benefits. (Socrates lists examples such as indulging in food or drink, or trying to avoid exercise or military service, or postponing uncomfortable medical procedures. Clearly human nature has changed little in over 2400 years!) Socrates suggests that the *amount* of pleasure or pain is really the only way that pleasure or pain can be assessed. On initial assessment, we may feel that an immediate reward differs significantly from a delayed reward but Socrates maintains that if we choose a small reward rather than a big reward, only because the smaller one is closer in time, then we have made an error. If we were to weigh them up properly, of course we would always choose the bigger reward, even if the smaller reward was immediate and the bigger reward involved delayed gratification.

Socrates suggests that a saving principle of human life is the ability to measure and not be tricked by appearances, and that this is an issue of knowledge – a knowledge of measuring. Someone who does the wrong thing in this way is lacking knowledge, so is merely ignorant. His conclusion is: 'This, therefore is the meaning of being overcome by pleasure: ignorance.' [3] Gerosimos Santas provides a detailed analysis of Socrates's argument. [4] He points out that if, as Socrates argues, weakness of will is only due to ignorance, then it would not be true to say that the agent truly *knows* what action is best. This then would not be genuine akrasia, and Socrates would be justified in concluding that akrasia, as he has defined it, does not exist.

Socrates' explanation of akrasia as being merely ignorance is disturbing, because our impression when we experience akrasia is that we *do* know perfectly well what we should do. We are even able to make an explicit statement to the effect that the action we should do is clearly the better choice of action! This would suggest that we are not committing an error of measurement: there is no confusion as to which is the bigger reward, just a question as to why we do not choose that one.

Donald Davidson attempts to address this problem by using a wider definition of weakness of the will. Adopting the translation 'incontinence', he then uses this term to refer to any situation where there is a conflict between the action and the relevant normative beliefs, not just situations where the appetites are concerned or where there are moral considerations. [6] (He gives a droll example of judging that it is better and more sensible not to get up and brush his teeth because he is already warm in bed, he needs to sleep, and it is late…then wearily getting up to brush his teeth anyway against his 'better judgement'.) Because Davidson's definition includes examples where one is not 'overcome' by appetitive urges, Socrates's arguments do not appear to apply here. There are still problems, however, because this picture of akrasia still conflicts with Davidson's own model of rational action.

Rational action is described by Davidson in the form of two principles that link making a judgement (about the better thing to do) with wanting (to do it) and then to acting (to do it). That is, in Davidson's model, every intentional action has a rational judgement embedded in it. His first principle, P1, expresses the idea that you will do the action you most want to do, while P2 says that your judgement or valuation of the action will be reflected in wanting to perform the action. [6] Thus we make an 'all-things-considered' judgement about what to do; this leads to an 'unconditional' judgement of what to do, which is effectively the *intention* to act. The existence of akrasia shatters this model by adding a third, incompatible principle: 'There are incontinent actions'. Other philosophers' solutions to this problem, Davidson notes, mostly seem to have involved giving up one of the three principles, most commonly P2.

An admirable example of rejecting P2 is presented by Gary Watson, who makes the distinction between the 'valuational system' of an agent, which is the set of considerations that yields all-things-considered judgements; and the 'motivational system' of an agent, which is the set of considerations or desires that motivate the action. [7] These systems normally overlap, so we usually equate the two as in P2, but they can sometimes diverge, leading to akrasia. This divergence can be extreme, as when a sudden surge of aggression makes us desire, despite ourselves, to hurt someone we love (when of course we do not value the pain of that person); or the divergence may be only partial, where our desire is greater for one valued thing than for another (more highly valued) thing. This latter phenomenon might occur when we want to eat all of the chocolate and also want to lose weight – we desire both (but desire the chocolate more strongly) and value both (but value losing weight more highly). Watson's approach is therefore to show how P2, although usually true, can still be false when there is a conflict between valuing and desiring. This is intuitively appealing, as it appears to be compatible with the naïve view of what is happening in a situation of akrasia.

Davidson's reply is that if someone sincerely believed an action to be better, then this belief would have to show itself in an inclination to act. If you perform the action, there must somewhere be an underlying intention to do that action (not the better one) and, behind that, some reasoning or judgement that the action performed is desirable. He suggests that P2 might be defended by pointing out that the term 'values' here is being used to express externally-derived norms and social conventions, not the agent's own sincere judgement, and 'desires' is being used to reflect a narrow sort of selfish attraction. [6] That is, this distinction between 'values' and 'desires' does not really affect P2, because the two terms do not both refer to the agent's internal states. This may be easy to argue in the case of the chocolate-versus-weight-loss conflict (where it might be the case that wanting to lose weight comes from some kind of social pressure), but it is less plausible that the angry, momentary desire to hurt one's child is suppressed only by convention and not by one's own true values. In any case, Davidson himself comes up with an explanation along Watson's lines when he suggests that akrasia results from having an all-things-considered judgement that differs from the unconditional judgement (that leads to action).

Davidson acknowledges that there is a strong desire (!) to alter the wording of the principles, to achieve the satisfaction of solving the problem, but reiterates his conviction that 'no amount of tinkering' with the wording will solve the underlying issue. For Davidson, the key problem is that our action comes from a judgement, so we cannot perform an action that conflicts with our judgement. Davidson's solution is to tinker with the definition of incontinence instead, since a different definition of incontinence might allow it to be compatible with P1 and P2. He describes a new model of incontinent action as follows: If we have reason r for performing action x, but reason r$^\text{l}$ (which includes r amongst other data) for doing y, we might judge action y to be the better action, based on r$^\text{l}$, yet do x, based on r. Our action therefore comes from a judgement (based on r), so it remains compatible with P1 and P2, yet it is still against our better judgement (based on r$^\text{l}$). The incontinent action is therefore compatible with Davidson's model of rational action, but is still not the best action because it is based on an incomplete set of data. Our all-things-considered judgement is in favour of the better action y, but our unconditional judgement is in favour of x, and leads to us doing x. This solution is similar to Watson's, in that both result in a conflict between our all-things-considered judgement and our action. In Watson's view the judgement and the motivation are conflicting, whilst in Davidson's view the conflict is between two different judgements, based on overlapping reasons. The main difference is that Davidson has had to work within the (self-imposed) constraints of his theory, resulting in what appears to be a weaker account of akrasia.

Davidson's solution does allow his three principles to coexist, but the distinction between the two kinds of judgement is not intuitively appealing, and raises the question of why it is necessary to have two kinds of judgement if just one is enough to cause action on its own in this model. Watson's description of desire as a force that is independent of our value judgements is a much more plausible approach, with the advantage of compatibility with folk impressions about how we behave. As Watson observes, the whole idea of appetites and passions in our culture is that 'desires... arise independently of the person's judgement and values...and it is because of this sort of independence that a conflict between valuing and desiring is possible.' [5] These desires need not be just physiologically-based drives (such as aggression or seeking food or sex) but can also involve some beliefs or internalised cultural norms, which means that this model makes sense even in Davidson's nocturnal tooth-brushing example (internalised norms could be responsible for Davidson's 'desire' to get up from his warm bed to brush his teeth, despite valuing staying in bed). Although Davidson claims that the problem of akrasia survives despite any amount of rewording of his principles of rational action, this is true only if we continue to accept the idea that intentional action always and only comes from judgement. It may be reasonable to allow, as Irving Thalberg says, 'other types of occurrences or states than our value judgements...as reasons why we act. Our emotions and cravings might be reasons.' [8]

After all his effort to make sure that akrasia can be compatible with rational action (action that is caused by reasoned judgement), Davidson appears in the end to conclude that akrasia is actually not rational anyway. He suggests that we do not recognise ourselves when we experience incontinence, seeing our own behaviour as absurd. [6] Watson's account of akrasia helps us to understand why. If our values and motivations *usually* overlap, as Watson suggests, then the normal feeling is that we are acting in response to our values, and the occasional incidence of akrasia seems strange.

CONCLUSION

Although on first glance akrasia seems trivial, it is much more than just a quirk of human behaviour. Instead it is significant because it creates difficulties for theories about the process of rational action, and helps us to test these in trying to explain the exceptions to everyday models of motivation and behaviour.

REFERENCES

[1]   Plato. (1972). *Phaedrus*. R Hackforth (trans.), Cambridge: University Press, p.69 and pp.103-104.

[2]   Plato. (1901). *The Republic*. H. Davis (trans.), London:M.Walter Dunne, pp.155-157.

[3]   Plato. (1891). Protagoras. In B. Jowett (trans.), *The Dialogues of Plato*. (5 vols, 3rd edn, pp.176-184). Oxford: The Clarendon Press.

[4]   Santas, G. (1966). Plato's Protagoras and explanations of weakness. *Philosophical Review 75*, 3-33.

[5]   Watson, G. (1977). Skepticism about weakness of will. *Philosophical Review 86*(July), 316-339.

[6]   Davidson, D. (2001). How is weakness of the will possible? In: *Essays on Actions and Events*, (2nd edn, pp. 21-42). Oxford: Clarendon.

[7]   Watson, G. (1975). Free agency. *Journal of Philosophy 72*(8), 205-220.

[8]   Thalberg, I. (1965). The Socratic Paradox and reasons for action. *Theoria 21*, 242-254.

INDEX

B

N

Q

R

S

Y

Z